SWIFT
AND HIS CONTEXTS

SWIFT
AND HIS CONTEXTS

Edited by
John Irwin Fischer • Hermann J. Real • James Woolley

AMS PRESS
New York

Library of Congress Cataloging-in-Publication Data

Swift and his contexts / edited by John Irwin Fischer, Hermann
    J. Real, James Woolley

    (AMS studies in the eighteenth century; no. 14)

    Includes index.

    1. Swift, Jonathan, 1667–1745—Criticism and interpretation.
2. Swift, Jonathan, 1667–1745—Contemporary England. 3.
England—Civilization—18th century. I. Fischer, John Irwin,
1940–. II. Real, Hermann Josef. III. Woolley, James D. IV.
Series.

PR3727.S95 1989   828′.509   89–107
ISBN 0-404-63514-8

All AMS books are printed on acid-free paper that meets the
guidelines for performance and durability of the Committee on
Production Guidelines for Book Longevity of the Council on
Library Resources.

AMS PRESS, INC.
56 East 13th Street
New York, N. Y. 10003, U. S. A.

Manufactured in the United States of America.

For David Woolley

Contents

Preface

SWIFT RESPONDED TO AND IMPINGED UPON a multiplicity of contexts. In this volume of contextual essays, all previously unpublished, we seek to shed new light on Swift's texts and procedures. The texts addressed include those of wide general interest (*Gulliver's Travels*, *A Tale of a Tub*, the poems) as well as others studied primarily by specialists. The contexts considered range from the most immediate—political controversy, interpersonal tensions—to broad matters of literary and religious ideology. Though the studies vary in method, they typically draw upon early documents for evidence.

Swift's contexts help to define him, as he helps to define his contexts. But with him, because he was a genius, the process of reciprocal definition is more intricate, enlivening, and ultimately hopeful than it might be with most of us. Swift is not bound by his contexts; rather, Houdini-like, he seems to escape from them. The more rigorous the effort to assemble Swift's contexts, the more delightful and meaningful his escapes become—to documentary scholars and also, we hope, to their readers.

These essays are meant not only to illuminate some of the pleasures of reading Swift but also to offer a token of esteem to one of the great Swift scholars of our own time. Having attained distinction as a book-collector and a musician, David Woolley in mid-life transferred his first Swift library to Monash University and left his native Australia for London, where he was solo oboist for the Royal Philharmonic Orchestra, the London Symphony Orchestra, and the Royal Covent Garden Orchestra. He began to amass a second important Swift library and to become, at the same time and entirely outside the conventional academic framework, a scholar supremely versed in the primary documents relevant to Swift. Some of the fruits of this other career can be seen in Swift's *Poetical Works*, which he brought to completion after Herbert Davis's death; in his revision of *The Correspondence of Jonathan Swift* (in progress); in the Oxford Authors *Jonathan Swift*, which he co-edited; and in such studies as the famed "Swift's Copy of *Gulliver's Travels*." The writers of the present essays are among the many who would wish to acknowledge not only David's published achievement but his generous sharing of information, advice, and criticism to benefit the work of others.

For many kinds of assistance the editors acknowledge their indebtedness to Charles Benson, Panthea Reid Broughton, Irvin Ehrenpreis (who did not live to write his intended contribution to this volume), A. C. Elias, Jr., Frank H. Ellis, Ian Maxted, Joan Peake, Emma Robinson, and Heinz J. Vienken. The editors used a computer to set the type, and gratitude is due to the contributors and to Gabe Hornstein of AMS Press for their cooperation in this still-unconventional method of book production.

J. A. Downie

The Political Significance of
Gulliver's Travels

SEVENTY YEARS HAVE PASSED since Sir Charles Firth first made use of the title I have chosen for my essay. "Political allusions abound in the *Travels*," Firth asserted in his lecture to the British Academy in 1919. In saying this, he was, in one respect, doing little more than endorsing the view which had been taken of Swift's masterpiece ever since its first publication. But Firth wished to codify such general perceptions. "In *Gulliver's Travels* many figures which seem to be imaginary are meant to depict real personages," he claimed, "or at all events are drawn from them."[1] Considering that nearly two centuries had passed since publication, Firth's assurance was breathtaking. It now seems almost incredible that his assertions could have influenced so profoundly the way succeeding generations have approached Swift's book, for Firth wasn't even an expert in eighteenth-century history. "To the politics of Walpole's day he brought only the superficial expertise of a gifted amateur," J. P. Kenyon has observed, "and the literary critics who followed him could contribute little more.[2]

But that was not how it seemed to Firth's immediate successors, and his casual observations were soon being treated as if they had been tablets of stone from Mount Sinai. In 1938, Godfrey Davies claimed that Firth's essay "*proved* that Swift often drew upon contemporary events in England for the parts of the book he first wrote," i.e., Parts I and II.[3] Perhaps it was a similar misplaced confidence in Firth's perspicacity which led Arthur E. Case to go one stage further and (among other things) put forward a sustained allegorical interpretation of Gulliver's experiences in Lilliput, centering on British politics between 1708 and 1715 and the fortunes (or misfortunes) of Swift's ministerial friends, Oxford and Bolingbroke, even though, as Kenyon remarks, "a trained historian...can casually make mincemeat of most of Firth's and Case's attributions."[4]

However, Case's views were accepted by the Swift establishment readily enough. Of *Four Essays on* Gulliver's Travels, Harold Williams wrote that "the third essay, on 'Personal and Political Satire' in the *Travels*, is the best in the book, displaying discernment and balanced thought."[5] For thirty years, the conviction that there was a consistent political allegory running through *Gulliver's Travels* was a critical commonplace. "Professor Case is ordinarily so authoritative," Edward Rosenheim, Jr., wrote in 1970, "that we tend to accept his information without question."[6] It was for that reason that Case's discussion of personal and political satire was reprinted in various collections of essays on Swift,[7] and editions of *Gulliver's Travels* dating from these years—in other words, the ones almost invariably used by students—are inevitably accompanied by notes informing the reader of the import of the alleged political allegory. Even today, critics are to be found who accept Case's views. "To a large extent," Hermann J. Real and Heinz J. Vienken asserted in 1985, " 'Gulliver in Lilliput' is a satirical vivisection of the intellectual and moral shortcomings of Whig politics between approximately 1708 and 1715."[8]

But what if, after all, Firth and Case were mistaken in assuming that *Gulliver's Travels* is a political allegory? Phillip Harth was the first to question the validity of the approach of the allegorical critics. In 1976, arguing that "Gulliver in Lilliput" is an "exemplary tale of the ingratitude of princes and the jealousy of ministers," Harth suggested that it was inappropriate to view Gulliver's adventures in Part I as an allegory of political events in early eighteenth-century Britain.[9] Reviewing Harth's essay, Ken Robinson agreed that "he has the support of eighteenth- and nineteenth-century critics for his contention that the first book is simply allusive." Yet Robinson went on to suggest that Harth's "terms are misleading": "He claims to be abandoning an allegorical reading but is in fact only abandoning a particularized political allegory."[10] For the first time, critics were beginning to argue about the terms used to describe what goes on in *Gulliver's Travels*. This was a significant development, to which I shall return.

The following year, 1977, I tried independently to emphasize the problems facing anyone wishing to argue that there is a consistent political allegory running through the book, or, indeed, any part of it, including "A Voyage to Lilliput."[11] What I did not suggest was that allusions to the politics of early eighteenth-century Britain could not be found. All I did was to question the approach of critics such as Firth and Case. Indeed, I concluded my essay by attempting to direct attention away from Part I and Gulliver's adventures in Lilliput—the traditional hunting ground for political allusions—to Part II and Gulliver's lengthy and meaty conversations with the King of Brobdingnag.[12]

By 1980, however, F. P. Lock was urging us largely to reject not only the specific identifications of Firth and the sustained political allegory of Case but "the accumulated weight of personal and particular allusions that has been read into the book by modern criticism."[13] In order to substantiate his thesis, Lock had to ignore or to reinterpret contemporary evidence bearing on the political significance of *Gulliver's Travels*.[14] Before we can evaluate "those puzzlingly particular annotations that have made generations of readers wonder why Swift clogs his general satire with so many topical references,"[15] therefore, it is necessary to go back to the beginning—that is, to the first publication of the two volumes of *Travels into Several Remote Nations of the World*.

II

"The clandestine comedy with which Swift surrounded the actual publication of *Gulliver* is well known," Lock writes.[16] Nevertheless, it must be rehearsed once more. Benjamin Motte, the publisher, was contacted on 8 August 1726 not by Swift *in propria persona* but by one Richard Sympson, whose covering letter, in the handwriting of John Gay, accompanied a copy of his cousin Mr. Lemuel Gulliver's manuscript. On receiving Motte's reply, Sympson asked for both volumes of Gulliver's account of his travels to "come out together and [to be] published by Christmas at furthest."[17] Two days later Swift left London en route to Ireland. "Motte receiv'd the copy (he tells me) he knew not from whence, nor from whom, dropp'd at his house in the dark, from a Hackney-coach," Pope informed Swift; "by computing the time, I found it was after you left England, so for my part, I suspend my judgment."[18] On 28 October 1726, *Gulliver's Travels* duly appeared.

Why did Swift go to the trouble of covering his tracks? "It was partly due to Swift's desire to preserve his anonymity," Lock suggests, "and partly out of his love of a good joke."[19] "I congratulate you first upon what you call your Couzen's wonderful Book," Pope wrote to Swift on 16 November 1726. "That countenance with which it is received by some statesmen, is delightful," he continued:[20]

I find no considerable man very angry at the book: some indeed think it rather too bold, and too general a Satire: but none that I hear of accuse it of particular reflections (I mean no persons of consequence, or good judgment; the mob of Cuticks, you know, always are desirous to apply Satire to those that they envy for being above them) so that you needed not to have been so secret upon this head.

How should Pope's words be interpreted? He rallied Swift upon what he took to have been the excessive secrecy surrounding Gulliver's appearance. Possibly he was also reassuring Swift about the personal nature of his satire: Pope felt that Swift's precautions were unnecessary in the event because no one "of consequence, or good judgment" had had the discernment (as yet) to apply the satire personally.

The next day, 17 November, Gay endorsed Pope's information:

The Politicians to a man agree, that it is free from particular reflections.... Not but we now and then meet with people of greater perspicuity, who are in search for particular applications in every leaf; and it is highly probable we shall have keys published to give light into Gulliver's design.[21]

Given twentieth-century approaches to *Gulliver's Travels*, Gay's percipience is impressive, even though (presumably) he had failed to keep up with events: a key had already been advertised in the *Whitehall Evening Post* for 8–10 November 1726.[22] My point is this: why should both Pope and Gay take the trouble to assure Swift, in words that are virtually identical, that *Gulliver* is without "particular reflections"?

Significantly, Swift used the same vocabulary in replying to Pope, emphasizing that, in Dublin, if not in London, "the general opinion is, that reflections on particular persons are most to be blamed."[23] Quite clearly, Swift and his friends had at least entertained the possibility that readers would try to find personal satire in *Gulliver's Travels*. The question is whether or not Swift intended that they should find allusions to contemporary events and politicians. Perhaps he had hoped to ruffle the feathers of those in high places, and had simply been trying to avoid any repercussions. When, over a year earlier, he had told Pope about the completion of his "newly Augmented" *Travels*, he had added the rider that they were "intended for the press when the world shall deserve them, or rather when a Printer shall be found brave enough to venture his Eares."[24] This being the case, it is interesting that Swift's letter to Pope of 27 November 1726 concluded:

Let me add, that if I were Gulliver's friend, I would desire all my acquaintance to give out that his copy was basely mangled, and abused, and added to, and blotted out by the printer; for so to me it seems, in the second volume particularly.[25]

Motte had bravely published *Gulliver's Travels* and had been rewarded by seeing the "whole [first] impression sold in a week."[26] But had he been brave enough?

III

The question of censorship is an important consideration when trying to assess the political significance of *Gulliver's Travels*. On a number of occasions Swift claimed that Motte had cut the manuscript he had been given to print. Pointing out that the first edition "abounds with many gross Errors of the Press," Charles Ford sent Motte a list of corrections on 3 January 1727.[27] It is beyond reasonable doubt that Ford was acting on Swift's instructions. David Woolley suggests that: "It is probable from its substance and phrasing that this letter, though in Ford's autograph, was entirely composed by Swift, and similarly the list."[28] Gay had transcribed "Richard Sympson's" earlier letter to Motte. Clearly Swift was determined to deal, for the time being, through intermediaries. In addition, we have the evidence of letters between Swift and Ford. "Now, you may please to remember how much I complained of Motts suffering some friend of his (I suppose it was M[r] Took a Clergy-man now dead) not onely to blot out some things that he thought might give offence, but to insert a good deal of trash contrary to the Author's manner and Style, and Intention," Swift reminded Ford on 9 October 1733, when George Faulkner was preparing his edition of Swift's *Works*. "I think you had a Gulliver interleaved and set right in those mangled and murdered Pages."[29] Ford's "interleaved" *Gulliver* is preserved in the Forster Collection in the Victoria and Albert Museum.[30]

F. P. Lock nonetheless discounts out of hand any suggestion that Motte censored Swift's text. "Certainty is impossible without new evidence, which is unlikely now to come to light," he suggests. "But reading Ford's letter in the light of Swift's love of jests and mystification makes it seem likely that the story of Motte's adulteration of the text of *Gulliver's Travels* was more of a joke than a serious complaint."[31] Fortunately, Michael Treadwell has been able to offer such new evidence. Explaining in detail why Motte would "have been cautious about issuing a work like *Gulliver*, particularly had it contained the manuscript passages preserved in Ford's interleaved copy," Treadwell shows "that the Reverend Andrew Tooke was indeed a specialist in the kind of copy editing Swift accuses him of in the case of *Gulliver's Travels*, that he had the closest possible ties with Benjamin Motte and was, in fact, a sleeping partner in Motte's firm.... Such evidence does not, of course, *prove* Swift's claim that Motte and Tooke altered the text of *Gulliver's Travels*," Treadwell concludes, "but I believe that it adds so greatly to the inherent probability of that claim as to make any other explanation impossible to credit."[32]

Therefore it seems we must take Swift seriously when he solemnly told Pope that he had "observe[d] several passages which appear to be patched and altered, and the style of a different sort" in Parts III and IV in particular.[33] In his corrected fourth octavo edition, published on 4 May 1727, Motte made all but three of the corrections listed in Ford's letter. However, even though Ford had also indicated where Swift's style had been tampered with, Motte failed to make any substantive additions to the text. This angered Swift more than anything else. "Had there been onely omissions, I should not care one farthing," Swift explained to Ford on 20 November 1733, "but change of

Style, new things foysted in, that are false facts, and I know not what, is very provoking.... Besides, the whole Sting is taken out in severall passages, in order to soften them."[34]

Let us examine in detail one of the passages which, to Swift's annoyance, was allegedly altered in the first edition. Modern readers know that when he visits the Academy of Lagado, Gulliver relates his experiences "in the Kingdom of *Tribnia*, by the Natives called *Langden*," in which "the Bulk of the People consisted wholly of Discoverers, Witnesses, Informers, Accusers, Prosecutors, Evidences, Swearers; together with their several subservient and subaltern Instruments; all under the Colours, the Conduct, and pay of Ministers and their Deputies."[35] Clearly *Tribnia* is an anagram of "Britain," *Langden* of "England," and it is generally accepted that Swift is referring here to the Atterbury case.[36] But this is the reading of editions of *Gulliver's Travels* published from 1735 onwards. In the first edition, this famous satire on the politics of the 1720s reads rather differently, as Gulliver merely explains what he would do "should [he] happen to live in a Kingdom where Plots, and Conspiracies were either in vogue from the turbulency of the meaner People, or could be turned to the use and service of the higher Rank of them" (p. 311). Not only is the passage narrated in the conditional; the obvious anagrams are not to be found.

According to Swift, Motte had deliberately tried to take the sting out of passages such as this, presumably to avoid possible repercussions in high places. Ford told Motte that it "seems to have much of the Author's manner of thinking, but in many places wants his Spirit."[37] F. P. Lock doubts the veracity of such statements. "Although the passages (in both versions) contain several possible references to the Atterbury plot," he argues, "the variants do not seem to be at all influenced by considerations of political caution. Instead, they read like stylistic improvements." Lock regards the version given by Faulkner in 1735 as a revision in which Swift tries unhappily to make his political satire more topical, rather than as a restoration. "Unfortunately," he suggests, "along with the sharpness we are given the crudely intrusive anagrams that make the satire...needlessly specific."[38]

But if it was Swift's *intention* all along to make specific allusions to the politics of the 1720s, then it simply won't do to complain that his satire is "needlessly specific." Such an objection is a perfectly proper criticism of *Gulliver's Travels*, of course, but there is the accompanying danger that, in refusing to acknowledge what Swift was doing, Lock may be distorting his meaning. Swift claimed that the sting had been removed from parts of *Gulliver's Travels*. If that were indeed the case, then, presumably, Motte had changed the political significance of his book. We can take such allegations *cum grano salis* if we wish, and present subsequent substantive alterations as revisions. But let us be aware of what we are doing: in reasoning in this way, we are making assumptions about Swift's intentions. Lock's contention that *Gulliver* "was not even primarily intended as a critique of the Whig government then in power"[39] is as much of an assumption as Firth's assertion that allusions to the events of the reigns of Queen Anne and George I "abound in the *Travels*" or Case's insistence on a sustained allegorical interpretation of Gulliver's experiences in Lilliput. The problem merits another look.

IV

Swift claimed that the text of *Gulliver's Travels* was cut because it "may be thought in one or two places to be a little Satyrical."[40] It is worth stressing that Swift's complaints related primarily to Parts III and IV, not to "A Voyage to Lilliput," which is where Firth and Case locate the book's major political significance. Soon after its publication, contemporaries were scrutinizing it not merely for "the Satire on general societies of men" but for "particular reflections." *A Key, Being Observations and Explanatory Notes, upon the Travels of Lemuel Gulliver* considered Part I in November 1726. It pointed out straightaway "that, under the Allegory of a Voyager, Mr. Gulliver gives us an admirable System of modern Politicks."[41] Note that the author of the *Key* (most probably Edmund Curll) is quite specific: the allusions in *Gulliver's Travels* are to *modern* politics, that is, to the politics of the early eighteenth century. Unlike Firth, however, the author makes no attempt at a systematic analysis of Gulliver's adventures in Lilliput. Usually, he contents himself with suggesting resemblances; thus the temple "*polluted some Years* ago *by an unnatural Murder*, bears so near a Resemblance to the *Banquetting-House* at *White-Hall*, before which Structure, King CHARLES I. was Beheaded," "the *Tramecksans*, and the *Slamecksans*, exactly resemble our *Whigs* and *Tories*," and "the Severities threatned against poor *Lemuel*, some here have resembled to the late Earl of *O—d*'s Sufferings."[42]

It might prove worthwhile to look at these three alleged resemblances once more, because they could be taken as typical of the sort of parallels Swift has been accused of drawing in *Gulliver's Travels*. Ever since the *Key* attempted to "mythologize" the temple in which Gulliver was housed, critics have been prepared to consider the possibility that, for some reason, it was meant to stand for an actual edifice. It is hard to see why such an assumption should be made. There has been no suggestion hitherto in the narrative that features of the Lilliputian landscape should be taken as allusions to contemporary England. Why, therefore, should we assume that the reference to the temple requires "deciphering"? Where, indeed, are the allegorical pointers in Gulliver's description of the "ancient Temple"? "From the earliest commentaries it has been suggested that this refers to Westminster Hall in which Charles I had been condemned to death, but the real explanation may be," John Chalker sensibly notes, "that Swift had to justify the existence of an empty building large enough to contain Gulliver."[43] As none of the suggestions put forward as a counterpart actually corresponds in any important detail to the description of "an ancient Temple, esteemed to be the largest in the whole Kingdom" (p. 27), narrative exigency rather than allegorical meaning seems a much sounder reason for Swift's reference to "an unnatural Murder."

Instead of proceeding on the assumption that features such as the temple are meant to suggest actual places in contemporary Europe, we should surely ask ourselves two questions. What is there *in the text* to indicate that such an allusion is being made? And what would be the point of the allusion? The author of the *Key* goes about his business in precisely the wrong way when he admits: "I must freely own I cannot find any other Pile in this Kingdom more *à propos* to Mr. *Gulliver*'s Allusion."[44] If he finds it difficult to identify what Swift is allegedly alluding to, then what put it into his head to suspect an allusion in the first place? His casual remark has influenced readers of *Gulliver's Travels* from 1726 to the present day. Had Swift *wished* to suggest the execution of Charles I, why did he mislead by housing Gulliver in a temple and not some more appropriate Lilliputian public building? Nor, seeing the alleged parallel is never developed, is it at all clear why Swift should wish to allude to Charles I's martyrdom in this way.

As far as the Tramecksan and the Slamecksan are concerned, there are no such difficulties. Gulliver reports Reldresal's description of Lilliputian party politics:

You are to understand, that for above seventy Moons past, there have been two struggling Parties in this Empire, under the Names of *Tramecksan*, and *Slamecksan*, from the high and low Heels on their Shoes, by which they distinguish themselves.

It is alledged indeed, that the High Heels are most agreeable to our ancient Constitution: But however this be, his Majesty hath determined to make use of only low Heels in the Administration of the Government, and all Offices in the Gift of the Crown; as you cannot but observe; and particularly, that his Majesty's Imperial Heels are lower at least by a *Drurr* than any of his Court....We compute the *Tramecksan*, or High-Heels, to exceed us in Number; but the Power is wholly on our Side. We apprehend his Imperial Highness, the Heir to the Crown, to have some

Tendency towards the High-Heels; at least we can plainly discover one of his Heels higher than the other...(p. 48).

In this passage there are not only clear pointers alerting us to a possible parallel between Lilliputian politics and British politics, there are also good reasons why Swift should wish to allude to the state of the nation in this way. In the early eighteenth century, there were indeed "two parties" in the nation. Alternative names for Tories and Whigs were the High Church and the Low Church parties. The preservation of the constitution in Church and State was a fundamental tenet of Tory dogma, yet the government of George I was dominated by Whigs. Despite being nominal head of the Church of England, George I was not an Anglican, and therefore most decidedly not a High Churchman. The Tories were generally thought to comprise the majority of Englishmen. And finally the Prince of Wales, the future George II, was thought in 1726 to favor the Tories to a certain extent.

The author of the *Key* was not the only contemporary to think that "the *Tramecksans*, and the *Slamecksans*, exactly resemble our Whigs and Tories." It did not require much perspicacity to make the connection, which was even being noted in Court circles. Mrs. Howard wrote to Swift in November 1726 to tell him that the Princess of Wales "thinks you can not in Cõmon Deciency appear in heels."[45] Quite clearly, the allusion had been understood. In this instance, we have not only a *general* reflection on political parties, which is at once universal as well as specific, but *particular* reflections on George I and his son, the Prince of Wales. Doubtless, as far as the high heels and the low heels are concerned, I am stating the obvious, but it is worth spelling out that they serve as a perfect example of the way in which *Gulliver's Travels* comments specifically on the politics of early eighteenth-century Britain.

Yet there are problems even here. Presumably, for the comments on the state of political parties to be appropriate, let alone the references to George I and the Prince of Wales, we are to take it that Swift is alluding to the Britain of 1726, even though Gulliver's sojourn in Lilliput and Blefuscu is from 5 November 1699 to 24 September 1701.[46] The dating causes difficulties. Reldresal says that "for above seventy Moons past, there have been two struggling Parties." "If one proceeds, as one surely must, on the assumption that the Voyage to Lilliput is a political allegory in which the events ending the War of the Spanish Succession are adumbrated, Gulliver's fire-extinguishing action stands for the Treaty of Utrecht, signed in April 1713," Vienken and Real contend (following Case). "Counting backwards seventy moons from 1713 lands one in the midst of the bitter party strife of 1707."[47] Once again, we are making assumptions. Why should we set

Reldresal's conversation with Gulliver in 1713 when, according to Gulliver, it actually took place some years earlier? Even if we suspect allegorical camouflage, why should we assume that Reldresal's figures are precise? After all, "above seventy Moons past" is scarcely specific.[48] And why, if we believe Swift is using an accurate time-scale, should he wish to locate the origins of political parties in 1707, when the Whigs and Tories had emerged almost thirty years earlier? Finally, how does all this square with the idea that, in the figure of the Emperor of Lilliput, Swift is alluding to George I? 1699–1701 or 1713? Both? Or neither?

The Emperor of Lilliput is "a renowned Patron of Learning" (p. 26) and "an excellent Horseman," "strong and masculine, with an *Austrian* Lip, and arched Nose, his Complexion olive." He is "twenty-eight Years and three Quarters old, of which he had reigned about seven, in great Felicity, and generally victorious" (p. 30). Gulliver refers to him as "a most magnanimous Prince" (p. 36). Now Swift was not in the habit of praising the king, and this does not immediately strike one as a description of George I, who was 66 when *Gulliver's Travels* appeared. No amount of juggling with Swift's figures can make the Emperor of Lilliput's age correspond meaningfully with George I's (nor, indeed, with the age of any of the other candidates that have been put forward as the Emperor's original).[49] It is of course possible to fall back on that old device of the political satirist, irony. As Swift advised in his "Directions for a Birthday Song:"

> Thus your Encomiums, to be strong,
> Must be apply'd directly wrong:
> A Tyrant for his Mercy praise,
> And crown a Royal Dunce with Bays:
> A squinting Monkey load with charms;
> And paint a Coward fierce in arms.
> Is he to Avarice inclin'd?
> Extol him for his generous mind....[50]

It is for this reason that Case suggests that "the Emperor was described as being almost the exact antithesis of George [I]."[51]

By 1729, when Swift wrote his "Directions," the Scriblerians had made it their practice, in their onslaught on the Hanoverian Court, to "descant / On Virtues which they know they want."[52] Although Reldresal's description of the state of the parties in Lilliput does not seem appropriate either to the years around 1700 or to those around 1713, it corresponds quite strikingly with the situation in 1726. If the passage I have quoted is meant to allude to contemporary politics, surely the most obvious place to look for its significance is the era in which *Gulliver's Travels* was actually published.

To proceed otherwise seems perverse. Unfortunately, when Firth looked at Part I, he wrongly believed it had been written from 1714 onwards, rather than in the early 1720s; therefore he looked for allusions to the earlier period, and, in elaborating his sustained political allegory, Case seems to have followed suit.

Real and Vienken, on the other hand, would appear to want it both ways: in their view, although " 'Gulliver in Lilliput' is a satirical vivisection" of the politics of the years "between approximately 1708 and 1715,"[53] they nevertheless refer to "His Imperial Majesty, the Emperor of Lilliput, alias thick, awkward, ungainly George I,"[54] even though, as F. P. Lock has pointed out, such an interpretation "hopelessly conflates the reigns of Anne and George, making Anne (the Empress) George's wife"![55] This would seem to be a crucial consideration: can "Gulliver in Lilliput" be both a sustained allegory of "the joint political fortunes of Oxford and Bolingbroke during the latter half of Queen Anne's reign," as Case and Real and Vienken contend, and, at the same time, a satire of George I?[56] For all this to work, *Gulliver's Travels* would need a double, nay, a *treble* time scheme: in addition to the dates Gulliver supplies for his travels, and the actual date of publication, 1726, we would need, at least in the Lilliputian sequences, a further timescale.

This brings us to the third of the *Key*'s "resemblances":

The Severities threatned against poor Lemuel, some here have resembled to the late Earl of *O—d*'s Sufferings, and if you will allow any Parallel, then,
Skyris Bolgolam High Admiral.
Flimnap the High Treasurer.
Limtoc the General.
Lalcon the Chamberlain.
Balmuff the grand Justiciary, and the *Articles* of *Impeachment* by them exhibited, need no other Key than the Posts assigned them.[57]

Quite clearly, in their search for political allusions in *Gulliver's Travels*, contemporaries were prepared to look back to the events of the previous decade. But was that Swift's intention or merely another assumption? The author of the *Key* is much more tentative than Gulliver's twentieth-century commentators: "some here have resembled" virtually denies responsibility for drawing such a parallel.

The terminology he employs is interesting: Gulliver's experience is not described as an allegorical representation of Oxford's impeachment, simply as a possible parallel case. In other words, depending on one's politics, one could, if one was so disposed, see a similarity between Lilliputian ingratitude towards Gulliver and the disgraceful treatment meted out to the man who had successfully ended the War of the Spanish Succession. For this allusion to work, there is no need for an extended political allegory, no subtle representation of the impeachment of either Oxford or Bolingbroke or both: Swift has simply supplied an analogy to their predicament in 1715. If "you will allow any Parallel, then" the quaintly-named Lilliputian ministers refer to their actual counterparts in 1715. "As to *Limtoc* the General," the author of the *Key* continues, "I heard all his History at *Marlborough* in *Wiltshire*."

The three last-named Lilliputian ministers—Limtoc, Lalcon, Balmuff—are mentioned on this occasion only. However, the histories of Skyresh Bolgolam, the High Admiral, "a Person well versed in Affairs, but of a morose and sour Complection...[who] was pleased, without any Provocation, to be [Gulliver's] mortal Enemy" (p. 42), and Flimnap, the High Treasurer, who could "cut a Caper on the strait Rope, at least an Inch higher than any other Lord in the whole Empire" (p. 38), were developed by Swift at greater length. To what end? The opportunity for political characterization has been too great for ingenious twentieth-century commentators to pass up. Given that Firth suspected that in *Gulliver's Travels* "many figures which seem to be imaginary are meant to depict real personages, or at all events are drawn from them," it is hardly surprising that he tried to identify the counterparts of Skyresh Bolgolam and Flimnap.

According to the *Key*, all that is necessary to interpret the allusion to Skyresh Bolgolam is the reference to his position in the government. He was High Admiral; therefore Swift must be alluding to his British equivalent in 1715, the First Lord of the Admiralty, Edward Russell, Earl of Orford. That was too simple for Firth. He felt Bolgolam was "clearly intended to represent the Earl of Nottingham. The 'morose and sour complexion' attributed to Bolgolam at once suggests the identification."[58] Case also plumps for Nottingham, though for different reasons.[59] But if Swift wished to suggest Nottingham, then why assign the post of High Admiral to him, when, under George I, Nottingham was Lord President of the Council? Once again, one wonders whether narrative exigency rather than political characterization is at the bottom of Swift's description of Skyresh Bolgolam as "morose," rather than an obscure attempt to allude to Nottingham. If Swift wished to allude to Nottingham, why, in describing Bolgolam, did he call him "morose" instead of clinching the point by making use of Nottingham's nickname of "Dismal"? And why did Swift not make Bolgolam chief amongst the Emperor of Lilliput's councillors, rather than High Admiral?

Flimnap also "had always been [Gulliver's] secret Enemy, although he outwardly caressed [him] more than was usual to the Moroseness of his

Nature" (p. 64). Once again, Swift draws attention to a Lilliputian's "Moroseness," and if "no other *Key*" is necessary "than the Posts assigned" the Lilliputians, then Flimnap must be identified as Charles Montagu, Earl of Halifax, First Lord of the Treasury in 1715. Yet, as Firth pointed out, Flimnap "was obviously designed to represent Walpole, as all commentators agree."[60] Even the author of the key made the identification, when he ended his account of the rope-dancing thus: "With how much Glee will a *T[ownshen]d*, or a *W[al]p[ol]e* read this Pygmaean Account of *Flimnap* and *Reldresal*."[61] What are we to make of it all? Walpole was not Lord Treasurer in 1715: he wasn't even a treasury commissioner! If Gulliver's impeachment is meant to be part of a consistent allegorical representation of the experiences of either Oxford or Bolingbroke or both, then there are serious difficulties over the characters of Skyresh Bolgolam and Flimnap.

When he put forward his thesis, Case admitted that "the burden of proof lies on the shoulders of anyone who argues that the political allegory is consistent," yet he concluded his discussion of "A Voyage to Lilliput" by asserting that the "strongest arguments in favor" of his interpretation were "its consistency and the exactness with which it follows the chronology of the events which it symbolizes."[62] Case's claims have been strongly disputed.[63] Why must we assume that "Gulliver in Lilliput" refers consistently to the latter half of the reign of Queen Anne, when the evidence points in a different direction? If Swift is somehow getting at George I when he describes the conduct of the Emperor of Lilliput, then two basic conclusions can be drawn: first, the Lilliputian characters are not really "drawn from" real personages, even if they are meant to call them to mind; and second, Swift's method of alluding to contemporary politics is not consistent. Once these reservations are conceded, things begin to slot into place. Despite the vast dissimilarities between the Emperor of Lilliput (as described by Gulliver) and George I, the odd detail is supplied to assist the contemporary reader to make the comparison.[64] In the same way, although Walpole was not Lord Treasurer in 1715, most references to Flimnap are meant to satirize Walpole.

After all, this is the basic technique used by the Scriblerians when they made their "particular reflections." When the government prevented *Polly*, the sequel to *The Beggar's Opera*, from being staged, Gay printed it. In a preface, he denied that his play was "fill'd with slander and calumny against particular great persons," much less that "Majesty it-self is endeavour'd to be brought into ridicule and contempt."[65] Notice once again the insistence that this "general" satire of British society is free of "particular reflections." "*Polly*, as it was eventually published," John Fuller suggests, "appears to be no more, indeed perhaps rather less, slanted against Walpole than" *The Beggar's Opera*.[66] However, in drawing attention to the alleged political significance of his play in his preface, Gay supervised the way in which it would be read by contemporaries. Whether or not they would otherwise have looked for "slander and calumny against particular great persons" or the "ridicule and contempt" of majesty, in the person of George II, Gay's denial alerted them to the possibility. And of course, in *Polly*, not only are there a number of implicit criticisms of Walpole as the "Great Man," George II's conduct is compared with that of Pohetohee.[67]

Our reading of *Gulliver's Travels* is not supervised in quite this way, but Gay had learned the technique of drawing parallels between actual persons and their fictional counterparts from Swift. The Emperor of Lilliput is not George I in any simple way: he is not, in Firth's terms, "meant to depict" the King of England, nor is he drawn from him. But Swift forces us to compare the two. His method is one of analogy: reasoning from parallel cases. There is no need for him to present a consistent allegory to score his political point. The Scriblerian technique of commenting on topical politics is not a complex one: it consists merely of implying criticism by drawing parallels between the existing situation and what might otherwise obtain. Swift makes this clear in the concluding chapter to *Gulliver*, when he asks us to compare the way the Houyhnhnms run their country with what tends to happen at home: "For, who can read of the Virtues I have mentioned in the glorious *Houyhnhnms*, without being ashamed of his own Vices, when he considers himself as the reasoning, governing Animal of his Country?" (p. 292).

The similarities or "resemblances" that exist between the Tories and Whigs and the High-heels and Low-heels are obvious. The same method can be seen at work when Gulliver describes the dispute between the Big-endians and the Little-endians. I prefer to call what Swift is doing "parallel history" rather than "allegory."[68] The technique is not vastly different from the polemical strategy Swift adopted in his first political work, *A Discourse of the Contests and Dissentions between the Nobles and the Commons in Athens and Rome*.[69] A clear example of this occurs in Part III when Gulliver, in Glubbdubdrib, compares "some *English* Yeomen of the old Stamp" with their grandchildren, to the detriment of the latter (p. 201). This incident might be said to epitomize his method: just as in conclusion he asks you to compare humans with Houyhnhnms as governing animals, so in Glubbdubdrib he holds up two examples for comparison.

In comparing "*English* Yeomen of the old Stamp" with their degenerate successors, Swift is implicitly condemning the Britain of the 1720s. In

Gulliver's Travels, he is concerned not so much with re-fighting the battles of the previous reign as attacking the system of Walpole. After all, that is the actual historical context of the book: he brought the manuscript to England in 1726 on a visit which was undertaken at least partly in order to confront Walpole personally with what Swift felt to be the deleterious consequences of his administration's policies. The political significance of *Gulliver's Travels*, in Firth's terms,[70] can, I think, be summed up readily enough: Swift comments in a number of ways on the state of the nation in 1726, satirizing the monarchy and the government of Walpole. From time to time he also alludes to the events of earlier years, such as the Atterbury affair of 1722. He even draws parallels with the divisions in religion and politics which by 1726 had been part of English life for so many years. If he alludes to contemporary figures, such allusions assume no more than local allegorical significance: the evidence for a sustained political allegory is strained and raises more questions than it attempts to solve. Many of those "puzzlingly particular annotations" which students find, to their undoubted surprise, in the notes to the various texts of *Gulliver* can be discounted. Swift's allusions to topical politics are rarely that obtrusive: because of the "general" character of much of the satire in *Gulliver's Travels*, it is more profitable, in the later twentieth century, to apply them generally as well.

[1] C. H. Firth, "The Political Significance of *Gulliver's Travels*," *Proceedings of the British Academy* (1919–1920), 237–59.

[2] *Times Literary Supplement*, 2 May 1980, p. 494.

[3] Davies, Preface to C. H. Firth, *Essays Historical and Literary* (Oxford, 1938), p. v, emphasis added.

[4] Arthur E. Case, *Four Essays on* Gulliver's Travels (Princeton, 1945), pp. 69–96; *TLS*, 2 May 1980, p. 494.

[5] *Review of English Studies*, 23 (1947), 368.

[6] Edward Rosenheim, Jr., "Swift and the Atterbury Case," in *The Augustan Milieu: Essays Presented to Louis A. Landa*, ed. H. K. Miller, Eric Rothstein, and G. S. Rousseau (Oxford, 1970), p. 194.

[7] See, for example, *Discussions of Jonathan Swift*, ed. John Traugott (Boston, 1962), pp. 105–20; *Jonathan Swift: A Critical Anthology*, ed. Denis Donoghue (Harmondsworth, Mddx., 1971), pp. 317–42.

[8] Hermann J. Real and Heinz J. Vienken, "The Structure of *Gulliver's Travels*," *Proceedings of the First Münster Symposium on Jonathan Swift*, ed. Hermann J. Real and Heinz J. Vienken (Munich, 1985), p. 203.

[9] Phillip Harth, "The Problem of Political Allegory in *Gulliver's Travels*," *Modern Philology*, 73 (1976), S40–47.

[10] *The Year's Work in English Studies*, 57 (1976), 223.

[11] J. A. Downie, "Political Characterization in *Gulliver's Travels*," *Yearbook of English Studies*, 7 (1977), 108–20.

[12] Downie, "Political Characterization," pp. 118–20.

[13] F. P. Lock, *The Politics of* Gulliver's Travels (Oxford, 1980), p. 3.

[14] For instance, Lock refused to consider the question of the "*Armagh*" *Gulliver*, which is treated magisterially by David Woolley in "Swift's Copy of *Gulliver's Travels*: The Armagh *Gulliver*, Hyde's Edition, and Swift's Earliest Corrections," in *The Art of Jonathan Swift*, ed. Clive T. Probyn (London, 1978), pp. 131–78. "The complexity of the evidence and arguments involved precludes my indicating in detail why I disagree with Woolley's conclusions," Lock claimed, "particularly since they affect my own only indirectly" (p. 75 n). This was a strange assertion to make, seeing that Lock was arguing that the first edition of Swift's book accurately represented his intentions. He returned to the subject in "The Text of *Gulliver's Travels*," *Modern Language Review*, 76 (1981), 513–33. For a critique of this article, see the *Scriblerian*, 15 (1982–83), 19.
I shall deal with Lock's re-interpretations in the body of my essay.

[15] Lock, *Politics*, p. 3.

[16] Lock, *Politics*, p. 70.

[17] *The Correspondence of Jonathan Swift*, ed. Harold Williams, rev. David Woolley, 5 vols. (Oxford, 1963–72), III, 152–55; hereafter cited as *Corresp.*

[18] *Corresp.*, III, 181.

[19] Lock, *Politics*, p. 70.

[20] *Corresp.*, III, 181.

[21] *Corresp.*, III, 182–23.

[22] *Gulliveriana VI: Critiques of "Gulliver's Travels" and Allusions Thereto: Book One*, intro. Jeanne K. Welcher and George E. Bush, Jr. (Delmar, NY, 1976), p. xiii.

[23] *Corresp.*, III, 189.

[24] *Corresp.*, III, 102.

[25] *Corresp.*, III, 190.

[26] *Corresp.*, III, 182.

[27] *Corresp.*, III, 194–95; cf. Woolley, pp. 161–65.

[28] Woolley, p. 144.

[29] *Corresp.*, IV, 197–98.

[30] Victoria and Albert Museum, Forster Collection, no. 8551.

[31] Lock, *Politics*, p. 78.

[32] Michael Treadwell, "Benjamin Motte, Andrew Tooke and *Gulliver's Travels*," *Proceedings of the First Münster Symposium*, pp. 288–89.

[33] *Corresp.*, III, 189.

[34] *Corresp.*, IV, 211–12.

[35] *Gulliver's Travels*, in [*The Prose Writings of Jonathan Swift*], ed. Herbert Davis et al., XI (rev. ed., 1959; Oxford, 1965), 191. Subsequent references are to this edition, and page numbers are supplied in the body of the text within parentheses.

[36] See Rosenheim, pp. 174–204; cf. Lock, *Politics*, p. 81.

37 Woolley, p. 164.

38 Lock, *Politics*, pp. 81–82. More recently, Brean S. Hammond has drawn attention to the same passage to argue that "at least one episode in *Gulliver's Travels*...does meet the most rigid conditions demanded by Lock" in order for the claim that political allegory is at work to be valid. Hammond, however, fails to take into account the discrepancy between Motte's edition and Faulkner's edition. See the *Clark Newsletter*, 12 (1987), 2–4.

39 Lock, *Politics*, p. 2.

40 *Corresp.*, III, 153.

41 *A Key, Being Observations and Explanatory Notes, upon the Travels of Lemuel Gulliver. By Signor Corolini, a Noble Venetian Now Residing in London. In a Letter to Dean Swift. Translated from the Italian Original* (London, 1726), p. 5.

42 *A Key*, pp. 7, 19–20, 26.

43 Jonathan Swift, *Gulliver's Travels*, ed. Peter Dixon and John Chalker, intro. Michael Foot (Harmondsworth, Mddx., 1967), p. 349.

44 *A Key*, p. 8.

45 *Corresp.*, III, 185.

46 There is confusion over the dating of Gulliver's sojourn in Lilliput. According to his own account, he left Bristol on 4 May 1699, was shipwrecked on 5 November, set sail from Blefuscu on 24 September 1701, and arrived in the Downs on 13 April 1702 (pp. 20, 78–79). Yet he refers to "a Residence of nine Months and thirteen Days" in Lilliput (p. 63). Clearly, there is a discepancy here, which is perhaps explicable by Gulliver's letter to Sympson: "Your Printer hath been so careless as to confound the Times, and mistake the Dates of my several Voyages and Returns; neither assigning the true Year, or the true Month, or Day of the Month" (p. 7). However, Case (p. 64) suggests that Gulliver arrived in Lilliput on 5 November 1700 (not 1699), although there is nothing in the text to suggest what happened between 4 May 1699 and 5 November 1700. One thing *is* clear: in the light of this initial discrepancy, it would appear to be unwise to construct elaborate allegories using the dates supplied by Gulliver.

47 Heinz J. Vienken and Hermann J. Real, "*Ex Libris* J. S.: Annotating Swift," *Proceedings of the First Münster Symposium*, p. 316.

48 It is also ambiguous. Vienken and Real assume that Swift is referring to "a 'moon', or lunar year...a period of thirty days" (p. 316), yet one can take the alternative view that, regardless of the "exotic" usage, a "moon" is meant to represent a calendar year. Lilliputian histories go back "six Thousand Moons": is this meant to suggest a period of less than 500 years (if a "moon" is thirty days) or 6,000 years—often cited as the traditional age of the earth? Whichever conclusion we choose to draw, one more thing is clear: unless we can be certain that Swift is talking about lunar years, it would appear to be unwise to "proceed...on the assumption" that we are to count backwards from April 1713 for "above seventy" periods of thirty days.

49 On account of his "*arched Nose*," William III was first suggested as the original of the Emperor (*A Key*, pp. 8–9). Lock plumps for Louis XIV (*Politics*, p. 116).

[50] *The Poems of Jonathan Swift*, ed. Harold Williams, 2nd ed., 3 vols. (Oxford, 1958), II, 464; hereafter cited as *Poems*.

[51] Case, p. 71.

[52] *Poems*, p. 391.

[53] Real and Vienken, "Structure," p. 203.

[54] Vienken and Real, "*Ex Libris J. S.*," p. 313.

[55] Lock, *Politics*, p. 107.

[56] Case, p. 70.

[57] *A Key*, p. 26.

[58] Firth, p. 242.

[59] Case, p. 72.

[60] Firth, p. 244.

[61] *A Key*, p. 13.

[62] Case, pp. 70, 79.

[63] Downie, "Political Characterization," pp. 109–15; Lock, *Politics*, pp. 106 ff.

[64] Vienken and Real, "*Ex Libris J. S.*," p. 313.

[65] John Gay, *Dramatic Works*, ed. John Fuller, 2 vols. (Oxford, 1983), II, 70.

[66] Gay, I, 53.

[67] On this point, see J. A. Downie, "Gay's Politics," *John Gay and the Scriblerians*, ed. Nigel Wood, forthcoming.

[68] The terminology is important only insofar as it relates to the political significance of *Gulliver's Travels*. The word *allegory* derives from the Greek, and means "speaking otherwise than one seems to speak" (*allos*, other; -*agoria*, speaking). In that many episodes in *Gulliver's Travels* are extended metaphors carrying one or more sets of meanings *in addition* to the apparent and literal ones, in this sense they are perforce allegorical. In *Gulliver's Travels*, as I have argued, Swift alludes to topical politics in a number of ways. However, as there is no extended, particularized political allegory, such allusions are not sufficiently developed to assume more than local allegorical significance. In one sense, therefore, it might be misleading to use the term *allegory*. Hence my preference for the more precise *parallel history*, a phrase which Swift's contemporaries would undoubtedly have comprehended. See, for example, the *London Magazine*'s résumé of an essay appearing in the *Free Briton* no. 124 (13 April 1732): "THE *Craftsman* has lately had Recourse to his ancient Method of defaming by *Parallel History*...wherein, as of old in the Tyrant's Bed, all Characters are rack'd and tortur'd, to make them agree to his political Standard." In its own précis of the same article, the *Gentleman's Magazine* also refers to "*Parallel History*" as the *Craftsman*'s "ancient Method."

It is hardly worth pointing out that the early *Craftsman* was largely responsible for drawing attention to the possible political significance of *Gulliver's Travels*.

[69] J. A. Downie, "Swift's *Discourse*: Allegorical Satire or Parallel History?" *Swift Studies*, 2 (1987), 25–32.

[70] In this essay, I have restricted myself to consideration of the political significance of *Gulliver's Travels* in the sense intended by Sir Charles Firth, who was not concerned with the distinction made by hermeneuticians between *Sinn* and

Bedeutung—terms that have been Englished by E. D. Hirsch, Jr., as "meaning" and "significance" (see *Validity in Interpretation* [New Haven, 1967], pp. 211–12). In that Firth was concerned with Swift's intentions in *Gulliver's Travels*, what he was actually considering was the work's *Sinn* or meaning, and not, in Hirsch's terms, its *Bedeutung* or significance.

It could be argued that any discussion of the political significance of *Gulliver's Travels* should take into account its meaning to us today, either instead of or as well as its meaning to Swift's contemporaries. Perhaps this is what F. P. Lock is primarily concerned with when he writes that "*Gulliver's Travels* remains surprisingly relevant to the politics of the twentieth century" (*Politics*, p. 35).

John Irwin Fischer

The Legal Response to Swift's
The Public Spirit of the Whigs

I HAVE FOUND a number of heretofore unreported documents germane to the publication of Jonathan Swift's *The Public Spirit of the Whigs* and to the legal response that pamphlet provoked. These documents witness diversely. They render doubtful some matters we thought were certain, notably the publication date of *The Public Spirit of the Whigs*. They add information to our understanding of the roles played by Robert Harley and Henry St. John, Lord Oxford and Lord Bolingbroke, in this episode of Swift's career. They reverse our understanding of the role played by John Erskine, Lord Mar. And they prompt reflection on the relationship between literary interpretation and historical research.

The effects of these documents show best against a summary of our established understanding of the publication and consequences of Swift's pamphlet.[1] We have supposed that *The Public Spirit of the Whigs*, Swift's reply to Richard Steele's *The Crisis*, was published on 23 February 1713/14. The uncensored copies of Swift's first and second editions include a five-paragraph attack on the Scots peerage, the Scots nation, and the union between England and Scotland. This attack angered the Scots lords in Parliament, most of whom supported Robert Harley's Tory administration. The attack thus supplied to English Whig lords a means to embarrass Harley's government.

On 2 March, Queen Anne opened Parliament with a speech that expressed displeasure at seditious papers and factious rumors, and particularly at such as "insinuate that the Protestant Succession in the House of Hanover was in danger under [her] Government." Swift probably influenced or at least polished this passage,[2] which seems in part to have been designed, and was in fact used, to expel Richard Steele, as author of *The Crisis*, from the House of Commons. Before the Tories wielded this passage as a spear, however, they suffered it as a boomerang. Upon the completion of the Queen's speech and her withdrawal from the House of Lords, the Earl of Wharton rose to produce a copy of *The Public Spirit of the Whigs*, and, having affirmed it to be just such a libel as the Queen had complained of, he read out Swift's attack on Scotland and on the Union. The House declared the pamphlet to be libelous, and ordered that its publisher, John Morphew, be attached. On 3 March, Morphew informed the House that John Barber was also concerned in printing and publishing the pamphlet, and on 5 March both Morphew and Barber were questioned to discover the pamphlet's author. On 6 March, the Earl of Mar, Secretary of State for Scotland, informed the Lords that he had instituted criminal proceedings against Barber. We have supposed this announcement to be an administrative ploy to stymie further parliamentary examination of witnesses.

The ploy, we have recognized, did not wholly gag the Whig peers. On 9 March, under the direction of the Earl of Nottingham, the House was persuaded to ask the Queen to issue a proclamation offering a reward and a pardon to any person able to make true proof against the author of *The Public Spirit of the Whigs*. On 11 March, the House considered, but rejected, a proposal to include within the petition the following passage, embarrassing to Harley and possibly dangerous to Swift: "And we are the rather induced to lay our humble Address before Your Majesty, because the Author of the said seditious Libel pretends to know the Secrets of Your Majesty's Administration."[3] On 15 March the Queen issued her proclamation without this final charge. The proclamation did include a £300 reward for information leading to a successful prosecution of the pamphlet's author. Swift later claimed that the reward was kept small because "the Queen and Ministry had no Desire to have our supposed Author taken into Custody."[4] Whether for that reason or not, no one came forward to offer information and claim the reward.

The earliest information to perplex the over-tidy story just summarized emerges from the contents and dating of prepublication newspaper advertisements for *The Public Spirit of the Whigs*. The first advertisements for Swift's pamphlet appear on 30 January 1713/14 in two newspapers, the *Post Boy* and the *Mercator*. The advertisements are substantively identical to an advertisement appearing on 1 February in the *Examiner*:

In a few Days will be publish'd,

The Publick Spirit of the *Whigs*, set forth in their generous Encouragement of the Author of the Crisis: With some Observations on the Seasonableness, Candor, Erudition and Stile of that Treatise. Price 6d. but to the Subscribers Half a Crown. Note, This Work will be Printed in Quarto, fit to be bound up with the Crisis. As also, A Modest Enquiry into the Reasons of the Joy expres'd by a certain Sett of People, upon the spreading of a Report of Her Majesty's Death. Price 3d. Both Printed for John Morphew, near Stationers-Hall.

In their edition of *The Public Spirit of the Whigs*, Herbert Davis and Irvin Ehrenpreis remarked, but did not print, the 1 February instance of this advertisement. The date of the advertisement interested them. Mrs. Manley's *Modest Enquiry* appeared, as promised, on 4 February. But Swift's pamphlet was not advertised as published until 23 February. To explain this delay, Davis and Ehrenpreis commented that Swift "took longer with his reply than he had expected."[5] This supposition overlooks and obscures the information offered by the advertisement itself.

When published, *The Public Spirit of the Whigs* sold for 1*s.*, not 6*d.* Apparently, then, on or shortly before Monday, 1 February, Swift underestimated the size, and hence the cost, of his answer to Steele's pamphlet. By no later than Thursday, 4 February, however, Swift knew the size of his task. On that day, the advertisements in the *Mercator* and *Post Boy* set the price of *The Public Spirit of the Whigs* at 1*s.* and set the date of publication as "next Week." On Friday, 5 February, the *Examiner* advertisement effected the same price change but promised the pamphlet "in a few Days." The following Monday and Tuesday, 8 and 9 February, the *Examiner* and *Mercator* advertisements agreed that the pamphlet would appear "in a few Days."

This pattern of advertisements suggests that although Swift initially misjudged his task, he recovered quickly and was prepared to publish his pamphlet sometime during the week of 8 February. Apparently, he did not do so. For the next four numbers, issued over a week and a half, the *Mercator* droned on, promising that *The Public Spirit of the Whigs* would appear "in a few Days." More interestingly, all advertisement of the pamphlet ceased in the *Examiner* from 8 until 19 and 22 February and in the *Post Boy* from 4 until 23 February. These final three advertisements establish 23 February as the publication date of Swift's pamphlet. But they do not explain the interim between the first run of advertisements and the second.

Several explanations may be offered. Each depends on the assumption that Swift himself wrote the original advertisement of 30 January and controlled the changes in it through 23 February. My evidence for this assumption is internal and circumstantial but convincing, I think.

Steele published *The Crisis* by subscription. That method, as Swift caustically remarks in *The Public Spirit of the Whigs*, "was a little out of Form; because Subscriptions are usually begged only for Books of great Price...."[6] The aggressive bumptiousness of Steele and his patrons is as nothing, however, when compared to the bull that in every instance of the advertisement for *The Public Spirit of the Whigs* is attached to its price: "Price 6*d.* [later, 1*s.*] but to the Subscribers Half a Crown." Only Swift, I believe, possessed the authority to pretend to offer his pamphlet to subscribers at five times its street price. And only Swift, I believe, would have aimed at Steele's gracelessness a solecism so obliquely ironic.

Similarly, only Swift could have known, before its completion, the probable length and publication date of his pamphlet. Thus, the major shifts in his advertisement must derive, proximately or at a distance, from his instructions. I do suspect that, as the effects of his control were not uniform, so its exercise was not complete. Because the hiatus of advertisement in the *Examiner* and the *Post Boy* probably required active intervention, I attribute the hiatus to Swift. The *Mercator*, which, I suppose, remained for some reason uninstructed, mindlessly reiterated its fruitless promise.

But again, what prevented, until 23 February, the publication of a pamphlet that on 8 February Swift apparently thought could appear "in a few Days"? One grotesque explanation is prompted by Swift's convoluted parody of Steele's subscription scheme. Steele's pamphlet was first advertised on 22 October 1713 and repeatedly promised thereafter until its publication on 19 January 1713/14. One might read Swift's on-again off-again advertisement as a further parody of *The Crisis*'s prepublication hoopla. Finally, however, the jest seems pointless. A more pedestrian explanation is weightier.

In late January, rumors were common that Queen Anne was mortally ill. On 2 February, however, Swift anticipated, as a vindication of her vitality, Anne's return from Windsor to London in order to open Parliament.[7] Even if *The Public Spirit of the Whigs* was complete by 10 February, Swift might plausibly have withheld it from publication until that triumphant appearance. On 16 February, however, ill health prevented the Queen from delivering her opening speech. Parliament was adjourned for one week to Tuesday, 23 February. Swift, one supposes, had advance knowledge of this adjournment and rescheduled the publication of *The Public Spirit of the Whigs* for 23 February.

That some such sequence constitutes the actual order of events is suggested by Swift's response to Steele's publication on Monday, 15 February, of *The Englishman: Being the Close of the Paper So Called*. In most ways, the response is awkward and minimal. Swift merely tacked three new paragraphs to the tail of *The Public Spirit of the Whigs*, already brought to a close by two powerful summary paragraphs. The method is that of an author who believes himself done with his task, and Swift says as much in the suture that holds his new material to his old.

I have now finished the most disgustful Task that ever I undertook: I could with more Ease have written *three* dull Pamphlets, than remarked upon the Falshoods and Absurdities of *One*. But I was quite confounded last *Wednesday* when the Printer came with another Pamphlet in his Hand, written by the same Author, and entituled, *The Englishman, being the Close of the Paper so called*, &c. He desired

I would read it over, and consider it in a Paper by it self; which last I absolutely refused.[8]

Despite its brusqueness, this passage permits us two inferences beyond our awareness of Swift's impatience. The first is that, as Swift wrote this passage, possibly on 17 or 18 February, he knew that the publication date of his pamphlet was firmly set within the first three days of the next week. This inference depends upon the single rhetorical nicety Swift employs to blend his old material with his new. By designating as "last *Wednesday*" the day that his printer, John Barber, putatively handed to him Steele's new work, Swift projects all his material forward to the day on which all of it was first to be read, Tuesday, 23 February. The second inference is that on 17 February, Swift's "last *Wednesday*," John Barber held some or all of *The Public Spirit of the Whigs* save the final three paragraphs that Swift subsequently wrote. This inference depends upon the fact that, without it, one cannot easily explain Barber's care to show Steele's pamphlet to Swift and his request that Swift answer the new pamphlet "in a Paper by itself." Speculatively, one might even read Barber's request as the wish of a printer to produce a new paper rather than to cancel and reset the last sheet of one already printed.

Of course, if, as I think, the odd prepublication history of *The Public Spirit of the Whigs* derives from Swift's delays and maneuvers to publish his pamphlet coincidentally with the opening of Parliament, then Swift's efforts failed comically. *The Public Spirit of the Whigs* finally appeared, as advertised, on 23 February. The Queen did not. Parliament was again adjourned to "this day seven-night," that is, 2 March, when its session at last commenced.[9]

This outcome renders risible not only Swift's efforts but also my attempt to explain the fitful progress toward publication of *The Public Spirit of the Whigs*. But, pedantic or not, if my explanation is right, then the fourth of the pamphlet's seven sheets, the one containing Swift's attack on Scotland, could have been printed as early as 5 February. Indeed, the whole pamphlet, save only its last three paragraphs, could have been printed by 10 February, the publication date assigned to it in an information brought against John Barber in the Queen's Bench Court.[10]

Other documents precede that information, however. The first several of these recast the role of John Erskine, Lord Mar, from that of Swift's champion during the investigation precipitated by *The Public Spirit of the Whigs* to that of Swift's principal adversary. The tradition of Mar's advocative role derives from mistakes in, and misreadings of, part of a single sentence in a single contemporary report of the investigation written by the arch-Whig,

Abel Boyer, and published in the March 1714 number of the *Political State of Great Britain*. Boyer wrote, "On the 6th of *March* the Earl of *Marr*, One of Her Majesty's Principal Secretaries of State, acquainted the House, That he had already order'd *John Barber* to be prosecuted, which put a sudden Stop to all farther Inquiries about that Matter, in a *Parliamentary Way*."[11]

Boyer's statement can be corrected in several particulars by comparing it with the minutes of the Lords' proceedings kept by the Clerk of Parliament. First, on 5, not 6, March, Barber himself and Mar told the Lords of the prosecution brought against Barber. Second, the fact of that prosecution did not prevent the Lords from asking further questions of Morphew and Barber on that day and of their employees on 6 and 9 March. Third, the fact of that prosecution did permit Barber to refuse to answer potentially incriminating questions and did prohibit Mar, unless enabled by the Queen, from presenting to the Lords evidence proper to the Court.[12] So corrected, the one useful bit of information in Boyer's statement can be examined.

Boyer claims that Mar's announcement put an end to *parliamentary* inquiry. As we have just noted, that claim is not strictly true. Worse still, it has been misread to suggest that the purpose of Mar's announcement was to squelch *all* further inquiry about *The Public Spirit of the Whigs*. Irvin Ehrenpreis, for example, writes that "the Earl of Mar, as Secretary of State for Scotland, instituted a mock-prosecution of Barber, whereupon further parliamentary inquiries were stopped...."[13] As a Whig, Boyer might have delighted in Ehrenpreis's misreading. But Boyer is not responsible for it.

Fifty years ago Laurence Hanson taught us that, though the House of Lords could examine witnesses on oath, it had no prosecutorial powers. It might, and did, petition Anne "to issue a proclamation offering a reward of £300 for the discovery of the author [of *The Public Spirit of the Whigs*]. But it could not bring Swift into court...."[14] It could recommend to the Attorney General to prosecute Barber, but that step had already been taken by Mar. Legally, just as Boyer says, after Mar's announcement, Parliament had nothing further to do. Responsibility for Barber's case passed to Lord Mar, Attorney General Northey, and the procedures of the Queen's Bench Court. There, in the records of those officers and that court, we may trace the history of Barber's case.

We recall that on Friday, 5 March, Barber informed the Lords that he was under prosecution. The Lords' minutes appear to record Barber's words nearly as he spoke them: "On Saturday last [27 February] he was sent for in custody by the E. of Mar."[15] Taking Barber's hint, one finds in Mar's Secretaries' Letter Book for Criminal Entries the following copy of a warrant directed to John Davis, one of the Queen's Messengers:

You are hereby authorised and required, in her Ma.^{tie's} name, to take into your custody the body of John Barber Printer, and to keep him under safe guard, untill you receive farther orders herein from me. And for so doing this shall be your Warrant. Given at Whitehall the 27.th day of Febry 1713/14 and the Twelth Year of her Ma.^{tie's} Reign.[16]

Immediately below this copy one finds a copy of a letter that in the margin is noted as the "Earl of Mar's letter to the Attorney & Sollicitor General concerning his prosecution of Barber ye Printer":

Whitehall March 1.st 1713/14
Gentlemen

I send you herewith a Pamphlet, entitled the public Spirit of the whigs &c:, which is found to contain several passages, highly reflecting on her Maties Administration, and tending to creat uneasinesses in the minds of her Maties Subjects in both parts of the Kingdom, particularly in the 22.^d 23.^d and 24.th pages. And it appearing upon Examination, that the same hath been printed and publish'd by John Barber, Printer: I have by Her Maties express command, bound over the said Barber to appear before the Court of the Queen's Bench in Westminster Hall, the first day of next Terme; and am now to Signifie to you her Maties pleasure, that the Said Barber be prosecuted for this his said offence, according to due course of Law, and also for the discovery of the Author of the said Pamphlet. I am
      Gentlemen
Your most obedient & most hu.^{bl} Servt
        Mar [17]

    Taken together, these two documents suggest several points. First, either at least part of *The Public Spirit of the Whigs* was available to hostile readers earlier than 23 February or Mar moved against the pamphlet very rapidly indeed. If the latter, then, within four days the pamphlet was officially complained of, vetted by someone competent to judge it susceptible of prosecution, and, perhaps, submitted to the Queen and judged offensive by her. Additionally, Mar, anticipating the action taken in the House of Lords a few days later, interrogated Morphew and through him identified Barber as the man—next to the author, of course—most worth prosecuting in the case. It is possible that all this was done between 23 and 27 February, but, given bureaucratic cumbersomeness, I suspect it took longer. It is also possible that the Queen was not consulted and that Mar's references to her on both 27 February and 1 March constitute the same sort of legal fiction as that by which the monarch is always supposed to be present in King's or Queen's Bench Court. On the other hand, in passages I shall consider later, Swift twice describes Anne's role as decisive.[18] Further, Mar's words, "by Her Maties express command," seem specifically to reject formulaic legalism.

I am inclined to believe, therefore, that Anne played both an early and a major role in the prosecution occasioned by Swift's pamphlet.

Second, whether or not the Queen was consulted at this point in the case, Mar clearly chose to prosecute aggressively those concerned with Swift's pamphlet. The vigor of his wording alone seems sufficient to demonstrate that he intended no "mock prosecution." But there is also other evidence of his exasperated purposiveness. First, he, not the House of Lords, initiated prosecution against Barber, and he did so well before the opening of Parliament. Second, he proceeded against Barber with such confidence that he neglected to secure any but hearsay evidence to connect Barber with *The Public Spirit of the Whigs*. This failure proved to be legally significant. Third, he bound Barber over to the Court in a substantial sum. The printer himself was required to provide £400 in bail and to secure two sureties for his good behavior in the sum of £200 each.[19] Mar's procedures thus conform to what we know of the man. Loyal to Scotland and strong-willed, Mar was unlikely to play cat's paw in this case simply to save Harley from embarrassment. Rather, he played out his own game, just as he had when he broke with the administration's policy toward Scotland earlier in 1713.[20]

The next two documents generated by the case demonstrate how fully Mar and the opposition lords controlled the game. The first of these documents possesses an ironic poignancy. Mar had, we shall see, no secretary competent to take the recognizances necessary to guarantee Barber's bail and sureties.[21] Mar therefore borrowed the services of Erasmus Lewis, secretary to William Bromley, one of Mar's two fellow Secretaries of State. Lewis, of course, was Harley's long-time protégé and Swift's friend. But Lewis had no choice. He took the recognizances and forwarded them to Treasury Solicitor Borrett with an enclosed explanatory note. The note, a copy of which occurs in Bromley's letter book, is an instance of reluctant, but helpless, compliance.

Sir
Yesterday Morning I took the enclosed Recognizances for the Appearance of Mr Barber at the Queen's Bench Bar on the first Day of next Term, the Fact of which he is accused having been under the examination of the Earl of Mar, by whose Direction I took these Recognizances there is nothing farther incumbent on me than barely to transmit them to you.
I am &c.
E. Lewis
2ᵈ March 1713/14 [22]

The second document exhibits similar impotence. On 11 March, we recall, the Lords voted to petition the Queen to issue a proclamation for the discovery of the author of *The Public Spirit of the Whigs*. On 13 March, Lord Bolingbroke supplied to Attorney General Northey a copy of the petition along with enclosed directions. A copy of both the petition and the directions occurs in Bolingbroke's letter book. The petition can be read in *The Prose Writings of Jonathan Swift*.[23] The directions are as follows:

Whitehall 13th March 1713/14
Sir

    I transmit to you by the Queen's Command a Copy of an Address of the House of Lords to her Ma:^{ty}, that you may prepare a Draught of Such a Proclamation as is therein desired, and attend the Lords of the Councill with it at my Office tomorrow at Six in the Evening. You will be pleased also to inform your self what Rewards have been usually offer'd on the like occasions, and acquaint the Lords therewith. I am

          Sir   Your most humble Servant
                Bolingbroke.[24]

Swift, we recall, was pleased in 1738 to extract a little comfort from the size of the reward offered for his discovery: "The Reason for offering so small a Sum was, that the Queen and Ministry had no Desire to have our supposed Author taken into Custody."[25] It seems, however, that Swift was nearer the mark in his exasperated comment to Peterborough on 18 May 1714: "So well protected are those who scribble for the Government."[26]

    It seems also that once the storm in Parliament had thundered forth into the world as a royal proclamation against the author of *The Public Spirit of the Whigs*, neither Harley nor Bolingbroke much bestirred themselves about the legal case that pended against Barber and therefore still threatened Swift. So far as I can discover, the next move in that case belonged to Mar, who, on 29 March, addressed a second letter to Attorney General Northey. Mar failed to have a copy made of this letter, so its contents must be inferred from the answer Northey returned to it, on 2 April.[27] Such inference is easy. Northey answered letters in a lawyerly way, detailing what he supposed his correspondent had told him, and then answering what he believed he had been asked:

April 2^d 1714
My Lord

    In obedience to her Ma:^{ties} comands signified to me by your Lop: the first of March last, I have prepared an information, which may be exhibited the first day of next term against John Barber for printing a seditious Pamphlet entituled the publick Spirit of the whigs &c: your Lords^p is pleas'd in your letter of the 29th of March to take notice, that for the reasons therein mentioned, you were under a necessity of sending me a Book not markt, but that you Judg'd there were sufficient grounds for charging Barber, and therefore bound him to appear in the

Queen's bench the next terme, and that on the third of March it appearing before the house of Lords that Robert Lamburn and Freeman Collins knew most of that affair, your Lords? hath bound them to give Evidence, tho they declared they could not swear to any particular book, but as you really believe Barber to be guilty your Lop: hopes the Testimony of those men will [word omitted here: prove?] him so, and that if you conceived it would be of any service in order to a more effectual prosecution of Barber that his servants should be examined in your office, it should imediatly be done, and their informations transmitted to me, I beg leave to acquaint your Lop: that it will be necessary to have a farther Examination of that affair, and that without further Guidence than what your Lop: mentions, the Prosecution of Barber will be ineffectual, for that to convict Barber of printing that Libell, by the course of proceedings in Law the very Book to be produced in Evidence against him must be proved to have been printed by him, and his confession that he printed a book with that Title will not be sufficient. I am

My Lord Your Lords.ᵖˢ most
obedient humble Servant
Edw: Northey

With Northey's letter, we arrive at the legal nub of the matter. Mar knows that Barber is guilty of printing Swift's attack upon the Scots peerage. On 6 and 9, but not 3, March, Freeman Collins, a compositor employed by Barber, and Robert Lamborn (or Lambert), an occasional employee, or smooter, testified that each had set for Barber a part of *The Public Spirit of the Whigs* from manuscript copy.[28] Each was prepared to repeat his evidence, and Mar was prepared to secure further depositions. Indeed, either the close of Northey's letter is merely hypothetical, or Mar had already secured Barber's confession that he printed a book titled *The Public Spirit of the Whigs*.

But all of this evidence is worthless in law. Through the first two "editions" of *The Public Spirit of the Whigs*, Barber published at least five states of Swift's text. These states, usefully described by John Harris,[28a] consist of an uncensored "first edition," an uncensored "second edition," a lightly-censored "second edition," a heavily-censored "first edition," and a heavily-censored "second edition." All these states, uncensored and censored in both "editions," share substantially the same setting of type. Swift's attack on Scots and Scotland is incompletely suppressed in the lightly-censored state, and awkwardly excised in the heavily-censored state. Nevertheless, due to Mar's failure to secure a "markt" uncensored copy of *The Public Spirit of the Whigs*, the very existence of the censored versions sufficed to place Barber beyond prosecution.

Legal practice dictated that when a supposedly libelous pamphlet or newspaper was purchased as evidence for possible prosecution of its producers, the copy purchased was by its purchaser immediately inscribed with the date, place of purchase, name of vendor, and any other information pertinent to future legal action. As Secretary of State Townshend in 1729 instructed Samuel Gray, Messenger of the Press, publications were to "be marked by the Person or Persons who shall buy the same, to the end there may be sufficient Evidence against the Publisher thereof, in case such pamphlet or News Paper shall contain anything liable to a prosecution."[29] Mar neglected to take this crucial step. By the time he realized his error, he was apparently unable to purchase an uncensored copy of Swift's pamphlet in such a way as to inculpate Barber. In a deathbed biography of Barber, Edmund Curll, or his understrapper, claims that even Barber's printing house was searched.[30] If so, the search failed. Barber could safely claim that indeed he had published *The Public Spirit of the Whigs*. For his part, Mar could only fret and scurry.

Whatever else, Mar remained active. A week after receiving Northey's letter, he produced a dozen depositions and the following answer to Northey:

Whitehall April 9.th 1714
S.[r]

Understanding by yours of the 2.[d] Inst:, that before you could carry on an effectual prosecution against Barber, for printing that seditious pamphlet, entituled the publick Spirit of the whigs, it would be necessary that there should be a farther Examination into that affair, I accordingly gave directions for takeing the informations of the witnesses upon Oath; and recommended the care of it to M.[r] Lewis, my own Secretary not being as yet in the Commission of the peace. You'l receive therefore herewith the depositions of twelve persons who have been examined, most of them servants to Barber, and employ'd in his printing house. They seem all to agree, that a Book with this title was printed at Barber's printing house, and from a manuscript Copy. how far this Evidence will be sufficient in Law to convict Barber, I must leave it to you to Judge I am
S.[r]
Your most obedient
humble Servant
Mar.[31]

From a legal point of view, this letter contains no news. The depositions, which I have been unable to locate, could have had no legal weight. Despite their tantalizing bibliographical interest, apparently none of them affirmed that Swift's five offending paragraphs had been set or printed in Barber's shop. Therefore, even if one puts aside the particular politics of this case, one would not expect Northey to initiate a prosecution against Barber. "It was," as Hanson remarks, "vital to the prestige of government that it should not begin proceedings unless there was almost a certainty of securing a conviction, and the Attorney-General [i.e., Attorneys General] was not slow to point this out."[32] In this case, conviction appears to have been impossible to secure and also, from the government's viewpoint, undesirable. I take it as a measure, therefore, of Mar's hostile persistence and of the inattention or helplessness of Oxford and Bolingbroke that on the first day of Easter Term, 14 April 1714, Northey entered charges against Barber in the Queen's Bench Court.

These charges resulted in the generation of five records: two notices that John Barber was to appear on 14 April in the Queen's Bench Court to answer an information against him, the original information submitted by Edward Northey on 14 April, a court record of the events of 14 April, including a copy of the original information, and a jury summons to cause twelve good men to appear in court on the first day of Trinity term, 28 May, in order to try Barber.[33]

Like all informations for libel, the one entered against Barber is repetitive and methodically abusive. Barber is accused, among other things, of being

...a seditious malicious man and an assiduous Publisher of false and seditious libels and plotting and intending the greatest damage and wickedness to the Most Serene Lady the Queen and her Government [and] to scandalize and vilify the right honourable peers and nobles of the Kingdom of Scotland.

Such formulaic, if full-mouthed, imprecations aside, the legal effect of the information is to accuse Barber of breaking the Queen's Peace by having "both published and printed and caused to be published" a libel entitled *The Public Spirit of the Whigs*.

This charge is grave.[34] It is criminal in eighteenth-century common law and punishable by any or all of the following: fine, imprisonment, pillory, whipping, loss of ears, and branding. In this case, however, lack of evidence rendered the case flaccid. The court record indicates that the information against Barber was read out on 14 April, that Barber's attorney, Francis Pember, responded on his behalf with a plea of not guilty, and that a jury trial was agreed to by both the defense and the Crown. There the record ceases, with the exception of the jury summons.

Almost certainly, the Crown closed the case by declaring that it would not further prosecute Barber. *Nolle prosequi* declarations were commonly entered into the record of cases so terminated. But the practice was not invariable.[35] At all events, the interest of the case consists, not in its lame conclusion, but in what we learn from it about the facts and the meaning of the publication of Swift's pamphlet.

As to matter of fact, the documents generated by the case are provocative. Both the original information and the copy entered into court record agree that Barber published *The Public Spirit of the Whigs* "on the tenth day of February" 1713/14. This assertion may be an innocent mistake, but, for two reasons, it probably is not. First, owing to Mar's assiduity, Northey possessed by 14 April a sufficient number of depositions to avoid misdating Swift's pamphlet. Second, the consequence of misdating discouraged inadvertence. To cite Hanson again, "The slightest error in an indictment was sufficient to secure the acquittal of the prisoner. It was seriously maintained in [John] Tutchin's case [for libel, 1704] that he ought to be acquitted because he was not described as 'gentleman' in the indictment, and he finally owed his discharge to the fact that a mistake had been made in the date of the distringas."[36] Hanson's instance itself demonstrates that mistakes sometimes happened. Yet one supposes they were not common.

Knowing the consequence of an error in an indictment, one must acknowledge the grotesque possibility that *The Public Spirit of the Whigs* was purposively misdated in Northey's information in order to effect a last-ditch escape for Barber. But Northey's letter of 2 April demonstrates, I think, that he had no need for so brazen a ruse. Finally, therefore, the most likely explanation for the publication date supplied in the information is that some form of *The Public Spirit of the Whigs* did in fact enter into circulation 10 February 1713/14.

Additional evidence can be advanced to support this early publication date. From the Lords' minutes we learn that Barber employed Robert Lamborn (or Lambert) specifically to set *The Public Spirit of the Whigs*, that Lamborn began work on or about 2 February, and that Freeman Collins also set some of the pamphlet.[37] Nothing, therefore, appears to preclude the physical production of the pamphlet by 10 February. Second, on 11 February, Swift wrote to Joshua Dawson in Ireland asking him to renew Swift's Letter of Absence. In his request, Swift emphasized that the letter should "not be limited in point of Place." F. Elrington Ball supposed that Swift's emphasis might reflect "the need of refuge if the authorship of 'The Public Spirit of the Whigs'...became known."[38] Ball assumed Swift's pamphlet was not published until 23 February. But if, on 11 February, Swift could already anticipate something of the reaction his pamphlet would generate, Ball's supposition becomes more apposite. Third, on 20 February, Robert Harley recorded the following memorandum:

feb:20
    1713/14   Scotland
      I have done the utmost to support the

Peers—& at the same
time to secure their Reputation.

They do all they can by their distrust
to authenticate all the Scandals
that their enemys cast
on them.[39]

Many Caledonian improprieties might have occasioned Harley's exasperated scrawl. But among them, certainly, is the self-righteous over-reac-
tion Swift described in 1738: "Upon the first Publication of [*The Public
Spirit of the Whigs*], all the *Scotch* Lords, then in *London*, went in a Body,
and complained to Queen *Anne* of the Affront put on them and their Nation
by the Author of this treatise."[40] Because of its date, it is hard not to read
Harley's memorandum as further evidence that Swift's pamphlet was
known before 23 February.

Nevertheless, though I am inclined to believe that Swift's pamphlet was
in some sort available on or about 10 February, this belief raises problems
that I cannot resolve. First, any version of *The Public Spirit of the Whigs*
published before 15 February must lack those three paragraphs in which
Swift answers Steele's *The Englishman: Being the Close of the Paper So
Called*. No such version of Swift's pamplet has ever been described. Second,
though the pattern of advertisements for Swift's pamphlets is provocative,
as detailed above, the fact is that advertisements continue to appear beyond
10 February, suggesting that the pamphlet had not yet been published. Third,
if a version of Swift's pamphlet appeared on 10 February and gave offense,
the offensive paragraphs could readily have been excised by 15 February.
Yet the offense is repeated in copies of the putative first and second editions
of *The Public Spirit of the Whigs*, copies that could not have been published
prior to 15 February. One might offer hypothetical resolutions to these
problems, but with no further evidence to offer, I am unwilling to do so. It
seems better to remark that the contradictory import of the evidence I have
presented finally suggests that *The Public Spirit of the Whigs* was produced
and circulated in ways too complicated to reconstruct from the remaining
evidence and too mercurial to fix within a single publication date.

Similarly, the documents I have found dissolve, not correct, the meaning
previous scholars educed from the events surrounding the publication of
Swift's pamphlet. Partly, I suspect, Swiftians constructed the fable of Mar's
clever ploy out of love for simple conflicts and neat endings. The documents
offer neither pleasure. In place of a strong administration, unified in its
desire to protect Swift, we find only the everydayness of cabinet infighting,

inattention, and misunderstandings. In place of a defined ending, we read a case that dribbles on for months and, to speak strictly, never ends. Even the delight of éclaircissement eludes us. Only an ironist can enjoy the fact that Swift appears never to have grasped the role that Mar played in the prosecution against Barber. On 19 February 1728/29, Swift listed Mar third among nineteen "men of distinction and my friends who are yet alive."[41]

Finally, however, the story of Mar's ploy probably owes less to our literary imaginings than to our wrong use of Swift's literary imagination. Swift did not know all the facts of the prosecution occasioned by his pamphlet. More importantly, even the facts that he knew are altered in his narration of them. Thus, in the advertisement he appended to Faulkner's 1738 publication of his pamphlet, Swift, having described the Scots lords' visit to Queen Anne, affirms that because of that visit "a Proclamation was published by her Majesty, offering a Reward of three hundred Pounds...." One presumes that Swift knew that Anne's proclamation was effected through the petition of the entire House of Lords, not the wishes of the Scots lords alone. But Swift liked the story better as he told it.

Closer to the event, in 1714, Swift altered the story more radically still. In "The Author upon Himself" he wrote:

> Now, Madam *Coningsmark* her Vengeance vows
> On S—'s Reproaches for her murder'd Spouse
> From her red Locks her Mouth with Venom fills;
> And thence into the Royal Ear instills.
> The Qu— incenc'd, his Services forgot,
> Leaves him a Victim to the vengeful *Scot*;
> Now, through the Realm a Proclamation spread,
> To fix a Price on his devoted Head.
> While innocent, he scorns ignoble Flight;
> His watchful Friends preserve him by a Sleight.[42]

In these lines, the very occasion of the proclamation is almost suppressed. The Queen's willingness to abandon Swift to Scots vengeance is attributed to Coningsmark's resentment over "The Windsor Prophecy." *The Public Spirit of the Whigs* descends to a footnote. Swift's lines offer experiential truth, I believe, extracted from historical circumstance. But the process is not reversible. To Irvin Ehrenpreis as well as to others, Abel Boyer's slippery report appeared to answer the question posed by the last line of this passage: what "Sleight" did Swift mean? The appearance deceived. Boyer's report is itself bad history, and it cannot be proved to be an accurate gloss even of Swift's perception of fact.

On the other hand, "The Author upon Himself" is illuminated by the mundane, fragmented documentary story that we have traced. The poem is about the fate in politics of high gifts and noble aspirations. It is strongly overwritten: contrasts are heightened; particulars drop out. What remains is a heroically innocent Swift, preserved, not by his truth or righteousness, but by a "Sleight" that defines the world that he hoped to reform. The same intractable world emerges from Mar's letters, Northey's legalisms, Lewis's impotence. Swift's lines do not correspond to historical events on a piecemeal basis. Yet, ironically, they are more true to Swift's experience, I believe, than our over-tidy reading of them had allowed us to see.

[1] The fullest narrative of the events I summarize is that of Maurice J. Quinlan, "The Prosecution of Swift's *Public Spirit of the Whigs*," *Texas Studies in Literature and Language*, 9 (1967), 167–84. See also Herman Teerink, *A Bibliography of the Writings of Jonathan Swift*, ed. Arthur H. Scouten, 2nd ed. (Philadelphia, 1963), pp. 299–302; *The Rothschild Library: A Catalogue of the Collection of Eighteenth-Century Printed Books and Manuscripts*, 2 vols. (Cambridge, 1954), 2056; *The Correspondence of Jonathan Swift*, ed. Harold Williams, rev. David Woolley, 5 vols. (Oxford, 1963–72), II, 11, n.4, 12, n.1, 15, n.2 (hereafter cited as *Corresp.*); [*The Prose Writings of Jonathan Swift*], ed. Herbert Davis et al., 14 vols. (1939–68; various reimpressions, sometimes corrected, Oxford, 1957–69), VIII, xv–xxii, 201 (hereafter cited as *Prose*); *The Poems of Jonathan Swift*, ed. Harold Williams, 3 vols., 2nd ed. (Oxford, 1958), I, 179–80 and n., 195 n., 196 n. (hereafter cited as *Poems*); Irvin Ehrenpreis, *Swift: The Man, His Works, and the Age*, 3 vols. (London, 1962–83), II, 702–13. These accounts depend on some or all of the following documents: County Record Office, Leicester, England, Finch Manuscripts, Box XI, Bundle 150; *Post Boy*, 20–23 Feb., 23–25 Feb.; *Examiner*, 29 Jan.–1 Feb.; *The Wentworth Papers: 1705–1739*, ed. J. J. Cartwright (London, 1883), pp. 359–61; *Manuscripts of the House of Lords: 1712–1714*, ed. Maurice F. Bond, n.s. X, in continuation of the volumes issued under the authority of the Historical Manuscripts Commission (London, 1953), 226–29; *Journal of the House of Lords*, XIX, 628–36; *Political State of Great Britain*, 7 (1714), 215–23; Ebenezer Timberland, *The History and Proceedings of the House of Lords*, II (London: Timberland, 1742), 404–08; Nicholas Tindal, *The Continuation of Mr. Rapin's History of England*, vol. XVIII (vol. VI of *Continuation*), 5th ed. (London, 1763), 149–53; William Cobbett, *Parliamentary History of England*, VI (London, 1810), cols. 1259–65.

[2] See J. A. Downie and David Woolley, "Swift, Oxford, and the Composition of Queen's Speeches, 1710–1714," *British Library Journal*, 8 (1982), 121–46.

[3] *Journal of the House of Lords*, XIX, 635.

[4] *Prose*, VIII, 30.

[5] *Prose*, VIII, xvii.

[6] *Prose*, VIII, 32.

[7] *Corresp.*, II, 10.

[8] *Prose*, VIII, 66–67.

[9] *Manuscripts of the House of Lords: 1712–1714*, p. 224.

[10] Like an indictment, an information is a formal presentment of charges against an accused. Unlike an indictment, an information does not require the action of a grand jury but may be preferred in Queen's Bench Court by any one of several of the queen's legal officers; see Sir James Fitzjames Stephen, *A History of the Criminal Law in England*, 3 vols. (London, 1883), I, 249, and also Francis Ludlow Holt, *The Law of Libel*, 2nd ed. (London, 1816), pp. 251–64.

[11] *Political State of Great Britain*, 7 (1714), 220–21.

[12] *Manuscripts of the House of Lords: 1712–1714*, pp. 227–28.

[13] Ehrenpreis, II, 710.

[14] *Government and the Press: 1695–1763* (Oxford, 1936), p. 75.

[15] *Manuscripts of the House of Lords: 1712–1714*, p. 227.

[16] PRO, Scotland, Secretaries' Letter Book, Earl of Mar, S.P. 55/2, p. 25.

[17] Pp. 25–26.

[18] *Poems*, I, 195; *Prose*, VIII, 30.

[19] These sums do not appear in Mar's letters, of course. They can be found in E. H. Lushington's *An Account of Persons Held to Bail to Answer in the Court of the King's Bench for Libels from 1 Anne to 57 Geo. 3, both Inclusive* (Ordered to be Printed 3d March 1818), p. 6. A copy of the printed report and manuscripts pertinent to its preparation are contained in PRO, K.B. 33/24/2. Additional collateral manuscripts exist in K.B. 33/5/10.

[20] *DNB*, Erskine, John, 6th or 11th Earl of Mar of the Erskine line (1675–1732).

[21] Generally, a recognizance is a legal instrument by which one acknowledges that one would incur a specified debt should one fail to perform a particular future action (such as appearing in court or causing another person so to appear). See Anthony Highmore's *A Digest of the Doctrine of Bail* (London, 1783), reprinted in 1978 by Garland Publishing along with Sir Edward Coke's *A Little Treatise of Baile and Mainprize* (1635).

[22] PRO, Secretaries' Letter Book, William Bromley, S.P. 44/115, p. 180.

[23] *Prose*, VIII, 198–99.

[24] PRO, Secretaries' Letter Book, Lord Bolingbroke, S.P. 44/114, p. 342.

[25] *Prose*, VIII, 30.

[26] *Corresp.*, II, 22.

[27] PRO, Scotland, Secretaries' Letter Book, Earl of Mar, S.P. 55/2, pp. 29–30.

[28] *Manuscripts of the House of Lords: 1712–1714*, pp. 227–28.

[28a] "Swift's *The Publick Spirit of the Whigs*: A Partly Censored State of the Scottish Paragraphs," *Papers of the Bibliographical Society of America*, 72 (1978), 92–94.

[29] PRO, K.B. 33/5/6.

[30] *An Impartial History of the Life, Character, Amours, Travels, and Transactions of Mr. John Barber, City-Printer, Common-Councilman, Alderman, and Lord Mayor of London. Written by Several Hands* (London: E. Curll, 1741), p. 6.

[31] PRO, Scotland, Secretaries' Letter Book, Earl of Mar, S.P. 55/2, p. 31.

[32] *Government and the Press: 1695–1763*, p. 55.

[33] All of these are in the Public Record Office. One of the two appearance notices occurs in a Rule or Order Book, K.B. 21/28, fol. 126; the other appears in a Controlment Roll, K.B. 29/373, membrane 7. The information is contained in Indictments, London and Middlesex, K.B. 10/15, part I, Easter term, London. The full court record occurs in Crown Roll, K.B. 28/49, case 19. The jury summons is noted on membrane 11 of the Controlment Roll already cited. I am grateful to James P. Derriman for aid in translating these documents.

[34] "The Government's Response to Swift's *An Epistle to a Lady,*" *Philological Quarterly*, 65 (1986), 50–51. In this essay, I erred in at least one point of law. On p. 51, I understood literally the following notation from K.B. 28/131, case 13: "On which said Thursday next after the Octave of St. Hilary…the sheriffs of London sent not their writ for the purpose.…" In fact, the notation is a fiction for a grant of continuance. See R. J. and A. B. Corner, *The Practice of the Crown Side of the Court of Queen's Bench, with an Appendix containing the New Rules of Practice* (London, 1844), pp. 144–47.

[35] "The Government's Response," p. 52.

[36] *Government and the Press: 1695–1763*, p. 57.

[37] *Manuscripts of the House of Lords: 1712–1714*, p. 228.

[38] *The Correspondence of Jonathan Swift*, ed. F. Elrington Ball, 6 vols. (London, 1910–14), II, 126, n. 3.

[39] BL, Portland Loan, MS Loan 29/10, Harley memorandums, section 11.

[40] *Prose*, VIII, 30.

[41] *Correspondence*, ed. Ball, V, 466.

[42] These lines are quoted from the English Faculty Library, Oxford, uncanceled copy of the second volume of *The Works of J.S, D.D, D.S.P.D.* (Dublin: Faulkner, 1735), pp. 346–47.

I gathered much of the information included in this essay while I held a grant from the National Endowment for the Humanities. I most gratefully acknowledge that support.

Frank H. Ellis

Swift's Phillis, or, The Progress of Self-Deception

> The heart is deceitful above all things.
> Jeremiah 17:9

THE ROAD FROM LONDON TO WINDSOR begins in Piccadilly, skirts Hyde Park, winds southwest through Kensington, Hammersmith, Hounslow, and then proceeds straight as a Roman road to Staines. At Staines the road crosses the Thames, turns sharp right, and in three miles reaches Windsor. Back and forth over this road in the Lord Treasurer's coach Swift and Oxford traveled twelve times between July 1711 and October 1713 while Swift was writing *The Conduct of the Allies* and *The History of the Four Last Years of the Queen* and Oxford was dancing attendance upon the Queen.[1] Swift and Oxford recalled these junkets with evident pleasure, first in May 1714 in "The Author upon Himself":

> And, *Harley*, not asham'd his Choice to own,
> Takes him to *Windsor* in his Coach, alone;[2]

then in "Horace, Lib. 2. Sat. 6. Part of It Imitated," written in July 1714:

> HARLEY...
> Would take me in his Coach to chat,
> And question me of this and that;
> As, "What's a-Clock?" And, "How's the Wind?"
> "Whose Chariot's that we left behind?
> Or gravely try to read the Lines
> Writ underneath the Country *Signs*;...
> As once a week we travel down
> To *Windsor*, and again to Town;[3]

next in Oxford's letter of August 1717:

Two years retreat [in the Tower] has made me taste the conversation of my Dearest Friend with a greater relish, than even at the time of my being charm'd with it in our frequent journeys to Windsor;[4]

and again in the last lines of "Phillis, or, The Progress of Love":

> For John is Landlord, Phillis Hostess;
> They keep at Stains the old blue Boar,
> Are Cat and Dog, and Rogue and Whore.[5]

Aside from its memorialization in Swift's poem, Staines's fame is geological. "Staines is the only place west of London where it is possible to cross the Thames without leaving gravel for alluvial soils."[6] The annual flood in the Thames valley makes this an important consideration for traffic between London and the southwest. So the bridge at Staines is the most important structure in the town. The design of the two lower stories of the west tower of St. Mary's Church turns out *not* to be the work of Inigo Jones.[7] But the bridge at Staines, mentioned in Roman times, was blown up during the Civil Wars and rebuilt in 1684–87. In Swift's day and for a hundred years thereafter it was still made of wood (fig. 1).

Both the Queen and her Lord Treasurer were notoriously thirsty, so traffic between London and Windsor required an unusually large number of inns at Staines. "There were between 12 and 20 licensed houses in the 18th century."[8] One of these was the Blue Anchor, "a stately inn of c. 1700 with red and vitrified bricks in a chequerboard pattern."[9] It may be the historical counterpart of the old Blue Boar.[10] Even today "a room on the first floor has early 18th-century panelling and a fireplace with brackets and panelled overmantel."[11]

Although Swift's poem that mentions Staines could have been written any time after July 1711, Stella's fair copy is headed "Written A.D. 1719."[12] Unfortunately there is no evidence to confirm Stella's date. But neither is there any reason to doubt it.[13] In May 1719 Swift bought himself an expensive horse and set off on a summer ramble.[14] Vanessa in Dublin was complaining bitterly of neglect and refusing "to sitt down contented with this treatment."[15] Swift may have been glad to get away. "Quand j'auray mes pensees et mes tems libre, la Muse viendra," he told her.[16] "Fair Maidens all attend the Muse" (73) becomes one line in "Phillis, or, The Progress of Love." During his summer ramble Swift stayed in country houses, including Gaulstown in Westmeath and Camolin Park, County Wexford, where gossip about servants was a staple of conversation. But he also liked to stay in bush taverns, where "Lodgings for a penny" were advertised, to enjoy "the vulgar dialect" of wagoners and hostlers.[17] After a long hiatus between May and December of 1719 Swift's correspondence picks up again back in Dublin, where he is recovering from a bad attack of labyrinthine vertigo and "a pitifull broken shin." "I write nothing but Verses of late," he tells Charles Ford, "and they are all Panegyricks."[18] "Panegyricks" is not improbably an ironic surrogate for three poems with the word "Progress" in the title,

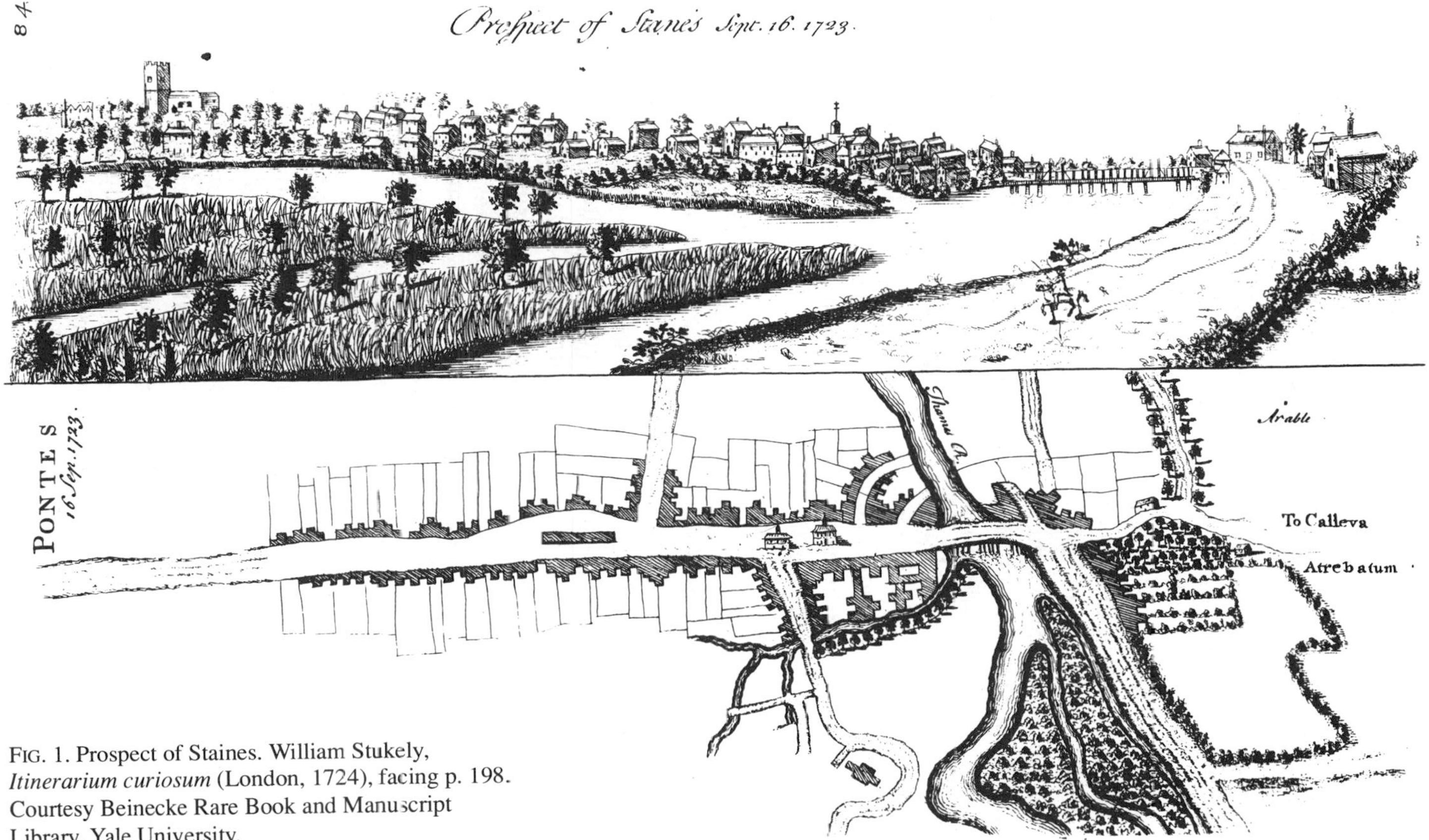

FIG. 1. Prospect of Staines. William Stukely, *Itinerarium curiosum* (London, 1724), facing p. 198. Courtesy Beinecke Rare Book and Manuscript Library, Yale University.

in which the progress is always a downfall, or at least an eclipse, which, as Francis Bacon observed, is a melancholy thing. But this is all speculation. Stella's date for the poem remains unconfirmed.

The juxtaposition of "Phillis" and "Love" in the title of the poem may not, however, be fortuitous. It already existed in a popular tune title. Swift was a schoolboy in 1681 when Thomas D'Urfey set "An Excellent New Ballad" attacking Shaftesbury to the tune of "How unhappy is Phillis in love." As little as he liked music, Swift could hardly have avoided this tune: "An Excellent New Ballad" was thrice anthologized (the third time in 1719–20), and nine other broadside ballads were set to the same tune.[19]

The poem that Swift wrote in 1711–19 only ends in Staines. It begins somewhere else, possibly in England but more likely in Ireland, in the possibly existential but more likely notional country house of some innominate squire. Generically the poem is a comedy. It is worked up from that paradigmatic family embarrassment, the daughter who elopes with the butler. Swift designates the plot a "Farce" (96), and it conforms exactly to Northrop Frye's formula for New Comedy (C_n):

$$C_n = GMB \rightarrow GWB \mid BLOCK \mid COMIC\ PERIPETEIA \rightarrow GGB^{20}$$

The action begins when Phillis meets John, her father's butler (GMB). The complications begin when Phillis wants John (GWB). Of blocks there is a sufficiency of two kinds: (1) socio-economic (Phillis and John belong to different social classes and different economic levels) and (2) cultural (Phillis is engaged to marry the man of her father's choice and her wedding day arrives, to the "happy rustle of bridal gowns and banknotes," in Frye's phrase). The comic peripeteia begins when Phillis absconds on her wedding day and ends with her mother reading the letter to the father left on Phillis's dressing table. Despite a degree of irony sufficient "to get the audience confused about its sense of the social norm," the story ends as a comedy should: Phillis gets John (GGB).[21] The comic plot is generated by the opposition of self-deprecating eirons and self-important alazons. The comic tone is generated by assorted clowns (a Fortune-teller, an unfee'd Vicar, a redundant Bridegroom, "Swains unwholsome") and by alazons repeating the obsession that holds them in bondage: "the Bride was missing, / The Mother scream'd" (26–27); the Father orders John to "bring her back, alive or dead," but "John was missing too" (38–40).

The plot of the poem may also be expressed in terms of folklore motifs:[22]

Motif	Phillis, or, The Progress of Love
J2521: Extreme prudery.	Desponding Phillis was endu'd With ev'ry Talent of a Prude,
K2051: Adulteress feigns unusual sensitiveness.	She trembled when a Man drew near;
K2051.3: Adulteress feigns great disdain of men.	Salute her, and she turn'd her Ear:
K2051.1: Adulteress pretends shame before male.	If o'er against her you were plac't She durst not look above your Wast;
	She'd rather take you to her Bed Than let you see her dress her Head;
K2058: Pretended piety.	In Church you heard her thrô the Crowd Repeat the Absolution loud; 10
T55: Girl as wooer.	In Church, secure behind her Fan She durst behold that Monster, Man: There practic'd how to place her Head, And bit her Lips to make them red:
T55.6: Woman exhibits figure.	Or on the Matt devoutly kneeling Would lift her Eyes up to the Ceeling, And heave her Bosom unaware For neighb'ring Beaux to see it bare.
T131.1.2.1: Girl must marry father's choice.	At length a lucky Lover came, And found Admittance from the Dame. 20 Suppose all Partyes now agreed, The Writings drawn, the Lawyer fee'd, The Vicar and the Ring bespoke: Guess how could such a Match be broke. See then what Mortals place their Bliss in!
R225.2: Lovers elope to prevent girl's marriage to undesired fiancé.	Next morn betimes the Bride was missing, The Mother scream'd, the Father chid,
T133.4: Bridegroom… come[s] for the bride.	Where can this idle Wench be hid? No news of Phil. The Bridegroom came, And thought his Bride had sculk't for shame, 30 Because her Father us'd to say The Girl had such a Bashfull way.
H1385.2: Quest for vanished daughter.	Now, John the Butler must be sent To learn the Way that Phillis went; The Groom was wisht to saddle Crop, For John must neither light nor stop; But find her where so'er she fled, And bring her back, alive or dead.

See here again the Dev'l to do;
For truly John was missing too: 40
R225.1: Elopement on   The Horse and Pillion both were gone
  winged horse.   Phillis, it seems, was fled with John.
K1271.2: Lovers...make   Old Madam who went up to find
  absurd excuses.   What Papers Phil had left behind,
                          A Letter on the Toylet sees
                          To my much honor'd Father; These:
                          ('Tis always done, Romances tell us,
                          When Daughters run away with Fellows)
                          Fill'd with the choicest common-places,
                          By others us'd in the like Cases.   50
T11.7: Love through sight That, long ago a Fortune-teller
  in magic mirror.   Exactly said what now befell her,
                          And in a Glass had made her see
                          A serving-Man of low Degree:
T22.3: Predestined   It was her Fate; must be forgiven;
  husband.   For Marriages are made in Heaven:
                          His Pardon begg'd, but to be plain,
                          She'd do't if 'twere to do again.
T91: Unequals in love.   Thank God, 'twas neither Shame nor Sin,
                          For John was come of honest Kin: 60
                          Love never thinks of Rich and Poor,
                          She'd beg with John from Door to Door:
                          Forgive her, if it be a Crime,
                          She'll never do't another Time,
                          She ne'r before in all her Life
                          Once disobey'd him, Maid nor Wife.
                          One Argument she summ'd up all in,
                          The Thing was done and past recalling:
                          And therefore hop'd she would recover
                          His Favor, when his Passion's over.   70
                          She valu'd not what other thought her;
                          And was—His most obedient Daughter.
                            Fair Maidens all attend the Muse
                          Who now the wandring Pair pursues:
                          Away they rode in homely Sort
T69.5: [Daughter   Their Journy long, their Money short;
  punished by marrying   The loving Couple well bemir'd,
  poor man.]   The Horse and both the Riders tir'd:
                          Their Vittells bad, their Lodging worse,
T481.1: Adulteress   Phil cry'd, and John began to curse;   80
  roughly treated by her Phil wish't, that she had strained a Limb
  lover.   When first she ventur'd out with him.

John wish't, that he had broke a Leg
When first for her he quitted Peg.
　But what Adventures more befell 'um
The Muse has now not time to tell 'um.
How Jonny wheadled, threatned, fawnd,
Till Phillis all her Trinkets pawn'd:
How oft she broke her marriage Vows
In kindness to maintain her Spouse;　　　　90
Till Swains unwholsome spoyld the Trade,
For now the Surgeon must be paid;
To whom those Perquisites are gone
In Christian Justice due to John.
　When Food and Rayment now grew scarce

**N130: Changing of luck
or fate.**

Fate put a Period to the Farce;

N400: Lucky accident.

And with exact Poetick Justice:

**Q481: Princess compelled
to keep an inn.**

For John is Landlord, Phillis Hostess;
They keep at Stains the old blue Boar,

**T256: The quarrelsome
wife and husband.**

Are Cat and Dog, and Rogue and Whore.　　100

This analysis suggests that Phillis is a gentrified version of the forthputting woman (T55). Her counterparts in Old Irish story were fairy princesses who wooed mortal men (F302.3) and by the same wiles: "At the neck-opening of her shirt [Finnabair] offered him certain fragrant sweet apples."[23] There was even a subgenre of Old Irish story called *aitheda* or elopements. Gentrification does not seem to have upset the sexual hierarchy implied in the forthputting woman motif. The perceived superiority of fairy princesses to mortal men in eighth-century Ireland may not have been any greater than the actual superiority of mistress to servant in eighteenth-century Ireland. But the fact of female sexuality upset the Victorian sensibilities of a whole generation of scholars:

These ladies [in Old French *lais*], who so boldly offer themselves to men, have long since reminded scholars of the forth-putting women with which [sic] the pages of early Celtic literature are filled.... As Heinrich Zimmer showed in one of his latest discussions, the women of early Irish saga exhibit a freedom in sexual matters which is quite foreign to the great Aryan people—a situation which points to a high degree of antiquity for the traditions recorded, and may even reflect a pre-Celtic (non-Aryan) culture.[24]

Swift did not find "freedom in sexual relations...foreign to the great Aryan peoples" who were his parishioners. He represents Phillis neither as Aryan nor atypical but as self-deceived.

"The Reader truly *Learned*" will have remarked two notable silences or lacunae in the plot of this poem. The first is The Consummation and the second is The Elopement. The second desideratum is easily supplied in a graphic medium (fig. 2). The artist evidently was a man, for Phillis has modestly turned her back. The first desideratum however is both more interesting and more difficult to illustrate—"*Hic multa desiderantur.*" But it can be supplied from the imagination of an authority on self-deception, Jean-Paul Sartre:[25]

Take the example of a woman who has consented to go out with a particular man for the first time.

Sartre tells us exactly what happened when Phillis "first...ventur'd out with" John (82):

She knows very well the intentions which the man...cherishes regarding her. She knows also that it will be necessary sooner or later for her to make a decision. But she does not want to realize the urgency; she concerns herself only with what is respectful and discreet in the attitude of her companion.

John, after all, "was come of honest Kin" (60).[26]

She does not apprehend this conduct as an attempt to achieve what we call "the first approach;" that is, she does not want to see the possibilities of temporal development which his conduct presents. She restricts this behavior to what is in the present; she does not wish to read in the phrases which he addresses to her anything other than their explicit meaning. If he says to her, "I find you so attractive!" she disarms this phrase of its sexual background; she attaches to the conversation and to the behavior of the speaker, the immediate meanings, which she imagines as objective qualities. The man who is speaking to her appears to her sincere and respectful as the table is round or square.... The qualities thus attached to the person she is listening to are in this way fixed in a permanence like that of things, which is no other than the projection of the strict present of the qualities into the temporal flux. This is because she does not quite know what she wants.

Phillis "ne'r before in all her Life / Once disobey'd" her father, "Maid nor Wife" (65–66). The full form of this phrase, "neither wife, maid nor widow," which is proverbial for "whore" (Tilley M26), seems to compromise Phillis.

She is profoundly aware of the desire which she inspires, but the desire cruel and naked would humiliate and horrify her.... In order to satisfy her, there must be a feeling which is addressed wholly to her *personality*—i.e., to her full freedom— and which would be a recognition of her freedom. But at the same time this feeling must be wholly desire; that is, it must address itself to her body as object.

FIG. 2. T. C., couple on horseback. The Bettmann Archive, Inc.

"She'd rather take you to her Bed / Than let you see her dress her Head"
(7–8).

This time then she refuses to apprehend the desire for what it is; she does not even
give it a name; she recognizes it only to the extent that it transcends itself toward
admiration, esteem, respect and that it is wholly absorbed in the more refined forms
which it produces, to the extent of no longer figuring any more as a sort of warmth
and density. But then suppose he takes her hand. This act of her companion risks
changing the situation by calling for an immediate decision. To leave the hand there
is to consent in herself to flirt, to engage herself. To withdraw it is to break the
troubled and unstable harmony which gives the hour its charm. The aim is to
postpone the moment of decision as long as possible. We know what happens next;
the young woman leaves her hand there, but she *does not notice* that she is leaving
it. She does not notice because it happens by chance that she is at this moment all
intellect. She draws her companion up to the most lofty regions of sentimental
speculation; she speaks of Life, of her life, she shows herself in her essential
aspect—a personality, a consciousness. And during this time the divorce of the
body from the soul is accomplished; the hand rests inert between the warm hands
of her companion—neither consenting nor resisting—a thing.

We shall say that this woman is in [self-deception].[27] But we see immediately
that she uses various procedures in order to maintain herself in this [self-decep-
tion].

"Desponding Phillis was endu'd / With ev'ry Talent of a Prude" (1–2).

She has disarmed the actions of her companion by reducing them to being only
what they are; that is, to existing in the mode of the in-itself. But she permits herself to enjoy his desire, to the extent that she will apprehend it as not being what it
is, will recognize its transcendence. Finally while sensing profoundly the presence
of her own body—to the degree of being disturbed perhaps—

"She trembled when a Man drew near" (3)

—she realizes herself as *not being* her own body, and she contemplates it as though
from above as a passive object to which events can *happen*

"Would lift her Eyes up to the Ceeling, / And heave her Bosom unaware"
(16–17)

but which can neither provoke them nor avoid them because all its possibilities are
outside of it.

"It was her Fate" (55), "The Thing was done" (68).

What unity do we find in these various aspects of [self-deception]? It is a certain
art of forming contradictory concepts which unite in themselves both an idea and
the negation of that idea.

"She'd do't if 'twere to do again.... She'll never do't another Time" (58, 64).

The basic concept which is thus engendered, utilizes the double property of the human being, who is at once a *facticity* and a *transcendence*.

Before she flees from home, Phillis flees from herself.

The first act of [self-deception] is to flee what it can not flee, to flee what it is (p. 70).

What is it then that Phillis is? One thing that she may not be when she appears "in Church" (9) is *virgo et intacta*. Church? "Where are more Appointments and Rendezvouzes of Gallantry?...Where more Bargains driven of all Sorts?"[28] Suspicions are aroused by Phillis's letter to her father: "She ne'r.../ Once disobey'd him, Maid nor Wife" (65–66). Wife? It would have been extremely difficult for John and Phillis to marry, but it cannot be assumed to have been impossible.

It would have been illegal for a priest to marry them without banns or a license. Licenses cost 17 or 18 shillings, more money than John made in two months. A dispensation to waive proclamation of the banns cost even more. But clandestine marriages without banns or license were solemnized every day in privileged chapels in London. In one of these, Swift remembered, a court lady was married to her footman.[29] In another of these, St. James's in Duke Place, Waitwell and Foible "were rivetted in a trice." In Hampstead clandestine marriages were performed at Sion Chapel for five shillings, and the countryside was full of marrying parsons.[30] Phillis calls herself "Wife" (66), and the narrator mentions "her marriage Vows" (89). The evidence of the poem confirms Lawrence Stone's observation that the years 1677 to 1714 were "a period when parent-child tensions over control of marriage were rising and when commercialized clandestine marriages were becoming a public scandal (and were the theme of over one third of all comedies played on the London stage)."[31] So it is at least possible that John and Phillis were clandestinely married and that the elopement was precipitated by the threatened marriage of Phillis to "a lucky Lover" (19) of her father's choice.

Suspicion that Phillis is no longer *virgo et intacta* when she absconds seems confirmed by the conclusion of Phillis's letter: "The Thing was done and past recalling" (68) and might have been aroused much sooner. "She'd rather take you to her Bed," the narrator tells us, "Than let you see her dress her Head" (7–8), which is the same kind of joke as Pope's in *The Rape of the Lock*: "Oh hadst thou, Cruel! been content to seize / Hairs less in sight, or any Hairs but these!" And whether we construe "She'd rather take you to her Bed" as the narrator's assessment of Phillis's forthputting character or as Phillis's own words overheard by the narrator, the phrase is confirmatory of "Wife" (66) and "The Thing was done" (68). With this hypothesis firmly in mind, we can now ask the question, How soon do we learn that Phillis is in a state of self-deception?

The talents of Swift's prude differ somewhat from the talents of Pope's prude, Clarissa:[31a]

> *Some Nymphs there are, too conscious of their Face,*
>
>> ...practic'd how to place her Head,
>> And bit her Lips to make them red (13–14).
>
> *For Life predestin'd to the Gnomes' Embrace.*
> *These swell their Prospects and exalt their Pride,*
> *When Offers are disdain'd, and Love deny'd.*
>
>> Salute her, and she turn'd her Ear (4).
>
> *Then gay Ideas crowd the vacant Brain;*
> *While Peers and Dukes, and all their sweeping Train,*
> *And Garters, Stars, and Coronets appear,*
> *And in soft Sounds, Your Grace salutes their Ear.*
>
>> ...a Fortune-teller
>> ...in a Glass had made her see
>> A serving-Man of low Degree (52–54).

Eaten up with Schelerian *ressentiment*, Clarissa is a social climber who rejects love. Free from *ressentiment*, Phillis is a forthputting woman who embraces love. Clarissa's talents are duplicity (III, 127) and Pollyannish platitude: "Merit wins the Soul" (V, 34). Phillis's talents are deception and self-deception. "In Church you heard her thrô the Crowd / Repeat the Absolution loud" (9–10), hypothetically because she had something to conceal that required absolution:

A general Confession to be said of the whole Congregation, after the Minister, all kneeling.
Almighty and most merciful Father; we have erred and strayed from thy ways like lost Sheep. We have followed too much the devices and desires of our own hearts. We have offended against thy holy laws....We have done those things which we ought not to have done ["The Thing was done" (68)].... But Thou, O Lord, have mercy upon us miserable offenders. Spare thou them, O God, which confess their faults. Restore thou them that are penitent.

> Or on the Matt devoutly kneeling
> Would lift her Eyes up to the Ceeling,
> And heave her Bosom unaware
> For neighb'ring Beaux to see it bare (15–18).

"Unaware" (17) establishes Phillis as self-deceiver, or in Sartre's enigmatic definition, "a being which is what it is not [a transcendence] and which is not what it is [a facticity]."[32] Here is Phillis thinking of herself as pure transcendence—another St. Agnes whose honor is preserved by a miracle (fig. 3)—while exhibiting herself as pure facticity of which she is "unaware" (17).

The self-deception is even more obvious in the contradictions of her letter:

> She'd do't if 'twere to do again....
> She'll never do't another Time (58, 64).
>
> ... disobey'd him...
> And was—His most obedient Daughter (66, 72).

To this point in the poem the narrator addresses an undifferentiated male reader, "you" (5, 7–9), directing him to "Suppose...Guess...See" (21, 24, 25, 39). Now, with the conclusion of Phillis's letter to her father, a more focused readership is addressed: "Fair Maidens all attend the Muse" (73). At this point a reader of either sex might fear that Dean Swift is about to unload moral platitudes. And this is exactly what happens—up to a point. The wages of sin turn out, not surprisingly, to be poverty, hunger, prostitution, and disease, in that order. But no reader could anticipate the surprising conclusion to the poem:

> When Food and Rayment now grew scarce
> Fate put a Period to the Farce;
> And with exact Poetick Justice (95–97).

"Fortune turns on a Wheel"[33] was one of Swift's favorite clichés. And here he turns the wheel to end the poem. Swift evidently agreed with his friend Addison that poetic justice was a "ridiculous Doctrine."[34] "With exact Poetick Justice" but with a noticeable lack of moral justification, Phillis and John are allowed to achieve their "fundamental project":[35]

> For John is Landlord, Phillis Hostess;
> They keep at Stains the old blue Boar,
> Are Cat and Dog, and Rogue and Whore (98–100).

We catch a last glimpse of Phillis in 1725 through Defoe's eyes:

In Taverne, Coffee-Houses, and Places of publick Resort...there are handsome Barkeepers, &c. These Creatures being puff'd up with the fulsome Flattery of a set of Flesh-Flies, that are continually buzzing about 'em, carry themselves with the utmost Insolence imaginable.... I had bespoke a Dish of Rice-Tea; but Madam was so taken up with her Sparks, that she had quite forgot it.[36]

FIG. 3. Jusepe de Ribera, St. Agnes (1641). Courtesy Gemäldegalerie Alte Meister, Staatliche Kunstsammlungen, Dresden.

In realizing her fundamental project—whoredom—Phillis becomes an existential heroine; she achieves authenticity. But does she achieve grace?

However far this existentialist reading may open the poem to our understanding, sooner or later we have to face the fact that it is factitious and anachronistic. "A work of art is the product of a particular time and place," says Michael Dummett, "and cannot be fully understood save as being of that time and place."[37] This requires us to imagine how Defoe might have read the poem when it was first published in 1727. Fortunately self-deception is a topic in Puritan apologetics as well as in analytical philosophy and social psychology. Before this topic is undertaken, however, some concluding generalizations can be made about the poem.

One criticism of Swift's verse is its "failure to meet some kind of generic expectation."[38] But there is no failure of this kind in "Phillis, or, The Progress of Love." The supergenre is story; the genre is comedy *cum* moral allegory *cum* existentialist fable *cum* satire/panegyric; the subgenre is mock-romance. The three supergenres that subsume all literary works are song, story, and play (and may have evolved in this order). The assumption is that every literary work is more of one of the supergenres than the other two. "Phillis" is clearly more of a story.

While the concept of multiple genres is similar to the familiar concept of mixed genres, it is essentially different. Only the simplest literary confection—a riddle, for example—can exemplify a single genre. Every work of any complexity exemplifies two or more genres. Matthew Prior's "An Ode, Humbly Inscrib'd to the Queen" (1706) is a Horatian ode, a "Historical Poem" (like "Annus Mirabilis" [1667]), and a panegyric. The subgenre is a new variety of the advice-to-a-painter poem, *viz.* an advice-to-a-sculptor poem. The sculptor addressed is the imagined sculptor of an imagined Hadrian's column to be raised in London to celebrate the military victories of the reign of Queen Anne. Prior himself points out that "A Letter to M. Boileau" (1704) combines the "various Beauties of a familiar Epistle, a genteel Satire, and an epic Poem."[39] "Literary compositions run into each other, precisely like colours," Lord Kames observes: "we never can say where one species ends and another begins."[40]

"A Letter to M. Boileau" and "An Ode Humbly Inscrib'd to the Queen" require a subgenre because they are respectively a satire and the mirror-image of a satire, a panegyric. Generically as well as effectively satire is troublesome. The trouble is that, unlike comedy and tragedy, satire has no predetermined shape. Satire is like spat, the free-swimming oyster embryo that cannot grow into an oyster until it fixes itself to a grain of pre-existent shell. Similarly every verse satire requires a subgenre to give it shape.

Alternatively it may be said that satire is the cuckoo bird of the literary genres; it lays its eggs in other birds' nests. This explains why the great age of verse satire in England produced such a dazzling array of new subgenres: mock address-from-the-throne; mock Calves-Head-Club-hymn, mock-doxology, and the like.[41]

Because it is a satire/panegyric (subsequently to be determined), "Phillis, or, The Progress of Love" requires a subgenre. The subgenre that Swift uses is one that he had never used before, the mock-romance. Romances that roughly parallel "Phillis" are *The Squyr of Lowe Degre* (*c.*1520) and the story of Amyas in *The Faerie Queene* (1596), IV.viii.49–ix.16. The only structural parallel between *The Squyr of Lowe Degre* and "Phillis" is the unequals-in-love motif (T91). The squire of low degree falls in love with "the kings doughter of Hungre." But there the parallel ends. There is no forthputting woman and no elopement. The story of Amyas in *The Faerie Queene* is somewhat closer to "Phillis." The forthputting woman is not the fairy queen but a giant's daughter "given…to vaine delight, / And eke too loose of life." Her paramour is Amyas, the squire of low degree, whom she keeps in "captive hold" until he is freed by Prince Arthur himself (IV.viii.49, 52). There is also an elopement. Despite a possible allusion to *The Squyr of Lowe Degre* in "A serving-Man of low Degree" (54), there is no evidence that Swift read the romance. The mockery of romance is much more likely to derive from *Don Quixote* (1605–15), which Swift read repeatedly.

The style of "Phillis, or, The Progress of Love" reflects Swift's life-long interest in "the vulgar dialect." The diction is colloquial, slangy, vulgar: "the Dev'l to do" (39), "Vittells" (79). In his own copy of *Miscellanies. The Last Volume* (1727) Swift noted that "wisht" (35) was "a trades-men's Phrase" (cf. "bespoke").[42] The syntax is also conversational, almost without inversion, "Proper Words in proper Places."[43] But there is more parallelism than there is in "The Fable of Midas" (1712), for example.[44] It is a style almost without metaphor. Ninety-eight lines of non-figurative statement or narrative are broken only by Phillis's self-deceiving expletive, "that Monster, Man" (12) and the petrescent metaphor, "Cat and Dog" (100). "Dog and Cat?" Vanbrugh exclaims, "that sounds more like Man and Wife."[45] Phillis's epistolary style is distinguished from the rest of the poem by her use of the fashionable contractions that Swift feared were corrupting the language: "do't" (58, 64), "'twere" (58), "'twas" (59), "ne'r" (65). The whole poem, not just Phillis's letter to her father, is a confection of "the choicest common-places" (49).

Of these commonplaces three kinds may be distinguished. First, proverbs included in Morris P. Tilley, *A Dictionary of the Proverbs in England* (1950):

"Marriages are made in Heaven" (56) (M688), "Maid nor Wife [nor Widow]" (66) (M26). Since Tilley neglected to define *proverb*, the criteria for proverb remain as mysterious as Francis J. Child's criteria for *ballad*. This creates a second class of "choicest common-places" in "Phillis," expression in other words of proverbial sentiments or ideas: Phillis and John eloped "in homely Sort / Their Journy long, their Money short.... Phil cry'd, and John began to curse" (75–80), which rephrases such proverbs as "Marry in haste and repent at leisure" (H196) and "Marry today repent tomorrow" (M694). A French visitor to England in 1692 deplored clandestine marriages: "Hence comes the Matches between Footmen and young Ladies of Quality, who you may be sure live no very easy Life together afterwards."[46] The third class, defined by Swift as "Sayings...which have a proverbial Air [but were] not originally Proverbs"[47] and with no foundation in Tilley, is the simple cliché: "alive or dead" (38). Some of these reflect the reduplicative tendency of common speech: "neither light nor stop" (36), "neither Shame nor Sin" (59). Theoretically it should be possible to write entire works of literature in commonplaces of these three kinds. Swift comes very close to accomplishing this in *A Complete Collection of Genteel and Ingenious Conversation* (1738). "Phillis" falls only a little short.

Everything that has been said so far could have been said of a prose work. The sound effects of "Phillis" have been ignored. But the feature of the poem that is most apparent upon first reading is the amazing regularity of the closed iambic tetrameter couplet sound pattern. Of the 500 metrical feet in the poem, 490 (98%) are iambs.[48] Of 100 lines in the poem, 87 (87%) are end-stopped; of 50 couplets in the poem, 38 (76%) are pure rhymes and 50 (100%) are closed. There are no triplets. The double rhymes capture some of the carelessness and leveling of actual speech: "all in, /...recalling" (67–68), "befell 'um /...tell 'um" (85–86). This is a constant feature of the sound effects of Swift's mature style: "bottom; /...caught 'um" makes a rhyme in "The Fable of Midas" (79–80).

The tight metrical pattern is further reinforced by simple repetition: "In Church...In Church" (9, 11), "See...see" (25, 39), "When first...when first" (82, 84), "Justice...Justice" (94, 97), and most remarkable of all, "now...Now...now...now...now...now...now" (21, 33, 52, 74, 86, 92, 95), which repeats a pattern used so successfully in "A Description of the Morning" (1709): "Now...Now...Now...now."[49] The almost unbroken regularity of the sound effects is played off against the relaxed, colloquial irregularity of the style (diction *plus* syntax): "But what Adventures more befell 'um / The Muse has now not time to tell 'um" (85–86). The result, something like syncopation in music, is one of the most attractive features of the poem.

The closed iambic tetrameter couplet pattern asserts itself so strongly that any variation in the pattern calls loud attention to itself. Of the two principal kinds of metrical variation, double rhymes ("places /...Cases" [49–50]) and slant rhymes ("scarce /...Farce" [95–96]), there is more than the usual number in "Phillis": 22% and 2%, compared with 15% and none in "The Fable of Midas." The metrical variations bunch up at three places in the text, the beginning and ending of Phillis's letter to her father (47–56, 67–72) and the last lines of the poem (95–100). Half a dozen irregularities in the sound pattern of lines 67–72 focus attention on these lines: three successive double-rhymed couplets (repeating the same effect in lines 47–56), a grammatical inversion, "One Argument she summ'd up all in" (67), an unusual example of something like internal half-rhyme, "recover...Favor...over" (69–70), enjambment, "recover / His Favor" (69–70), slant rhyme, "recover /...over" (69–70), and an unusual caesura, "And was—His most obedient Daughter" (72). The sound effects of these lines slow down the reading and allow more time for the irony to take effect: the daughter who disobeys her father (65–66), in her state of self-deception signs herself and believes herself to be her father's "most obedient Daughter" (72).

The number of run-on lines in "Phillis" is just about average, 13%, to 11% in "The Fable of Midas." Most of the run-on lines, by reducing the emphasis on the last accented syllable of the first line of the couplet and increasing the emphasis on the first accented syllable of the second line of the couplet, emphasize adjectives and adverbs, modifiers and qualifiers: "EV'ry TALent" (2), "NEIGHb'ring BEAUX" (18), "exACTly SAID" (52), "a SERVing-MAN" (54), "ONCE DISoBEY'D" (66). Repeated qualifying of the bare narrative may have the effect of suggesting something important beyond or beneath the story, something pointing toward an underlying allegory.

Now we must turn back to grace. Daniel Dyke, who was suspended for non-conformity in 1583 and died in 1614, was one of the most popular Puritan preachers of his time. His posthumous book, *The Mystery of Selfe-Deceiving. Or A Discourse and Discovery of the Deceitfullnesse of Mans Heart*, was one of the most popular books of its generation. The demand for copies required eight editions between 1614 and 1634 (STC 7398–7406); it was included in an edition of Dyke's collected works in 1635 (STC 7394), and one more separate edition was published in 1642 (Wing D2959). It is a remarkable book, apparently the first separate study of the phenomenon of self-deception. "What was new in Dyke," says an analytical philosopher today, "was the extent to which he tried to explain virtually all sin as the result of self-deception. Self-deceit was for him the primary explanation of why people...misunderstand divine grace, refuse to repent, and dismiss their sins by blaming external forces."[50]

Dyke's analysis of the "deceits of the heart...perswading to sinne"[51] affords some access to Phillis's thought processes *before* "she ventur'd out with" John (82):

May I not give mine eye libertie to wander a little in wanton glaunces? may I not loose the reines to my tongue to friske it out a little in some idle and lascivious speeches? may I not unshakle my feete, and give them leave to carry mee to such and such places (p. 192)?

"Over shooes, over bootes" is Dyke's comment on this passage (p. 194). Phillis may have deceived herself into thinking that fornication is "judged but a tricke of youth" (p. 185): "And is it...but a tricke to goe to Hell?" Dyke asks (p. 186). Phillis may have presumed "the rather to sinne" because she could "make amends for it afterward by some good deeds, as ...confession" (p. 209) repeated "loud" (10). She may have noticed that Acts 15:20 seems to include fornication among "things indifferent" (pp. 219–21).

Dyke's analysis of prudery provides some insight into Phillis's behavior *after* "she ventur'd out with" John (82). Dyke describes the mechanism: we "cover...many, not sleighter infirmities onely, but even grosser deformities...under some one, poor, petty...show of vertue, rather then vertue it selfe" (pp. 205–06)—"She'd rather take you to her Bed / Than let you see her dress her Head" (7–8). "This is the deceit of our hearts," Dyke says, "to shape out divers vices unto us, like those vertues to which they are most extreamly contrary. For example, not onely base *dejection* of mind goes under the account of true humility, but even *pride* it selfe: as in those that seek prayse by disabling and dispraysing themselves" (p. 183), which helps explain that strange word "Desponding" that begins the poem. Dyke even provides a plausible conjecture for the content of Phillis's mind as she repeats the service of General Confession on her knees: "in hearing of the word," Dyke says, "there come into our mindes such and such thoughts and good purposes of doing this or that good worke; sometimes also many good affections, as of griefe for our sins, and such like.... Here our deceitfull hearts will be ready to thinke these come from the spirit of grace, but the truth is they come from our owne carnall hearts" (p. 288).

Dyke's analysis of "colourable excuses and extenuations" (p. 145) enables us to understand exactly how Phillis justifies herself in her letter to her father. Phillis does not plead "the *corruption of nature*" or "the *examples* of the...godly" or "*Ignorance*" (pp. 146–48). It is clear that Phillis was corrupted by her own concupiscence (James 1:14), by her own "vile thoughts, desires, and affections," not by the precedent of Potiphar's wife (pp. 7, 147). Phillis's letter provides several examples of what Dyke calls "*Translation*, when by laying the fault upon some other cause, wee would altogether disburthen our selves thereof."[52] She blames "a Fortune-teller" (51) and "Fate" (55) and "Heaven" (56). She deceives herself about "a setled and immovable continuance of...outward prosperity" (p. 256) by hoping to regain her father's favor "when his Passion's over" (70). She knows her father as little as he knows her; he thinks his forthputting daughter is "Bashfull" (32); she thinks her implacable ("alive or dead" [38]) father is forgiving. Instead of regaining her father's favor, Phillis pawns "all her Trinkets" (88). She does not plead "the *Times*, and places where we live" nor the Devil nor the stars nor custom (pp. 156–57, 163, 164, 174). But she is guilty of what Dyke calls "double deceitfulness": "Though our hearts deceived us at first to make us *sinne*, yet let us not suffer them to deceive us further, to make us *defend* our sinne: This is to add deceit to deceit. This is *double* deceitfulnesse" (pp. 179–80). Yet this is exactly what Phillis pleads:

> She'd do't if 'twere to do again.
> Thank God, 'twas neither Shame nor Sin (58–59).

"If we say that we have no sin, we deceive ourselves, and the truth is not in us" (1 John 1:8), which Dyke paraphrases, "If we say we have no deceitfulnesse of heart, wee deceive our selves" (p. 33). It is clear that in Dyke's eyes, and Defoe's, Phillis would be an impenitent sinner: "When we ...presume to goe on in our sinnes," Dyke says, "...to continue also in the practice of godlinesse, [is] as it were parting stakes betwixt God and the Devill" (p. 215). Defoe called the practice of occasional conformity "*playing Bo-peep* with God Almighty."[53] "Grace must have all or none," Dyke concludes (p. 216).

Such all-or-nothing simplicities are not for Swift, however. Instead of "Christian Justice" (94) he imposes "Poetick Justice" (97) upon the little world of the poem, while at the same time laughing at poetic justice. Dyke's argument converges upon the solid, bourgeois, commercial virtue of "just cautelousnesse" (p. 33), the exact equivalent of Melville's "ruled, undemonstrative distrustfulness" in *Billy Budd*.[54] But Swift's values are not the bourgeois values of Defoe. They are much closer to the aristocratic values of John Wilmot, Earl of Rochester: "Wit is the noblest and most useful Gift of humane Nature"; "RAILLERY is the finest Part of Conversation."[55] Swift's verse repeatedly demands to be read as the farthest fallout of Restoration comedy. Steele's sentimental comedy *The Conscious Lovers* was written partly in 1719, the year that Stella assigned to the writing of "Phillis, or, The Progress of Love," but the difference between the two works is two different chapters in the history of English literature.

Swift is not the narrator of "Phillis." The narrator is a reader of romances (47) and sentimental tragedies, like Nahum Tate's *King Lear*, that traffic in poetic justice (97). His understated character is summarized in the phrase "it seems" in the line, "Phillis, it seems, was fled with John" (42), and collapses into "the Muse" (73) in the last quarter of the poem. Swift may have missed a great opportunity in "Phillis." The triumphant examples of "The Humble Petition of Frances Harris" (1701) and "Mary the Cook-Maid's Letter to Dr. Sheridan" (1718) might have inclined him to tell the story in the person of Peg, whom John "quitted" (84) for Phillis. Peg's perspective would have been unique. If he thought about it, however, Swift may have decided that he wanted something less colored. The present narrator allows us to see Phillis plain. And, since he fails to interpret the story or to point the moral, the reader must make up his own interpretation. This necessity draws the reader further into the story than Peg's interpretation might have done.

Although he is not the narrator, Swift is still the poet. And we cannot help asking in conclusion why Swift chose to write this particular poem in 1711–19. One clue may lie in Richard Ellmann's lecture at the Library of Congress upon the occasion of Samuel Beckett's 80th birthday. Ellmann isolates "a moment of revelation" in the lives of Beckett, Joyce, Yeats, and Wilde, when they "came to a realization of [their] nature and direction," when they "must have made a crucial choice."[56] For Swift the crucial choice was made in 1711–12. In September 1711 he received two letters from Archbishop King in Dublin. With more than usual obtuseness King urged the vicar of Laracor "to make use of the favour and interest you have at present to procure…some preferment" in the Church. "I know you are not ambitious," the Archbishop bumbled on, but "I advise you, and believe it to be your duty" to write on "some new Subject in Divinity not handled by others," as Swift reported to Stella.[57] This advice must have galled Swift. He was desperately hoping for preferment in England. Congreve had just been provided for, and Swift was on tenterhooks. St. John tortured him further by telling him that he had refused a very good living for Swift because "it was in a place *he* did not like."[58] Swift was dying to be appointed a canon or prebendary of Windsor. "Windsor is a delicious situation," he told Stella, but he also told her that he "had no offers of any living."[59] Harold Williams observes that Swift's written reply to King's gratuitous advice is "a model of dignified restraint."[60] But Swift's real answer to the Archbishop is contained in what he wrote in 1711–12. Instead of elaborating "a subject of weight and learning," as the Archbishop recommended, Swift wrote hoaxes, like *A New Journey to Paris* (1711), and political ballads, like "The Description of Dunkirk with Squash's and Dismal's Opinion How Easily Prince Eugene May Retake It, and Many Other Matters of the Last Importance" (1712), only "two degrees above Grubstreet."[61] In October 1711 Stella teased Swift for "writing merry things, and not upon divinity."[62] "Phillis, or, The Progress of Love" is a product of Swift's "crucial choice" of wit and raillery and irony and paradox instead of "something new and surprizing" in divinity.[63] Late in life Swift encouraged his friends to believe that nearly everything he wrote was a concealed sermon.[64] But as a sermon on the consequences of rebellion, the poem is a failure. Phillis finally is not punished but rewarded. So much irony tends to confuse the parishioner, as Northrop Frye observes.[65] "Phillis, or, The Progress of Love" is a squib that blows up in the Archbishop's face.

But the simplest answer to the question is that Swift wrote "Phillis, or, The Progress of Self-Deception," in 1711–19 because he was himself in a sorry state of self-deception in those years. "How he reconciled his two devotions [to Stella and to Vanessa]," Irvin Ehrenpreis writes, "was a process to be adjusted within his own breast. But to accomplish it, he must have drained his considerable powers of self-deceit."[66] Self-deception involves paradox, not literary paradox but logical paradox or contradiction. The self-deceiver is required simultaneously to believe *p* and also to believe not-*p*. "All Deans naturally fall into paralogysms," Dr. Arbuthnot observes.[67] Among the social psychologists who have studied self-deception Kenneth J. Gergen takes an extreme view. Gergen denies that self-deception is a constituent of individual psychology. "The concept of self-deception," he says, "is a constituent of the culture's ethno-psychology—or system of folk beliefs about the nature of human functioning at the psychological level." Gergen finds the great social utility of the *concept* of self-deception to be its ambiguousness: "it enables the individual to be held responsible for his or her actions, but simultaneously holds the person blameless. The individual is responsible inasmuch as he or she voluntarily originates the action in question, but is forgiven to the degree that the voluntary system was misled, influenced, or otherwise constrained by mental events obscured from consciousness."[68]

This is precisely the ambiguity that is needed to solve the satire/panegyric genre problem in "Phillis, or, The Progress of Love." As forthputting woman Phillis "voluntarily originates the action" and must be blamed. As existential heroine creating her own values in a repressive society Phillis must be praised. "Christian Justice" (94) requires that Phillis be shown on the dung heap muttering, "Behold, I am vile" (Job 40:4). Swift shows her as "Hostess...at...the old blue Boar" (98–100). The final irony of course is that Phillis's fundamental project is whoredom. Even Sartre might have been confused by this development, and it seems momentarily to tip the scale to the side of blame. There is one more fact, however, that redresses the balance. While no one today would dare to confound the biographical figure of the poet with his literary creature, the fact that Swift and Phillis share a common protein—like histone in green plants and mammals—cannot be ignored. Phillis "valued not what others thought her" (71). By 1726, with *Gulliver's Travels* ready for the press and Vanessa dead, Swift had reached the point where he could finally say, "Let people think of me as they please."[69] If Phillis could have read her poem, I think she would smile, knowing that Swift had forgiven her.

[1] *Journal to Stella*, ed. Harold Williams (Oxford, 1948), I, 318, 321–32, 335–36, 349–51, 353–57, 360–66; II, 372–79, 550–52, 556–561 n. (hereafter cited as *Journal*); *The Account Books of Jonathan Swift*, ed. Paul V. and Dorothy J. Thompson (Newark, DE, 1984), pp. 160–61.

[2] *The Poems of Jonathan Swift*, ed. Harold Williams, 2nd ed. (Oxford, 1958), I, 194; hereafter cited as *Poems*. Line numbers in parentheses in the text of this article are the line numbers of "Phillis, or, The Progress of Love."

[3] *Poems*, I, 201.

[4] *The Correspondence of Jonathan Swift*, ed. Harold Williams, rev. David Woolley (Oxford, 1963–72), II, 282; hereafter cited as *Corresp.*

[5] *Poems*, I, 225.

[6] Susan Reynolds, ed., *A History of the County of Middlesex*, The Victoria History of the Counties of England (London, 1962), III, 13; hereafter cited as *VCH*.

[7] *VCH*, III, 18; Nikolaus Pevsner, *Middlesex* (Harmondsworth, Mddx., 1951), p. 143.

[8] *VCH*, III, 15.

[9] Pevsner, p. 144.

[10] In 1636 there was reported to be a Blue Boar tavern in St. Albans, a village in Hertfordshire through which Swift passed every time he traveled between Dublin and London and between Leicester (where his mother lived) and London (*Middlesex and Hertfordshire Notes & Queries*, 4 [1898], 203).

[11] *An Inventory of the Historical Monuments in Middlesex* (London, 1937), p. 113.

[12] Poems, I, 221.

[13] ED. NOTE: On Stella's datings see the article by James Woolley elsewhere in this volume.

[14] *Corresp.*, II, 322.

[15] *Corresp.*, II, 335.

[16] *Corresp.*, II, 325.

[17] *Corresp.*, II, 322; John Boyle, Earl of Orrery, *Remarks on the Life and Writings of Dr. Jonathan Swift*, 3rd ed. (London, 1752), p. 21; Patrick Delany, *Observations upon Lord Orrery's Remarks* (London, 1754), p. 73.

[18] *Corresp.*, II, 329–31.

[19] Claude M. Simpson, *The British Broadside Ballad and Its Music* (New Brunswick, 1966), pp. 320–22.

[20] Northrop Frye, *Anatomy of Criticism* (Princeton, 1957), pp. 43–49, 163–77.

[21] Frye, p. 176.

[22] *Motif-Index of Folk-Literature*, ed. Stith Thompson, 2nd ed., 6 vols. (Bloomington, 1966).

[23] *The Táin*, tr. Thomas Kinsella (London, 1970), pp. 168–69.

[24] Tom Peete Cross, "The Celtic Elements in the Lays of *Lanval* and *Graelent*," *Modern Philology*, 12 (1915), 611–12.

[25] Jean-Paul Sartre, *Being and Nothingness*, tr. Hazel E. Barnes (New York, 1956), pp. 55–57.

[26] "Mrs. Harris records without surprise in one of her letters, 'Lady Harriet Wentworth has married her footman. She left a letter for her sister in which...she said: "though John was ignoble, yet he was honest" ' " (Dorothy Marshall, "The Domestic Servants of the Eighteenth Century," *Economica*, 9 [1929], 34).

[27] For the translator's rendering of *mauvaise foi* as "bad faith," I have substituted "self-deception" at four points.

[28] [*The Prose Writings of Jonathan Swift*], ed. Herbert Davis et al., 14 vols. (1939–68; various reimpressions, sometimes corrected, Oxford, 1957–69), II, 31; hereafter cited as *Prose*.

[29] *Prose*, XIII, 42.

[30] John Ashton, *Social Life in the Reign of Queen Anne* (London, 1904), pp. 28–31; John R. Gillis, *For Better, for Worse: British Marriages, 1600 to the Present* (New York, 1985), pp. 90–98.

[31] Lawrence Stone, *The Family, Sex and Marriage in England 1500–1800* (New York, 1977), p. 35.

[31a] *The Rape of the Lock*, IV, 174–75; I, 79–86 (*The Poems of Alexander Pope*, ed. John Butt et al., 11 vols. [New Haven, 1939–69], II, 194, 151.

[32] Sartre, p. 58.

[33] *Prose*, XIII, 43; Morris P. Tilley, *A Dictionary of the Proverbs in England in the Sixteenth and Seventeenth Centuries* (Ann Arbor, 1950), F617.

[34] *The Spectator*, ed. Donald F. Bond (Oxford, 1965), No. 40 (16 April 1711), I, 168.

[35] Sartre, p. 480.

[36] Defoe, *Every-Body's Business, Is No-Body's Business: or, Private Abuses, Publick Grievances*, 4th ed. (London: Warner, Dodd, and Nutt, 1725), p. 23.

[37] "The Ethics of Cultural Property," *Times Literary Supplement* (25 July 1986), p. 809.

[38] Louise K. Barnett, "Swift's Poetry and the Critics," *Review*, 2 (1980), 41.

[39] Matthew Prior, *The History of His Own Time* (London, 1740), p. 232.

[40] Henry Home, Lord Kames, *Elements of Criticism* (Edinburgh, 1762), III, 219.

[41] *Poems on Affairs of State: Augustan Satirical Verse, 1660–1714*, ed. George deF. Lord (New Haven, 1963–75), VI, xxix–xxx.

[42] *Poems*, I, 223 n.

[43] *Prose*, IX, 65.

[44] *Poems*, I, 155–58.

[45] *The Relapse* (1696), V.i.

[46] Henri Misson, *M. Misson's Memoirs and Observations in his Travels over England*, tr. John Ozell (London: Browne et al., 1719), pp. 183–84.

[47] *Prose*, IV, 102.

[48] The first feet in lines 24, 25, 39, 42, 49, 61, 66, 96 are not iambs, and the last two feet in line 50 scan irregularly, "in the LIKE CASes."

[49] *Poems*, I, 124 (1, 3, 7, 15).

[50] Mike W. Martin, *Self-Deception and Morality* (Lawrence, KS, 1986), p. 33.

[51] *The Mystery of Selfe-Deceiving* (London: Stansby, 1633), p. 181; hereafter cited by page number.

[52] P. 150, mispaginated "138."

[53] Defoe, *An Enquiry into the Occasional Conformity of Dissenters* (London, 1697), p. 17.

[54] Cf. "The deceitfulnesse of our hearts must cause us daily to keepe an audit in our owne conscience, ever and anone calling them to their accounts" (p. 367). Melville, *Billy Budd*, ed. Raymond Weaver (London, 1924), p. 59.

[55] *Prose*, I, 10; IV, 91.

[56] Richard Ellmann, *Samuel Beckett, Nayman of Noland* (Washington, D. C., 1986), pp. 10–14.

[57] *Corresp.*, I, 254–55; *Journal*, I, 358–59.

[58] *Journal*, I, 314, emphasis added.

[59] *Journal*, I, 314, 323.

[60] *Journal*, I, 359 n.

[61] Frank H. Ellis, "Swift's Seventh Penny Paper," *Times Literary Supplement* (10 May 1974), p. 506; *Journal*, II, 431.

[62] *Journal*, II, 391.

[63] *Corresp.*, I, 255.

[64] *Poems*, II, 565; *Corresp.*, IV, 52.

[65] Frye, p. 176.

[66] Irvin Ehrenpreis, *Swift: The Man, His Works, and the Age* (Cambridge, MA, 1962–83), III, 98.

[67] *Corresp.*, II, 306.

⁶⁸ Kenneth J. Gergen, "The Ethnopsychology of Self-Deception," in Martin, pp. 236, 239. The idea of self-deception as a conceptualization of demonic possession is an attractive one. Jacques Abbadie could write about "the *Demon* of Concupiscence" in 1692 (*The Art of Knowing One-Self: or, An Enquiry into the Sources of Morality*, tr. T[homas] W[oodcock] [Oxford: Lichfield, 1695], p. 95), but Satan is not a term in Swift's theological vocabulary.

⁶⁹ *Corresp.*, III, 130.

Hermann J. Real

"An horrid Vision": Jonathan Swift's "(On) the Day of Judgement"

IN THE SUMMER OF 1752, Philip Stanhope, the son of Lord Chesterfield, visited Voltaire in Berlin, bearing an introductory letter from his father.[1] Complimenting Voltaire on his criticism of the follies of religious sectarianism in the *Histoire du Siècle de Louis XIV* (1751), Chesterfield sent Voltaire a copy of a poem by Swift which purportedly bore on Voltaire's subject. For obvious reasons the poem had never been published, he claimed, but there could be no doubt that it was authentic: "J'en ai l'original écrit de sa propre main."[2] The poem dealt with the Day of Judgment, and when it was finally printed in the mid-1770s, little was revealed as to its genesis and provenance.[3] More than two hundred years later, Swift scholars are still in the dark. While they are at odds about the poem's date of composition,[4] about the occasion which led to it,[5] and even about the wording of the title,[6] the majority seem at least agreed that the most authoritative of the five versions uncovered so far is the twenty-two line text published by the *St. James's Chronicle* in April 1774.[7]

Like the scholars, the poem's critics are divided. Although there has been little sustained scholarship on "The Day of Judgement," strong feelings abound in the critical history of the poem. For one group of readers, the poem is "profane," "irreverent," and "hair-raising,"[8] its "correlative indignation against mankind [mounting] into something like the rage of a madman."[9] Matthew Weld Hartstonge, Sir Walter Scott's literary agent in Dublin, was so horrified at this "infamous paper" that he thought it "impossible wholly to have been the Deans."[10] A second group, however, considers Swift's lines "tremendous," "magnificent," and "wonderful."[11] The poem is not only "an intellectual effort of a high order";[12] it is also so clever that "the reader can deflect the satire...by pure admiration of the skill."[13] To these critics, in short, "(On) the Day of Judgement" is Swift's "greatest" poem.[14] As in the case of *Gulliver's Travels*, the critical history of the poem seems to have given rise to two "schools" or interpretative extremes: "(On) the Day of Judgement" is a poem which critics either hate or love.

Whichever way they feel, however, they are united in the belief that the poem is impossible to ignore.

Given the "grim force"[15] of Swift's lines, emotional outbursts do not come entirely unexpectedly, of course. After all, "(On) the Day of Judgement" belongs to a clump of "vexatious" poems which all originated in the early 1730s.[16] We know that, at this stage of his life, Swift was an old man, disillusioned, lonely, and bitter. We do not know, however, *what exactly* sent the old man, a writer of occasional verse throughout his life, "on such a rip in the first place."[17] While it is safe to assume that the misogyny of the Dean's obscene verses sprang from circumstances in his daily environment, the occasion of his eschatological poetry is shadowy and at issue. As it will turn out, "(On) the Day of Judgement" is a subversive scrawl, much of the kind which became a hallmark of Swift's poetry after the early "Verses Wrote in a Lady's Ivory Table-Book" (*c*.1698), yet with this difference, that it is a subversive scrawl of unperceived proportions.

However, the poem is not subversive in the sense that it sabotages the religious convictions of Swift and the teachings of his Church. The Dean's target is the presumptiousness of contemporary eschatology, both sacred *and* profane, which, "(On) the Day of Judgement" shows, was in the habit of generating more darkness than light on the most fundamental question a Christian could possibly ask: the final relationship of man to God. Not surprisingly for readers of Swift's verse, there is the familiar sense of impasse, the sense that the Dean has once again exhausted the catalogue of logical, *theo*-logical possibilities by "vexing" his fellow eschatologists with the one "solution" which no one had ever thought of before: the Day of Judgment will be a day *without* a verdict. In fact, there is no poem "of graver import" in the whole of Swift's work.[18]

II

"(On) the Day of Judgement" has a double theme—the *eschata* of history, the Resurrection, Judgment, Heaven, and Hell, that is, as well as the contemporary obsession with these events. It is no exaggeration to say that, until the 1740s, the Age of Reason was less reasonable in its rage for eschatology[19] than perhaps befitted it,[20] even if it has to be conceded that there was a whole cluster of causative factors, religious, philosophical, and scientific, for this preoccupation.

For one thing, in the Christian interpretation of history, there cannot be a more significant event than the Second Coming of Christ.[21] Of this event not even "the meanest Soul, and the lowest Imagination [can] think

...without the greatest Emotion, and the deepest Impression," as a contemporary of Swift enthused.[22] In this Last Day, all history culminates and reveals its divine purpose. On this Last Day, "Christ shall come from heaven to judge the living and the dead, and this is what we mean when we speak of the last day and the day of divine judgement, that is, the last period of time," St. Augustine exclaimed in *The City of God*.[23] For Augustine, as for other Fathers of the Church,[24] the course of history was linear, finite, and providential.[25]

The conviction that God's sovereignty and rule over the universe climaxes in a final intervention involving a judgment and the advent of a new heaven became the orthodox, the Anglican, position in due course. In his *Exposition of the Thirty-Nine Articles*, Gilbert Burnet, the Bishop of Salisbury, pronounced categorically:

Then shall [Christ] pass a final Sentence upon all that ever lived upon Earth, according to all they have done in the Body, whether it be good or bad.[26]

The number of voices reduplicating statements like this is legion. If there is anything uncontested in the spectrum of latter-day thought since the Reformers, it is the conviction that "the Lord Jesus Himself would assuredly come again."[27] The belief in the immortality of the soul and the resurrection of the body, as well as in a future assize, belonged, as John Wallis (1616–1703) "demonstrated" in a sermon to his university in 1679, to "the Fundamentals in the Doctrine of Christianity, well setled long agoe."[28] Along with many others, William Sherlock (1641–1707), Dean of St. Paul's, followed suit. In his popular *Practical Discourse Concerning a Future Judgment* (1692), Sherlock endeavored to prove, both "by the Principles of Reason" and "by Revelation," that God had indeed "appointed a Day for Judgment" since man was by nature "*an Accountable Creature*."[29]

Thus much, the certainty of the event, as well as the rationale of its happening, was not controversial. Everything else was in dispute. In fact, there does not seem to have been another field of theology which was as marred by confusion and logomachy, by self-righteous intolerance and dogmatic arrogance, as eschatology. From the Fathers of the Church to the eighteenth century, theologians and preachers alike wrangled over such questions as whether the Kingdom of God would be terrestrial or transcendental, whether it would be external and manifest or inward and spiritual, and also whether it was already present, imminent, or uncertain. In addition, they were at variance over whether the *parousia*, the advent, of Christ would be catastrophic, preceded by both cosmic conflagration[30] and the coming of Antichrist, or gradual, whether there would be one resurrection of the dead or two,[31] and whether the Son or the Father would preside over the assize. Finally, they clashed on whether his judgment was to be individual and/or universal and whether the divine verdict would be finite and temporary or definitive and everlasting.[32] In short, "no Subject whatever has more entangled and ruffled the Thoughts of the wisest Men, than this concerning our Future State," as the Deist Charles Blount (1654–1693) summed up the state of the debate at the turn of the century. "It has been controverted in all Ages, by Men of the greatest Learning and Parts."[33]

Among all these questions, three appear to have been more urgent than others to seventeenth- and eighteenth-century thinkers:

(1) the nature of reward and punishment;
(2) the sense of (an) impending doom; and
(3) the expectation of the millennium.

The majority of biblical commentators were agreed that the notion of an all-knowing and all-just God made a just judgment inevitable. Protestant eschatologists would insist, Puritans perhaps more stridently than their brethren in enmity, the Anglicans,[34] that the Day of the Lord was the day of divine retribution. "The Righteous shall be rewarded with eternal Happiness," Archbishop Tillotson conceded in a sermon on the famous verse in Matthew (25:46), yet there could not be any doubt either that the reprobate would be sentenced to "everlasting Punishment."[35] If the good, like pious and accomplished young ladies, were "call'd to more Superiour Bliss,"[36] "*impious Wretches*," Thomas Harrison warned, "*must for ever dwell in Flames below*; / *Incessant Torments there with* Satan undergo."[37] Throughout the seventeenth and eighteenth centuries, the torments of Hell, both physical and spiritual, were painted in such lurid and glaring colors that the faithful were almost frightened into Heaven.[38]

The notion of a vindictive, if "righteous," Lord entailed a host of delicate theological issues, however. For one thing, if righteousness always signified "strict and severe Justice," William Sherlock asked, "who then could be saved?"[39] For another, it was difficult to see how the orthodox doctrine of eternal damnation was to be reconciled with the traditional image of a benevolent, merciful, and all-embracing God.[40] Moreover, since "among all the Arguments to Repentance and a good Life, those have the greatest Force and Power upon the minds of Men, which are fetch'd…from the final state of good and bad Men after this Life," as Archbishop Tillotson claimed,[41] the chief value of hell consisted in its deterrence. In this view, the observance of God's ordinances was traded in for man's future happiness, and the relationship between God and man became a commercial venture.[42] Finally, there were the awesome questions of theodicy, inquiries into the destiny of those who had never been converted to the Christian faith and the fate of children who die in infancy.[43] Indeed, "the doctrine of future rewards and punishments [posed] fundamental questions about the nature of man and God."[44]

The pressure exerted by some of these problems led to quite heterodox, even radical, solutions in the course of the seventeenth century. The Ranter Richard Coppin, for example, interpreted the biblical passages concerning the Day of Judgment not as pointing towards a factual event terminating world history but as an allegory which involved "no resurrection of 'this earthly body,' "[45] and the Digger Gerrard Winstanley countered the postulate of eternal damnation by resuscitating the pre-Nicene fallacy of "universal salvation" (including that of Satan), which was also made actionable by the Ordinance for the Punishing of Blasphemies and Heresies (1648).[46] Similarly, English Arians like John Locke, Samuel Clarke, and William Whiston simply "disbelieved in eternal torment."[47] A fourth group of commentators, Henry More among them, found consolation in the thought that God was not obliged, after all, "to execute what he [had] threatened."[48]

Both the anxiety and casuistry manifest in this contentious debate on the future rewards and punishments were conditioned by the sense of impending doom pervading eschatological thinking from the sixteenth to the eighteenth centuries. Although Scripture sounded elusive and self-contradictory on the precise day of Judgment—according to St. Mark, it was only known to the Father (13:13), according to Revelation, it was near "at hand" (1:3; 22:10)—Protestant theologians usually showed themselves convinced that the Second Advent was imminent. Like many others, Thomas Flatman expected Doomsday to occur during his own lifetime:

> 'Tis not far off; methinks I see
> Among the Stars some dimmer be;
> Some tremble, as their Lamps did fear
> A neighbouring Extinguisher.
> The greater Luminaries fail,
> Their Glories by Eclipses vail,
> Knowing e'er long their borrow'd Light
> Must sink in th' Universal Night.[49]

In this chorus, a voice like that of Henry More, who warned that "the approach of this Day is very uncertain, (by reason of the obscurity of Prophecies),"[50] was the exception to the rule.

There are at least two reasons for this far-flung expectation of the coming of end-time. Because "the circumstances of secession called for profound second thoughts about the destiny of man and God's final purposes,"[51] the Reformers, and especially Luther, began to attach greater significance to Revelation, which had been something of an embarrassment to a philosophically-minded interpreter of the Bible like St. Augustine,[52] than to the apocalyptic passages of the Synoptic Gospels.[53] In Revelation, a seer prophesies the arrival of a millennium, an earthly kingdom in which resurrected saints will reign with Christ for a thousand years (20:4–6).

In Luther, the millennium is an interval *before* the last judgment, and it is succeeded by a period of excruciating tribulations in which the forces of Antichrist hold sway. If this period is interpreted not as a prediction concerning the future, but as an event of the past, it is easy to associate with the persecutions the Church had to suffer under the papal regime. In other words, Luther identified Antichrist with the evils he saw emanating from the papacy. Man lived, he concluded, in the last days.[54]

The literalist biblical chronology prevalent throughout the sixteenth and seventeenth centuries seemed to lend credence to this interpretation. According to Fathers of the Church like St. Augustine, the world had been created about the year 4000 BC. Like many chronologers of the Renaissance, Christopher Helvicus (Helwig), of whose *Historical and Chronological Theatre* Swift had two editions in his library,[55] calculated the year of the creation at precisely 3948 BC.[56] If to this the threefold division of universal history was added[57]—there being "2000. yeares of nature, between the Creation, and the giving of the Law by *Moses*, and 2000. yeares of the Law between that, and the comming of Christ, and 2000. yeares of Grace and Gospell between Christ first, and his second comming"[58]—time was indeed drawing to its close, even if end-time was not yet *immediately* imminent.

If, in the eyes of the many, the history of man remained what had been uncontested since St. Augustine and the Fathers of the Church, namely a course of events ruled by a single, all-embracing Providence operating in time, as well as a progression toward the one inexorable goal, there was no religious movement since the Reformation that contributed more to the prevalence of this feeling than millenarianism. As John Graunt summarized it in 1645, this was the belief in "the glorious reigne of Christ upon the earth," according to which "all the Martyrs and holy Prophets shall rise from the dead, and reigne with Christ a thousand yeares in all prosperity, peace, riches, plenty, wealth, and glory, with such supreme power and Majesty, as never any Monarch in this world had before."[59] Rejected by the "orthodox apologists of the faith" after ever so many expectations of the approaching millennium had been frustrated in the history of the church,[60] millenarian or chiliastic fervor became a powerful force in the political, social, and intellectual history of the sixteenth and seventeenth centuries.

More often than not, it is true, it was associated with the sectarian zealotry of radical "saints" like the Münster Anabaptists or the Fifth Monarchy Men,[61] not to mention the "enthusiastic" Puritan preachers of the Civil War.[62] Nonetheless what used to be considered "the ideology of lunatic-fringe 'fanatics' and uprooted classes"[63] was at one stage also adopted by "respectable" theologians and scientists in the course of the seventeenth century. Among these were the celebrated biblical scholar, Joseph Mede (1586–1668), Professor of Greek at Cambridge,[64] as well as ecclesiastical leaders like Archbishop Thomas Tenison and William Lloyd, Bishop of St. Asaph.[65] In his *Sacred Theory of the Earth* (1684–90), Thomas Burnet, Master of the Charterhouse, interpreted the general progress of learning brought about by the New Science of the seventeenth century as a preparation for the millennium.[66] To cut a long list of believers short, those strange bedfellows John Milton and Thomas Hobbes both held chiliastic views.[67]

Millenarianism, however heretical it was thought to be in some quarters, also became widespread among ordinary people in the seventeenth century. In fact, "the excitement arising out of the Reformation and intensified by the civil war…created millenarian hopes at all levels of society."[68] At the same time, however, millenarians presented the same sad spectacle of warring prophets, proud, intolerant, and uncharitable, as their less radical brethren had done. Admittedly, all were united in the vision of the New Jerusalem, a holy *eu*topia, as it were, soon to be established upon earth. Yet there were "enormous differences" as to the precise dates of its arrival and "the method chosen by God for its enactment" as well as to the beneficiaries in the new heaven.[69] Inevitably, the central issue in this debate was whether the Scriptures were to be interpreted literally or allegorically. While the followers of the pre-millennialist camp assumed the Second Coming of Christ would precede the millennium, no matter whether Christ's reign was regarded as personal or spiritual, their post-millennialist rivals placed it *after* the millennial age.[70] For Gerrard Winstanley, for example, the Kingdom of Christ had already been inaugurated by transforming the conditions of this world, by "the casting out of covetousness and the establishment of a classless society."[71] On the other hand, Thomas Brightman (1562–1607), author of a commentary on Revelation, and Thomas Hobbes thought that it followed the end of history, ushering in "a world-wide paradise on earth for the Saints."[72] The war of words became so heated and acrimonious at times that Bishop Joseph Hall exclaimed in exasperation in 1650, "Now, Lord, where are we? what Reader doth not find himselfe lost in this wildernesse of opinions?"[73]

III

By the mid-seventeenth century, the poets had climbed aboard the theological bandwagon.[74] Until then, for almost 150 years after the eschatological frenzy had re-erupted at the beginning of the sixteenth century, they had largely ignored the *eschata* of history as a poetic theme. After 1650, the new poetic genre developed rapidly. Spurred on by the predictions of Christ's imminent Advent in 1649–50 and 1666, Henry Vaughan and Thomas Flatman, for example, composed verses on *The Day of Judgment* which in mood and message anticipated many a future poem on the *novissima*.[75] At the turn of the century, the number of eschatological poems swells. In 1696, Nahum Tate's *Miscellanea Sacra* appeared, containing not only Tate's own "The Last Trumpet" but also a free translation of the medieval Dies Irae, "On the Day of Judgment," by Wentworth Dillon, Earl of Roscommon.[76] John Pomfret (1667–1702), the Bedfordshire vicar, soon followed suit. His two pindaric odes, "On the General Conflagration, and Ensuing Judgment" and "Dies Novissima: or, The Last Epiphany," are animated, as Pomfret's editor marveled, by such a "Holy Warmth" as was seldom found in the "many excellent Pens [that] have exercised their Talents upon this Subject."[77] The same year, 1702, saw the publication of a ponderous epic in five parts, Marshall Smith's Miltonic *The Vision, or a Prospect of Death, Heav'n, and Hell: With a Description of the Resurrection and the Day of Judgment.*[78] *The Vision* is indicative not only of the growing influence of *Paradise Lost* at the beginning of the eighteenth century but also of the effrontery with which the poetic dabblers determined the protocol of man's final rendezvous with his Creator. To what extent they claimed to be privy to the secrets of the divine plan becomes evident from the argument prefixed to the fifth part:

The Signs forerunning the Day of Judgment. The Procession of the Son of Man from Heav'n, to sit in Judgment. The Judgment Seat fixed in the Air. The manner of the Resurrection. The Saints are first Rais'd. Try'd and Sentenc'd. Then they ascend up to the Judgment Seat, and assist in the Tryal of the Wicked. The Wicked are Rais'd, Try'd and Condemn'd. The general Conflagration describ'd. The Wicked surrounded with the Flames, sink into the Abiss of Hell, whilst the Righteous ascend into the Heav'n of Heav'ns. The Subject Matter of their Felicity there.[79]

Between 1702 and 1735, there is probably not a single year which did not witness the appearance of at least one eschatological poem.[80] In 1707, for example, Isaac Watts (1674–1748) published the first edition of his *Hymns and Spiritual Songs*, which was studded with poems on the Last Day.[81] The Sapphic ode, "The Day of Judgment," from Watts's *Horae Lyricae*, published a year earlier, even became a minor classic of the genre.[82] By 1713, two more noted poets, Nicholas Rowe, in a short orthodox piece celebrating the felicity of the Saints in heaven,[83] and Edward Young, in a long and rambling though influential *Poem on the Last Day*,[84] had also responded to the appeal of the theme.

The first apex of the poetic mania for the *novissima* was reached in 1720 when no fewer than four poems on the Last Day came out in one year. Among these were Samuel Catherall's *Essay on the Conflagration*, written with the "usual minatory intentions" and little more than a versification of ideas from Burnet's *Sacred Theory of the Earth* and William Sherlock,[85] as well as John Bulkeley's pompous epic on *The Last Day*, which despite its unreadability was reissued twice by 1722.[86] The fact that the topics of reward and punishment, of heaven and hell, of eternal happiness and misery were indeed "the inexhaustible Stores of a Christian Orator," as Henry Felton had proclaimed in 1715,[87] is moreover evinced by the eschatological verses of Richard Daniel, the Dean of Armagh,[88] whom Swift was to denounce as the "vilest Poet alive" and "consequently a public enemy to mankind."[89] The one poetic endeavor generally considered to excel the usually mediocre output on the subject is Aaron Hill's *The Judgment-Day*,[90] which presents the destruction of the material universe as a nightmarish cacophony orchestrated for earthquake, volcano, thunder, and lightning:

> Torn from their roots, the groaning forests lie,
> And hills leap headlong and invade the sky:
> Mankind now, first united, join in prayer,
> Shrieks from a thousand kingdoms rend the air,
> And ghastly horror stalks o'er all, and leads on pale despair.
> See, how destructive flashes wind their way!
> And point the following thunder where to rend.
> Mark! how the sprouted rivers upward stray,
> And hiss against the light'nings which descend.[91]

The preoccupation with the *eschata* of history continued throughout the 1720s. The degree to which the contemporary consciousness of the coming of end-time, punctuated by calls for the necessity of repentance, haunted the imagination of virtually all strata of society is perhaps chronicled best in an incident related in the diary of John Byrom (1692–1763), virtuoso and fellow of the Royal Society. Returning home one night in November 1727 from a visit to Sir Hans Sloane, Byrom found himself "much diverted with the bellman's verses":

> If that we do believe a future state,
> Let us repent before it is too late;

> Although we now may be in health and strength,
> The life of man is but a span's length:
> Let's make our calling and election sure.
> *Past one o'clock!*[92]

The second climax came in the early 1730s, when Swift is thought to have written "(On) the Day of Judgement." In 1734, Joseph Trapp, whom Swift had befriended during his time as *chef de propagande* of the Harley-Bolingbroke administration,[93] published his gloomy *Thoughts upon the Four Last Things*, a metrical paraphrase of biblical passages, in four parts, describing at length the events surrounding death, judgment, heaven, and hell. In the same year, Edward Cave, the founder of the *Gentleman's Magazine*, decided to run a competition for eschatological verse. In an "Advertisement" of July 1734, he promised "*the sum of* FIFTY POUNDS" to that poet "*who shall make the best* POEM, Latin *or* English, *on* LIFE, DEATH, JUDGMENT, HEAVEN *and* HELL, viz. *all the said subjects jointly, and not any single one independent of the rest.*"[94] Sixteen of the submitted poems, totaling thirty-six in number, were published in an "extraordinary" issue in July 1735, several of the "learned and curious Readers [being] impatient to see the Produce of so *uncommon a Proposal.*"[95] The first prize of £50 was awarded to the seventh poem in the collection, "On *Life, Death, Judgment, Heaven* and *Hell*," ostensibly by Theophilus Philomel.[96] "Lemuel Gulliver, Jr.," who had also entered the competition, came away empty-handed, his contribution, like others, "*deem'd unnecessary to be printed.*"[97]

In the eschatological poetry between 1650 and 1740, the spectrum of themes, images, and motifs remained essentially unchanged even if their individual texture varied from poem to poem. Like Thomas Flatman, the majority of versifiers continued to be convinced that the end was near at hand. In *A Poem on the Last Day*, Edward Young, for one, emphatically proclaimed the proximity of the assize, and Thomas Harrison seconded in his own "On the Day of Judgment": "Behold! The great, the awful Day is near."[98] There could be no doubt either about the axiomatic certainty of the Last Judgment. The inescapability of the final verdict, Joseph Trapp argued, followed from the very justness and wisdom of the Creator. Being a lawgiver, the Lord had no choice but to reward "his Faithful, and confound the Proud":

> All Laws are vain,
> Unless enforc'd with Pleasure, and with Pain...
> From hence, 'tis prov'd We must to Judgment rise;
> Or God, in Legislature, is not Wise.[99]

Similarly, all poets were agreed that Christ's epiphany on the Last Day was to be preceded by a physical catastrophe of gigantic proportions. Echoing the description of the signs signaling the consummation of history in Revelation (6: 11, 19; 15: 1–16, 21), they painted the destruction and final conflagration of the universe as the short-lived, if God-willed, rule of Chaos over Order. The laws of nature were to be repealed,[100] thunder and lightning were to devastate the earth,[101] and burning planets to tumble one upon the other.[102] In a fit of *trepidatio christiana* common in the eschatological poetry of the age, Joseph Trapp lamented:

> Who can abide That great, That fearful Day,
> When Thou, as JUDGE, Thy Glory shall display?
> When all Things in Confusion shall be hurl'd,
> And Wreaths of Smoke involve the flaming World?
> When from Thy red Right-hand *new* Lightnings fly;
> And unfix'd Orbs rush clatt'ring thro' the Sky?
> The Universal Mass, from Pole to Pole,
> Burnt up, and shrivel'd, like a Parchment Scrole?[103]

The resurrection of the dead and the advent of the divine Judge in glory[104] follows the cosmic conflagration, which is succeeded, in turn, by the description of sinful mankind struggling with its anguish. The poets dwell in meticulously graphic detail on the terror of the sinners, "the shrill Outcries of the guilty Wretches," the timorous apprehension of the "pale offenders," and the "Conscious Sinners shiv'ring with Despair."[105] In view of the fact that the God of the poets, like that of the theologians, is an "angry, incensèd God," a "frowning Judge," in whose eyes flashes "almighty Vengeance" and who is "provok'd by wrath,"[106] reprobate man has reason, too, to fear the outcome of the divine tribunal.

If the catalogue of the poetic themes, images, and motifs remained essentially the same between 1650 and 1740, structure and point of view admitted of some variety. Yet choice was limited here, too. This is particularly true of narrative voice, not only the vantage point from which the poets presented the dramatic events surrounding the Last Day but also their source of revelation for an occurrence that was supposed to be concealed to all but God. While some of the versifiers like Edward Young and Aaron Hill "solved" the problem by ignoring it, simply imploring some otherworldly mediator like a muse or an angel for illumination,[107] the majority resorted to the time-honored device of vision.[108] Visions had been associated with eschatological themes since the Middle Ages,[109] and had become extremely popular in the course of the seventeenth century. This popularity was due not least to the influence of Francisco de Quevedo Villegas (1580–1645), the Spanish satirist, whose *Sueños* (*Visions*) were translated into English by Sir Roger L'Estrange, among others, and with whom Swift seems to have been familiar.[110] This is Quevedo's report of how he came to learn of "*the Great Day of Account*":

HOMER makes *JUPITER* the Author or Inspirer of Dreams; especially the Dreams of Princes and Governors: and if the matter of them be Pious and Important. And it is likewise the Judgment of the Learned *Propertius*, That *Good Dreams came from above, have their weight, and ought not to be slighted.* And truly I am much of his Mind, in the case of a Dream I had the other Night. As I was reading a Discourse touching the *End of the World*, I fell asleep over the Book, and Dreamt of *the Last Judgment.*[111]

Clearly, this manner of revelation was too attractive, and too easy, for the rhymesters not to imitate it. Like John Pomfret and Marshall Smith,[112] G[eorge] L[arkin] displayed the glories of heaven and the terrors of hell "under the similitude of a vision" in 1711,[113] and in *An Essay on the Conflagration*, Samuel Catherall expressly rejected the artifice of an angel as mediator:

> But now my Earthly Senses overpowr'd
> In Conversation Heav'nly and Sublime,
> Sunk down, requiring sweet Repair of Sleep,
> Which fell upon me instantly, and clos'd
> My weary Eye-lids. But the Spatious Cell
> Of Fancy, *my internal Sight*, remain'd
> Still open, where the promis'd *Vision* strait
> Appear'd astonishing...
> > So I beheld
> Strange Things, as present, which are yet to come.[114]

Structurally, all these poems culminate in God's apostrophe to mankind. Having read out "the book of life," in which the thoughts and actions of each sinner are faithfully recorded,[115] an angry, impatient judge pronounces doom on "the daring sons of Infamy." With few exceptions, his speech is of denunciatory brevity.[116] Heeding John Dennis's dictum that no idea could produce greater terror in the minds of men than that of an angry God,[117] the poets show themselves eager to contribute their share to the stock of contemporary disquietude by descanting, in loving hyperbole, on the torments of the damned. There is literally Satan's plenty of "burning Darkness" and "Universal Night," of "that insatiable abyss" and "the Pit wide yawning," of "scenes of sorrow" and "the storms of wild despair."[118] Conversely, the bliss of the Saints is painted in ecstatic colors. In paradise, Nicholas Rowe, among countless others, promises his reader in "On the Last Judgment and

Happiness of the Saints in Heaven" that the joys of the Blessed "shall ne'er be done, / No Night shall rise, to shade Heav'ns glorious SUN, / But one Eternal HOLYDAY go on."[119]

IV

Not coincidentally, all these eschatological poets propounded the orthodox view of end-time. Whatever their differences in doctrine and emphasis, in their interpretation the course of history is finite, linear, and, above all, providential. This emphasis on the wisdom of Divine Providence suggests that the rise of the eschatological genre is connected, to some extent at least, with the growth of Deism and its particular, profane brand of eschatology, which was to become Swift's second object of attack in "(On) the Day of Judgement."

Deism posed an ever-increasing threat to all forms of theology from the middle of the seventeenth century when the rehabilitation of Epicurean philosophy gained momentum in English intellectual history.[120] Committed to a materialistic and mechanistic model of the universe, the Epicureans propagated the belief in the mortality of the soul. Their knowledge of natural law ("naturae species ratioque") caused them to abandon any idea of divine control or providence. "The gods," Lucretius explained in the *De Rerum Natura*, were "far off removed" from man and his affairs. As a consequence, they were "not pleased by good deeds, or provoked by bad."[121] Therefore, any notion of divine retribution and of life after death had to be discarded ("nil igitur mors est ad nos"). Life and death were but segments in the cycle of eternal return.

Although English Deism never succeeded in developing a coherent, consistent, and comprehensive system at any one stage in its history,[122] the movement did become associated in the eighteenth-century mind with two constituents of Epicurean thought. These were the rationalist account of the universe and, by implication, of religion,[123] as well as the rejection of the providential role of the Deity. The positions were logically interrelated, of course, yet in the consciousness of the poets, the problem of divine Providence and the issues it involved—the existence of God, the immortality of the soul, and the salvation of man—seem to have loomed larger.

"There are some infidels among us," Richard Bentley exclaimed in his Boyle Lectures of 1692, "that not only disbelieve the *Christian* religion, but oppose the assertions of *Providence*, of the *immortality* of the soul, of an universal *judgment* to come, and of any *incorporeal* essence; and yet, to avoid the odious name of *Atheists*, would shelter and screen themselves under a new one of *Deists*, which is not quite so obnoxious."[124] Significantly, when the seventeenth-century scientific "discoveries" seemingly anticipated by the Epicureans—such as the existence of atoms, the experimental proof of a vacuum, the infinity of space, and the plurality of worlds—forced men like Robert Boyle, Walter Charleton, and Isaac Barrow into "legitimizing" the Epicurean world view, the natural philosophers had taken exceptional care "to formulate a mechanical vision of the universe that emphasised at every turn the providential role of the Deity as the source of order and harmony imposed through laws at work in nature and capable of being imitated in society."[125]

Simultaneously, the unholy alliance betweeen Deism and Epicureanism was lambasted in contemporary eschatological poetry. It occurred as early as Sir William Alexander's *Dooms-Day* of 1614,[126] and it became a regular feature in the religious verse after the turn of the century. "My verse shall sound, shall make the atheist shrink, / And deist tremble," Samuel Catherall, for one, announced in the invocation of *An Essay on the Conflagration.*[127] And renewing Bentley's attack on the Deists, Joseph Trapp fumed in *Thoughts upon the Four Last Things*:

> ATHEIST I stile him; for He's much the Same;
> Tho' chusing DEIST'S somewhat milder Name.
> Speak then, dull Infidel, thy inmost Thought:
> Death's Nought, thou say'st, and after Death is Nought;
> A future State, vile Priestcraft's bugbear Theme,
> And all Reveal'd Religion is a Dream.[128]

The conclusion is obvious. If it is correct to assume that we serve Swift's verse best by "recovering the social, religious and literary history that verse responds to, records, and transforms,"[129] we have to take cognizance of two rival camps in English latter-day thought from the Renaissance to the Age of Reason. One, which is manned by hordes of cantankerous theologians, Bible commentators, and poets, proffers so *many* answers on the *eschata* of history as to present really *no* answer at all. As the Deist Charles Blount summed up in his commentary on Lord Herbert's *Five Catholick or Universal Articles of Religion*: "Concerning the Place, Quantity, Quality, Manner, or Duration of Reward or Punishment after this Life, there is no universal Consent or Agreement."[130] These are the ones who, in Jove's apostrophe in Swift's poem, are "blind by *Learning*" (12), *learning* being defined, in the words of Sir William Temple, as "the knowledge of the different and contested opinions of men in former ages, and about which they have perhaps never agreed in any."[131] The other camp, which is led by a couple of rationalist philosophers called Deists, brushes the "fact" of a future judgment aside. In their view, the great assize never happens. Having routed the terrors of superstition/religion ("vile Priestcraft's bugbear Theme"), they fall prey to the specter of eschatological hopelessness. These are the ones who, in Swift's poem, are "blind by *Reason*" (12), "*Free-Thinkers*" being, as the Dean had told the young gentleman lately entered into holy orders, "in Propriety of Speech...*no Thinkers at all.*"[132]

To complete the triad, the assumption that all of these eschatologists—theologians and commentators, as well as poets and philosophers—were also "blind by *Nature*" (12) was always taken for granted by Swift. "*Reason* itself is true and just," he stated in his sermon *On the Trinity*, "but the *Reason* of every particular Man is weak and wavering, perpetually swayed and turned by his Interests, his Passions, and his Vices," and "it must be allowed, that every Man is bound to follow the Rules and Directions of that Measure of Reason which God hath given him." Not only is man's reason perpetually "under the sway of subrational impulses and inclinations"; it is also "*only* a 'Measure of Reason' that man has."[133] A measure of reason indeed: *homo non est animal rationale.*

V

In "(On) the Day of Judgement," the Dean turns all the stereotypes on their heads, the theological and philosophical "myths" in the same way as the pious poetic cant. Since his early trifle, "Verses Wrote in a Lady's Ivory Table-Book," his satire was double-edged, simultaneously attacking the folly and vice around him as well as uttering pleas for an altered poetic vision.[134] That is why in Swift's verse distinct generic expectations—pastoral, georgic, or elegiac conventions—are provoked only in order to be sabotaged.[135] In his "inventiveness in discovering new uses for the ruins of the traditional form,"[136] "(On) the Day of Judgement" proves no exception to the rule.[137]

Not counting the introductory lines (1–3), the poem falls into two sections: a description of the apocalyptic turmoil preceding the Last Judgment (4–10) and Jove's apostrophe to sinful, trembling mankind (11–22).[138] In the first section, all the elements familiar from the intellectual and generic ancestry recur in admirable density and conciseness: the resurrection of the dead (4), the advent of an angry judge (5), the destruction of the material universe (6), and the terror of an anonymous mass of sinners trying to brace themselves for the divine verdict (7–8).

From the beginning, however, it is clear that the "awesome grandeur," "the genuine awe and fear at Jove's appearance"[139] promised by the title, is permeated by "signals of playfulness."[140] There is also, perhaps, an element of *serio ludere* in the echo of Pope's *Rape of the Lock*, where Ariel, like the speaker of Swift's poem (1) dreading "impending Woe," is described sitting "with careful Thoughts opprest."[141] Moreover, the traditional "vision," which is marked by physical and spiritual ecstasy, has deteriorated into a "Reverie" (2), which, by Swift's time, had acquired the meaning "fantastic, fanciful…idea" or "fit of abstracted musing."[142] "To say [God] hath spoken to [a man] in a Dream, is no more than to say he dreamed that God spake to him, which is not of force to win beleef from any man, that knows dreams are for the most part naturall, and may proceed from former thoughts," Thomas Hobbes commented drily in the *Leviathan*.[143] In this sense, it is possibly correct to say that the word vision is an "Augustan sneer."[144] Finally, there is the alleged mystery of "Jove," ostensibly a "deity from an outworn polytheism," playing here the role of "the Lord of all things visible and invisible."[145] Surely, the explanation is not that Jove is "a combination of traditional Christian and classically heroic elements," or that Swift was simply being "profane" or "ludicrous," or that he was indulging in some elaborate camouflage.[146] Since the beginning of the seventeenth century a fine was decreed against anyone who should "*jestingly* or *prophanely* speake or *use* the holy Name of God or Christ Jesus, or of the Holy Ghoste."[147] This being so, Swift did not have an alternative to "Jove": "Jove" simply appears where we should naturally expect "God." From the first lines, then, the odds are that, in "(On) the Day of Judgement," the Dean's tongue was in his cheek.[148]

Jove's apostrophe (11–22) is a stratified address which may be divided into two subsections. The first of these (11–18) opens with a seemingly general invective against mankind (" 'Offending Race of Human Kind" [11]), which in its second line specifies the vices which make the "Race of Human Kind" so offensive ("By Nature, Reason, Learning, blind" [12]); and it concludes with a hard-headed condemnation of those "Folks" who prided themselves on being privy to the secret operations of God. As Jove makes quite clear, however, this was but self-deception: "(So some Folks told you, but they knew / No more of Jove's Designs than you)" (17–18). There is a logical connection, then, between the beginning and conclusion of this subsection, the common denominator being blindness (11–12) and ignorance (17–18). The conclusion sums up once again the general indictment of the beginning: it targets, on the one hand, the nescience of theologians, Bible commentators, and poets, whose blindness in learning has left eschatology, the Christian interpretation of the purposiveness of history, in the state of "opinion," in a state of chaos, confusion, and doubt. On the other, it attacks rationalist philosophers like the Deists, whose blindness in reason likewise results in ignorance. As a consequence, "(On) the Day of Judgement" is not a satire upon the whole of mankind,[149] and it is not a satire upon "the paltry bickerings of the sects" either[150] (even if it *is* true that by the purported time of the poem's composition Swift felt "vexed" by the renewed brouhaha of the Dissenters).[151] Rather, the "intrinsic genre" of "(On) the Day of Judgement" is the whole spectrum of contemporary eschatological thought, sacred *and* profane.[152] If this assumption is correct, the poem is a satire on the arrant pretensions of the various religious *and* philosophical schools and on their proclivity to pass "judgment" on the other side. Swift does not have God ("Jove") put a fool's cap on the whole of mankind or on the divisive sectarians of his time. Instead, he has God ("Jove") put a fool's cap on the eschatologists, the men who make a show of knowing his final plan but who do not, the eternal shams and fake-redeemers of this world: "By Nature, Reason, Learning, blind" (12).

The brief middle section (13–16), sandwiched between the lines of hard-headed condemnation (11–12, 17–18), corroborates this interpretation. In it, each line exemplifies one facet of the general invective against the eschatologists: "*You* who thro' Frailty step'd aside" (13) spells out their "blindness by Nature," the weakness, that is, accruing from their subjection to "the miserable Condition of Man," in which reason is "discoloured by Passion and Interest."[153] The next group which Jove addresses, "*you* who never fell—*thro' Pride*" (14), personifies the pride, the "reas'ning Pride"[154] of philosophers like the Deists, who sin by pretending to probe deeper than they are given to know. "*Curiosity*," Bishop Edward Reynolds wrote in his *Works*, which were in the Dean's library, "may well be called the *pride* and the *wantonness* of knowledge, because it looketh after high things that are above us, and after *hidden things* that are denied us."[155] Finally, the last group, "*You* who in different Sects have shamm'd" (15), exposes the opinionativeness of "the Saints," not necessarily the rancor of the Dissenters only but also the uncharitableness of all denominations who show themselves avid to damn and to curse, even to rejoice at the suffering of the damned in hell ("And come to see each other damned" [16]). Thus faith, Pope might have written, like wit, "by each Man is apply'd / To *one small Sect*, and All are *damn'd beside.*"[156] *One* reason why the trial in Swift's poem is in fact a trial *without* judgment is that man, officious man, has already taken the work out of the Divine Judge's hands.

Yet, there is another, even weightier reason why the Lord ("Jove") falls silent at the end of his apostrophe, always supposing of course that the exclamation marks in the last two lines do not indicate exclamatory statements but incredulous questions: "I to such Blockheads set my Wit! / I damn such Fools!" (21–22).[157] The explanation is to be found in the Dean's attitude toward the mysteries of his faith, mysteries like the doctrine of the Trinity, the incarnation of Christ, the nature of transubstantiation, and the resurrection of the dead.[158] As he explained in *A Letter to a Young Gentleman*, and in his sermon *On the Trinity*, "Providence intended there should be Mysteries," it being impossible for man "to determine for what Reasons God thought fit to communicate some Things…in Part, and leave some Part a Mystery." Since this admitted of no doubt, it was fruitless for a clergyman to try to "explain" mysteries: "If you explain them, they are Mysteries no longer; if you fail, you have laboured to no Purpose."[159] As a consequence, Christians had to content themselves with the assurance that God did in fact exist but that nothing definitive was known of his essence or nature. God's essence, Hobbes, Locke, and countless others following in their wake proclaimed, was forever incomprehensible, unknowable, ineffable: "Therefore, when any thing [in God's word] is too hard for our examination, wee are bidden to captivate our understanding to the Words; and not to labour in sifting out a Philosophicall truth by Logick, of such mysteries as are not comprehensible," Hobbes had laid down in the *Leviathan*. However, he continued, "by the Captivity of our Understanding, is not meant a Submission of the Intellectuall faculty, to the Opinion of any other man; but of the Will to Obedience, *where obedience is due*."[160] Analogously, the impossibility of certain knowledge about the *novissima* made it imperative for man to stop his eternal prating, bickering, and fighting. It is significant that one poet who contributed to the competition for "*the best Poem on* LIFE, DEATH, JUDGMENT, HEAVEN *and* HELL" drove this very point home—by refusing to write about the Last Day. Confronted with the *eschata* of history, man, he declared, had but one choice, to be silent:

> Let the bold poet, aw'd, his pen lay by,
> Nor to explore these paths, forbidden, try,
> *Judgment, and heaven, and hell*, are themes too great
> For short ey'd mortals in our human state;
> Let things sublunary our genius prove,
> For *heav'n* is only truly known above.[161]

This is perhaps the deepest reason why Swift never *published* his poem: he would merely have joined in the chorus of those whose folly he had set out to expose.

One question remains to be settled, that of technique or rhetorical strategy. Given the lesson he wanted to teach and given the tactics he had resorted to in the past, Swift had (at least) two options: moralistic *adhortatio*, like that in "A Satirical Elegy on the Death of a Late Famous General,"[162] or "bite," the eighteenth-century catch phrase for "cheat, trick, or fraud,"[163] of which the "Elegy on Mr. Patrige" is perhaps the supreme example. In a *Spectator* essay, Addison defined "a biter" as someone "who thinks you a Fool, because you do not think him a knave";[164] and in a letter to William Tisdall, Swift similarly explained "a bite" as a joke at the cost of somebody's unsuspecting ignorance or naïveté:

I will teach you a way to outwit Mrs. Johnson: it is a newfashioned way of being witty, and they call it a *bite*. You must ask a bantering question, or tell some damned lie in a serious manner, and then she will answer or speak as if you were in earnest: and then cry you, 'Madam, there's a *bite*.'[165]

"(On) the Day of Judgement," then, is not a poem about the most horrifying of all visions, "the Almighty's refusal to make any distinctions."[166] Rather, it is a bite "selling" the ignoramuses in the "science" of eschatology, a hoax cheating the fools who make a show of being in the know about God's final plan, and it also beats them at a game they are particularly good at: "vexing" people. As the sneering mimicry of the fashionable society jargon ("Folks" [17], "Pranks" [20], "Blockheads" [21]) makes clear, too, the supreme judge does not suffer fools gladly; indeed, he does not suffer them at all.[167]

Even if this attitude is the universal pose of the satirist, this poem is a satire with a difference, the difference being that the tantrum-loving satirist-judge of "(On) the Day of Judgement" is a god who rules by *in*difference; that he turns out to be a judge whose utter dispassionateness is more wounding than savage indignation, contempt, or even hatred. No punishment is worse than indifference.[168] "I do not despise All Squires," Swift wrote to Robert Percival in 1730. "It is true I despise the bulk of them. But, pray take notice, that a Squire must have some merit before I shall honor him with my contempt. For, I do not despise a Fly, a Maggot, or a Mite."[169] And a little earlier, he had told Archbishop King that he "was not so liberal of [his] Contempt, nor would bestow it where there was not some Degree of Merit."[170] In other words, the "merit"-less absurdity of contemporary eschatology deserved neither Swift's laughter nor his indignation. While for a moment it seemed in "(On) the Day of Judgement" that satire had become God's own business,[171] the truth was that there was nothing left for God to say: the "World's *mad* [eschatological] Business" (19) was beneath his contempt.

At the beginning of the seventeenth century, Bacon had redefined man's relationship with God in the daring and influential metaphor of cosmic hide-and-seek:

'The glory of God is to conceal a thing, but the glory of the king is to find it out'; as if, according to the innocent play of children, the Divine Majesty took delight to hide his works, to the end to have them found out; and as if kings could not obtain a greater honour than to be God's playfellows in that game.[172]

Irrespective of the question whether this metaphor figured in Swift's thoughts as he pondered "(On) the Day of Judgement," the poem implicitly subverts God's relationship with man as envisaged by Bacon: there are areas of thought (like faith) which man is not supposed to penetrate; man is not supposed to be his playfellow in *this* game.

[1] See A. Owen Aldridge, *Voltaire and the Century of Light* (Princeton, NJ, 1975), p. 199.

[2] *The Poems of Jonathan Swift*, ed. Harold Williams, 2nd ed., 3 vols. (Oxford, 1958), II, 577; hereafter *Poems*. For proof that Chesterfield was familiar with Swift's hand, see *The Correspondence of Jonathan Swift*, ed. Harold Williams, rev. David Woolley, 5 vols. (Oxford, 1965–72), III, 419–20, 431–32; hereafter *Corresp.* For summaries of the complicated textual history of the poem, see *The Complete Poems*, ed. Pat Rogers (Harmondsworth, Mddx., 1983), pp. 863–64; hereafter Rogers; see also Milton Voigt, *Swift and the Twentieth Century* (Detroit, 1964), pp. 45–46. For details, see Sidney L. Gulick, Jr., "Jonathan Swift's 'The Day of Judgement,' " *PMLA*, 48 (1933), 850–55, and "No 'Spectral Hand' in Swift's 'Day of Judgement,' " *Papers of the Bibliographical Society of America*, 71 (1977), 333–36; Maurice Johnson, "Text and Possible Occasion for Swift's 'Day of Judgement,' " *PMLA*, 86 (1971), 210–17; George Mayhew, "Swift's 'On the Day of Judgement' and Theophilus Swift," *Philological Quarterly*, 54 (1975), 213–21; and Leland D. Peterson, "The Spectral Hand in Swift's'Day of Judgement,' " *Papers of the Bibliographical Society of America*, 70 (1976), 189–219.

[3] According to F. Elrington Ball, the original was in the possession of Swift's publisher, George Faulkner, "who passed [it] on to his patron Lord Chesterfield" (*Swift's Verse: An Essay* [London, 1929], p. 277), a view also taken by Gulick ("Jonathan Swift's 'The Day of Judgement,' " p. 851) but challenged by Mayhew (p. 218) and Peterson ("The Spectral Hand in Swift's 'Day of Judgement,' " pp. 201–08).

[4] Like Harold Williams (*Poems*, II, 577), Joseph Horrell tentatively suggests 1731 (*Collected Poems of Jonathan Swift*, 2 vols. [London, 1958], I, 98, 387); so does Ricardo Quintana (see *The Mind and Art of Jonathan Swift* [London, 1936], pp. 360–61). Maurice Johnson considers 1731 "a less likely date" than 1732 or 1733 ("Text and Possible Occasion," p. 215). This view has recently been endorsed by Leland D. Peterson, "Jonathan Swift and a Prose 'Day of Judgement,' " *Modern Philology*, 81 (1983–84), 401–06.

5 For two controversial statements, see Johnson, "Text and Possible Occasion," p. 214, and the rejoinder by W. B. Carnochan, "The Occasion of Swift's 'Day of Judgement,' " *PMLA*, 87 (1972), 518–20.

6 See Johnson, "Text and Possible Occasion," pp. 212–13.

7 Apart from *Poems*, II, 578, and *Rogers*, p. 864, see also Jonathan Swift, *Œuvres*, ed. Émile Pons et al. (Paris, 1965), p. 1848.

8 See "James Beattie…on *The Day of Judgment*," *Swift: The Critical Heritage*, ed. Kathleen Williams (London, 1970), p. 197 n.; Vivian Mercier, *The Irish Comic Tradition* (Oxford, 1962), p. 193; Donald Greene, "The Via Media in an Age of Revolution: Anglicanism in the 18th Century," *The Varied Pattern: Studies in the 18th Century*, ed. Peter Hughes and David Williams (Toronto, 1971), p. 318.

9 W. J. Courthope, *A History of English Poetry*, V (New York, 1962 [1925]), 138.

10 Mayhew, p. 219.

11 See Augustine Birrell, *Collected Essays*, 2 vols., 2nd ed. (London, 1902), II, 220; George Saintsbury, *A Short History of English Literature* (New York, 1900), p. 530; W. E. H. Lecky, "Biographical Introduction," in Swift, *Prose Works*, ed. Temple Scott, I (London, 1897), xl.

12 Ball, *Swift's Verse*, p. 262.

13 Nora Crowe Jaffe, *The Poet Swift* (Hanover, NH, 1977), p. 30.

14 Padraic Colum, "Swift's Poetry," *Dublin Magazine*, 6 (1967), 13.

15 G. F. Hamilton, "Dean Swift as a Churchman," *Irish Church Quarterly*, 10 (1917), 174.

16 See Richard H. Rodino, "Blasphemy or Blessing? Swift's 'Scatological' Poems," *Papers on Language and Literature*, 14 (1978), 153–54; "Varieties of Vexatious Experience in Swift and Others," *Papers on Language and Literature*, 18 (1982), 331–34.

17 I am indebted to a review by J. I. Fischer in the *Scriblerian*, 18 (1986), 195–97.

18 W. R. Irwin, "Swift the Verse Man," *Philological Quarterly*, 54 (1975), 234.

19 For discussion about the meaning of *eschatology* see, among others, Paul Althaus, *Die letzten Dinge: Lehrbuch der Eschatologie*, 9th ed. (Gütersloh, 1964), pp. 1–5. For my purposes, it is sufficient to take "eschatology" to mean "the expectation of an end of this earthly order," "an end that will be the accomplishment of God's world-plan," and the expectation of "a new order" which must "inevitably result" (Bruce Vawter, "Apocalyptic: Its Relation to Prophecy," *Catholic Biblical Quarterly*, 22 [1960], 37).

20 See John E. Groh, "The Kingdom of God in the History of Christianity: A Bibliographical Survey," *Church History*, 43 (1974), 257–67. Although more limited in scope, Hillel Schwartz, "The End of the Beginning: Millenarian Studies, 1969–1975," *Religious Studies Review*, 2, no. 3 (1976), 1–15, is also useful, and so is Bryan W. Ball, *A Great Expectation: Eschatological Thought in English Protestantism to 1660* (Leiden, 1975), in particular pp. 1–14.

21 The literature on this subject is vast, and I am indebted to more titles than I dare to remember; see, for example, Leon Morris, *The Biblical Doctrine of Judgment* (London, 1960); R. H. Charles, *Eschatology: The Doctrine of a Future Life in*

Israel, Judaism and Christianity (New York, 1963), in particular pp. 362–473; Peter Stockmeier, "Patristische Literatur und kirchliche Lehrdokumente als Zeugen der historischen Entwicklung der Lehre von Himmel, Hölle, Fegefeuer und Jüngstem Gericht," *Tod, Hoffnung, Jenseits: Dimensionen und Konsequenzen biblisch verankerter Eschatologie*, ed. Ferdinand Dexinger (Wien, 1983), pp. 41–60.

[22] See [George] Sewell in his "Life" prefixed to *The Whole Works of Mr. John Philips* (London: J. Tonson and T. Jauncy, 1720), p. xxix.

[23] *The City of God against the Pagans*, ed. and trans. William Chase Greene (London, 1960), XX. i (pp. 249–51); see also XX. iv–v (pp. 265–75).

[24] See, among others, Jaroslav Pelikan, "The Eschatology of Tertullian," *Church History*, 21 (1952), 108–22; Bernhard Kötting, "Endzeitprognosen zwischen Lactantius und Augustinus," *Historisches Jahrbuch der Görres-Gesellschaft*, 77 (1958), 125–39.

[25] See Grace E. Cairns, *Philosophies of History: Meeting of East and West in Cycle-Pattern Theories of History* (Westport, CT, 1971 [1962]), pp. 251–55; C. A. Patrides, *The Grand Design of God: The Literary Form of the Christian View of History* (London, 1972), pp. 16–18. On the transmission of the Augustinian view in the Renaissance, see Herschel Baker, *The Race of Time: Three Lectures on Renaissance Historiography* (Toronto, 1967), pp. 54–60. On Augustinianism in the Age of Reason, see Donald Greene, "Augustinianism and Empiricism: A Note on Eighteenth-Century English Intellectual History," *Eighteenth-Century Studies*, 1 (1967–68), 33-68.

[26] Quoted from the second edition (London: Ri. Chiswell, 1700), p. 67.

[27] Ball, *A Great Expectation*, p. 27.

[28] *The Resurrection Asserted* (Oxford: James Good, 1679), p. 27.

[29] Quoted from the fifth edition (London: W. Rogers, 1699), pp. 3–4.

[30] For a lovingly meticulous "painting" of the cosmic conflagration, see Henry More, *An Explanation of the Grand Mystery of Godliness* (London: by J. Flesher for W. Morden, in Cambridge, 1660), p. 445.

[31] The issue is elucidated in Fritz Heidler's *Die biblische Lehre von der Unsterblichkeit der Seele* (Göttingen, 1983), pp. 116–22. For a discussion nearer to Swift, see Thomas Burnet, *De Statu Mortuorum et Resurgentium Tractatus* (London: J. Hooke, 1727), pp. 41–103, 213–67.

[32] The structure of my account is to some extent indebted to Charles, *Eschatology*, in particular pp. 370–400.

[33] See *Oracles of Reason* (1693), Miscellaneous Works (New York, 1979 [1695]), p. 118.

[34] See John F. New, *Anglican and Puritan: The Basis of their Opposition, 1558–1640* (Stanford, 1964), pp. 76–81.

[35] *The Works of the Most Reverend Dr. John Tillotson*, 9th ed., 2 vols. (London: J. Round, J. Tonson, J. Darby, et al., 1728), I, 321.

[36] See *The Poems of John Dryden*, ed. James Kinsley, 4 vols. (Oxford, 1970 [1958]), I, 460.

[37] *Poems on Divine Subjects*, 2nd ed. (London: John Clark, 1721), pp. 70–72 (Foxon H91).

[38] See C. A. Patrides, *Milton and the Christian Tradition* (Oxford, 1966), pp. 279–80, and "Renaissance and Modern Views on Hell," *Harvard Theological Review*, 57 (1964), 217–36. The fullest and most systematic treatment is D. P. Walker's *The Decline of Hell: Seventeenth-Century Discussions of Eternal Torment* (Chicago, 1964).

[39] *A Practical Discourse*, p. 334.

[40] See New, *Anglican and Puritan*, pp. 77–78; Walker, pp. 51–53.

[41] See *Works*, I, 321.

[42] See William E. Alderman, "Shaftesbury and the Doctrine of Benevolence in the Eighteenth Century," *Wisconsin Academy of Sciences, Arts, and Letters*, 26 (1931), 137–59; Paul C. Davies, "The Debate on Eternal Punishment in Late Seventeenth- and Eighteenth-Century English Literature," *Eighteenth-Century Studies*, 4 (1970–71), 266–67.

[43] See Walker, pp. 34–40.

[44] Davies, "The Debate on Eternal Punishment," p. 257; see also E. R. Briggs, "Mysticism and Rationalism in the Debate upon Eternal Punishment," *Studies on Voltaire and the Eighteenth Century*, 24 (1963), 241–54.

[45] See Christopher Hill, *The World Turned Upside Down: Radical Ideas during the English Revolution* (London, 1972), pp. 177–79.

[46] See Walker, pp. 11–15, 104–05. In his list of sectarian heresies, *Gangraena* (1646), which was in Swift's library, Thomas Edwards refers to this belief several times; see George H. Sabine, ed., *The Works of Gerrard Winstanley* (New York, 1965 [1941]), pp. 25–26; and William LeFanu, *A Catalogue of Books belonging to Dr Jonathan Swift* (Cambridge, 1988), p. 17; see also C. A. Patrides, *Premises and Motifs in Renaissance Thought and Literature* (Princeton, NJ, 1982), pp. 200 17.

[47] See Walker, pp. 93–103.

[48] Davies, "The Debate on Eternal Punishment," p. 261; see also Anthony Collins, *A Discourse of Free-Thinking* (New York and London, 1978 [1713]), pp. 68–69.

[49] "A Dooms-Day Thought Anno 1659," *A Collection of English Poems*, ed. Ronald S. Crane (New York, 1932), p. 191; see also Ball, *A Great Expectation*, pp. 21–24, 89–125; Bernard Capp, *Astrology and the Popular Press: English Almanacs, 1500–1800* (London, 1979), pp. 164–79.

[50] See *An Explanation of the Grand Mystery*, p. 444.

[51] S. A. Burrell, "The Apocalyptic Vision of the Early Covenanters," *Scottish Historical Review*, 43 (1964), 3–4.

[52] See *The City of God*, XX. vii (pp. 283–93).

[53] See Katharine R. Firth, *The Apocalyptic Tradition in Reformation Britain, 1530–1645* (Oxford, 1979), pp. 6–31; Hans-Ulrich Hofmann, "Luther und die Johannes-Apokalypse, dargestellt im Rahmen der Auslegungsgeschichte des letzten Buches der Bibel und im Zusammenhang der theologischen Entwicklung des Reformators," Diss. Erlangen-Nürnberg 1982, in particular pp. 620–55.

[54] The last paragraph is a summary of Ernest Lee Tuveson, *Millennium and Utopia: A Study in the Background of the Idea of Progress* (New York, 1964 [1949]), pp. 22–30; see also B. S. Capp, *The Fifth Monarchy Men: A Study in Seventeenth-Century English Millenarianism* (London, 1972), pp. 23–32; and Jaroslav Pelikan, "Some Uses of Apocalypse in the Magisterial Reformers," *The Apocalypse in English Renaissance Thought and Literature: Patterns, Antecedents and Repercussions*, ed. C. A. Patrides and Joseph Wittreich (Manchester, 1984), pp. 81–92. Of course, Luther was not the first to identify Antichrist with the Church of Rome; see Marjorie Reeves, *Joachim of Fiore and the Prophetic Future* (London, 1976), pp. 136–39; and Richard Bauckham, *Tudor Apocalypse: Sixteenth Century Apocalypticism, Millennarianism and the English Reformation* (Oxford, 1978), pp. 91–112, 145–61, 208–32.

[55] See *Proceedings of the First Münster Symposium on Jonathan Swift*, ed. Hermann J. Real and Heinz J. Vienken (Munich, 1985), p. 367; hereafter *Proceedings*; see also pp. 383–84.

[56] I follow the English translation, *The Historical and Chronological Theatre* (London: George Wen and John Crosley, 1687), p. 1.

[57] See, among others, Klaus Scholder, *Ursprünge und Probleme der Bibelkritik im 17. Jahrhundert: ein Beitrag zur Entstehung der historisch-kritischen Theologie* (Munich, 1966), pp. 79–98.

[58] I am indebted to C. A. Patrides, "Renaissance and Modern Thought on the Last Things," *Harvard Theological Review*, 51 (1958), 169–74; and also to the fuller treatment in the same author's *Premises and Motifs in Renaissance Thought and Literature*, pp. 52–63.

[59] *Truths Victory against Heresie* (London: H. R., 1645), p. 44.

[60] See Peter Toon, ed., *Puritans, the Millennium and the Future of Israel, 1600–1660* (Cambridge, 1970), pp. 13–17; Patrides, "Renaissance and Modern Thought on the Last Things," pp. 182–83, and *Milton and the Christian Tradition*, pp. 278–79.

[61] On these topics, see in particular Norman Cohn, *The Pursuit of the Millennium* (London, 1957), pp. 272–306; P. G. Rogers, *The Fifth Monarchy Men* (New York, 1966), pp. 1–13, 28–46; Capp, *The Fifth Monarchy Men*; Tai Liu, *Discord in Zion: The Puritan Divines and the Puritan Revolution, 1640–1660* (The Hague, 1973), pp. 57–85; E. R. Chamberlin, *Antichrist and the Millennium* (New York, 1975), pp. 87–97.

[62] In addition to Capp, *The Fifth Monarchy Men*, pp. 36–42, and Liu, *Discord in Zion*, pp. 1–28, see also Keith Thomas, *Religion and the Decline of Magic: Studies in Popular Beliefs in Sixteenth- and Seventeenth-Century England* (Harmondsworth, Mddx., 1973 [1971]), pp. 166–71. For the interaction of the English Puritanical Revolution and Continental sectarians, see additionally Robert G. Clouse, "Johann Heinrich Alsted and English Millenarianism," *Harvard Theological Review*, 62 (1969), 189–207.

[63] Robert E. Lerner, "Medieval Prophecy and Religious Dissent," *Past & Present*, no. 72 (1976), 19.

[64] See Brian C. Cooper, "The Academic Re-Discovery of Apocalyptic Ideas in the 17th Century," *Baptist Quarterly*, 19 (1961), 29–34; Tuveson, *Millennium and Utopia*, pp. 76–85; Michael Murrin, "Revelation and Two Seventeenth Century Commentators," in *The Apocalypse in English Renaissance Thought and Literature*, pp. 125–46.

[65] See, among others, Margaret C. Jacob, "Millenarianism and Science in the Late Seventeenth Century," *Journal of the History of Ideas*, 37 (1976), 335–41.

[66] *Millennium and Utopia*, p. 117; see also M. C. Jacob and W. A. Lockwood, "Political Millenarianism and Burnet's *Sacred Theory*," *Science Studies*, 2 (1972), 265–79.

[67] See, among others, C. A. Patrides, " 'Something like Prophetick strain': Apocalyptic Configurations in Milton," in *The Apocalypse in English Renaissance Thought and Literature*, pp. 207–37; J. G. A. Pocock, "Time, History and Eschatology in the Thought of Thomas Hobbes," in *The Diversity of History*, ed. J. H. Elliott and H. G. Koenigsberger (London, 1970), pp. 149–98.

[68] Capp, *The Fifth Monarchy Men*, p. 45; see also Paul J. Korshin, "Queuing and Waiting: The Apocalypse in England, 1660–1750," in *The Apocalypse in English Renaissance Thought and Literature*, pp. 240–65.

[69] Jacob, "Millenarianism and Science," p. 336.

[70] For both views, see J. Dwight Pentecost, *Things to Come: A Study in Biblical Eschatology* (Edinburgh, 1966 [1958]), pp. 370–94.

[71] Hill, *The World Turned Upside Down*, p. 116.

[72] See Brian C. Cooper, "The Academic Re-Discovery of Apocalyptic Ideas in the 17th Century," *Baptist Quarterly*, 18 (1960), 352–53; Ball, *A Great Expectation*, pp. 160–71; Toon, pp. 26–32; Pocock, pp. 174–76.

[73] Ball, *A Great Expectation*, p. 160.

[74] In what follows, there seems little point in maintaining the distinction between "apocalyptic" and "eschatological" (see n. 19). I take "apocalyptic" writing to refer to an ideal state which is "attainable on earth" and which describes "a future state that will occur within the order of nature and within the ordinary temporal succession." When apocalyptic writing is concerned with a transcendental state, "outside of time, which will follow history," it becomes "eschatologically oriented" (Leland Ryken, *The Apocalyptic Vision in "Paradise Lost"* [Ithaca, 1970], p. 2).

[75] Both Vaughan and Flatman wrote several poems on eschatological themes; see *Henry Vaughan: The Complete Poems*, ed. Alan Rudrum (Harmondsworth, Mddx., 1976), pp. 151–55, 299–300; *A Collection of English Poems*, pp. 325–27.

[76] *Miscellanea Sacra: or, Poems on Divine and Moral Subjects*, 2nd ed. (London: Henry Playford, 1698), pp. 38, 138–40; for the text of "Dies irae, dies illa," see *The Oxford Book of Medieval Latin Verse*, ed. F. J. E. Raby (Oxford, 1966 [1959]), pp. 392–94.

[77] Quotations are from the seventh edition, *Poems upon Several Occasions* (London: D. Brown, J. Walthoe, A. Bettesworth, et al., 1727), pp. 121–32, bound

together with *Remains of the Revd. Mr. Pomfret* (London, 1727), pp. iii–iv, 8–17 (Foxon P721, P730).

[78] On the identification of the author, see Foxon S525 and headnote.

[79] See p. 133, and Raymond Dexter Havens, *The Influence of Milton on English Poetry* (Cambridge, MA, 1922), pp. 95–96.

[80] I here list a few titles which will not be mentioned later on: *Miscellanea Sacra: or, A Curious Collection of Original Poems, upon Divine and Moral Subjects* (London: Playford, 1705), pp. 31–33; *Omega: A Poem on the Last Judgment* (London: Edmund Parker, 1708), pp. 3–40 (Foxon O173); Michael Wigglesworth, *The Day of Doom: or, A Poetical Discription of the Great and Last Jud[g]ment* (Newcastle upon Tyne: printed by John White, 1711), pp. 1–50 (Foxon W457); William Bond, *A Description of the Four Last Things, viz. Death, Judgment, Hell, & Heaven* (London: John Clark, 1719), pp. 6–154 (Foxon B316–17); Joseph Addison, "Resurrectio Delineata ad Altare Col. Magd. Oxon.," *Works*, ed. Thomas Tickell, 4 vols. (London: Jacob Tonson, 1721), I, 413–17.

[81] See the edition by Selma L. Bishop, *Isaac Watts: Hymns and Spritual Songs, 1707–1748* (London, 1962), in particular pp. 22–23, 37–38, 39–40, 55, 59–60, 82–83, 87–88, 167–68, 204–05, 226–27, 242–43, 334–35. For the popularity of *Hymns and Spiritual Songs*, see Foxon, I, 872–73.

[82] See James Sutherland, ed., *Early Eighteenth Century Poetry* (London, 1965), pp. 25–26.

[83] See *Sacred Miscellanies: or, Divine Poems upon Several Subjects* (London: E. Curll, 1713), pp. 19–20. According to Hoxie Neale Fairchild, *Religious Trends in English Poetry, I, 1700–1740* (New York, 1958 [1939]), pp. 163–64, this poem is a translation from the Latin of "a well-known Lutheran theologian," Johann Gerhard (1582–1637). I have not seen the original.

[84] On the bibliography of this poem, see Foxon Y109–14; for its contemporary success, see *The Correspondence of Edward Young, 1683–1765*, ed. Henry Pettit (Oxford, 1971), p. 6, n. 1. For general criticism (and some analysis), see Erich König, *Edward Young: Versuch einer gedanklichen Interpretation auf Grund der Frühwerke* (Bern, 1954), pp. 14–22. Shortly after Young published his *Poem on the Last Day*, the first parody of the far-flung expectation of end-time was written; see "A True and Faithful Narrative," *John Gay: Poetry and Prose*, ed. Vinton A. Dearing and Charles E. Beckwith, 2 vols. (Oxford, 1974), II, 464–73; for this, see also Peterson, "Jonathan Swift and a Prose 'Day of Judgement,' " pp. 401–06.

[85] (Oxford: Anthony Peisley, 1720), pp. 1–65 (Foxon C76); see also Fairchild, *Religious Trends in English Poetry*, I, 119–20.

[86] *The Last-Day: A Poem, in XII. Books* (London: J. Peele, et al., 1720), pp. 1–389 (Foxon B561–63). A comparable enterprise was published three years later, *The Last Judgment of Men and Angels: A Poem in Twelve Books after the Manner of Milton* (London: William Mears, et al., 1723), by the prolific Thomas Newcombe (Foxon N254).

[87] *A Dissertation on Reading the Classics* (New York, 1972 [1715]), pp. 218–19.

[88] Pope, ed., *Miscellaneous Poems and Translations*, 3rd ed. (London: Bernard Lintot, 1720), pp. 279–85.

[89] *Corresp.*, III, 300, 312.

[90] The poem is advertised as published in the *Post Boy*, 9 March 1720/21. The preface to the second edition is dated 1 March 1720/21; see Foxon H222–23; Dorothy Brewster, *Aaron Hill: Poet, Dramatist, Projector* (New York, 1966 [1913]), p. 282.

[91] *The Works of the British Poets*, ed. Robert Anderson, VIII (London: J. and A. Arch, et al., 1795), 731.

[92] *The Private Journal and Literary Remains of John Byrom*, ed. Richard Parkinson, I, i (Chetham Society, 1854), 273.

[93] See *Journal to Stella*, ed. Harold Williams, 2 vols. (Oxford, 1948), II, 516, 550, 650–51.

[94] See 4 (1734), 382.

[95] See 5 (1735), headnote to May issue.

[96] *The Gentleman's Magazine Extraordinary* (July 1735), pp. 411–16 and *Gentleman's Magazine*, 6 (1736), 59.

[97] See p. 436.

[98] See *The Complete Works, Poetry and Prose, of the Rev. Edward Young*, ed. John Doran, 2 vols. (London, 1854), I, 281, l. 119; *Poems on Divine Subjects*, pp. 70–72.

[99] See *Thoughts upon the Four Last Things* (London: Lawton Gilliver, 1734), Part II, 6, ll. 35, 78–79, 84–85. Trapp is a late adherent of the "forensic theory of the Atonement" widely accepted by seventeenth-century theologians; see C. A. Patrides, "Milton and the Protestant Theory of the Atonement," *PMLA*, 74 (1959), 7–13.

[100] Pomfret, "Dies Novissima," *The Works of the British Poets*, VI, 503; see also, among others, Flatman, "A Dooms-Day Thought," *Collection of English Poems*, p. 191; Young, *The Complete Works*, I, 266. Another good example exhibiting the complete generic repertory of earlier eschatological verse is Elizabeth Rowe's "The Conflagration: An Ode," *The Miscellaneous Works in Prose and Verse*, ed. Theophilus Rowe, 2 vols. (London: R. Hett and R. Dodsley, 1739), I, 86–92.

[101] Hill, "The Judgement-Day," *The Works of the British Poets*, VIII, 731; see also Vaughan, *The Complete Poems*, pp. 153–54; Pomfret, *Poems upon Several Occasions*, p. 122; *The Gentleman's Magazine Extraordinary*, p. 423.

[102] Tate, *Miscellanea Sacra*, p. 38; Pomfret, "Dies Novissima," *The Works of the British Poets*, VI, 504; Hill, "The Judgement-Day," *The Works of the British Poets*, VIII, 730–32; *The Gentleman's Magazine Extraordinary*, p. 413.

[103] *Thoughts upon the Four Last Things*, Part II, 3, ll. 5–12.

[104] Trapp, *Thoughts upon the Four Last Things*, Part II, 4, ll. 19–20.

[105] Watts, "The Day of Judgment," *Early Eighteenth Century Poetry*, p. 26; Roscommon, "On the Day of Judgment," *The Works of the British Poets*, VI, 433; Trapp, *Thoughts upon the Four Last Things*, Part II, 4, l. 26.

[106] *The Gentleman's Magazine Extraordinary*, p. 401; Watts, "The Day of Judgment," *Early Eighteenth Century Poetry*, p. 26; Pomfret, *Poems upon Several Occasions*, p. 132; Alexander, *Dooms-Day, or, The Great Day of the Lords Judgment*, p. 151 (44).

[107] See *The Complete Works*, I, 263, ll. 19–21; 265, ll. 143–46; 279, ll. 5–16; "The Judgment-Day," *The Works of the British Poets*, VIII, 730.

[108] I have adopted Peter Dinzelbacher's definition of *vision*; see *Vision und Visionsliteratur im Mittelalter* (Stuttgart, 1981), p. 29.

[109] In addition to Dinzelbacher, I have found useful Howard Rollin Patch's *The Other World according to Descriptions in Medieval Literature* (Cambridge, MA, 1950), in particular pp. 80–133.

[110] The first edition appeared in 1667, and there were numerous reprints, the eleventh edition coming out in 1715. Although Quevedo was not in Swift's library, there is some internal evidence that the Dean read him; see Irvin Ehrenpreis, *The Personality of Jonathan Swift* (New York and London, 1969 [1958]), pp. 43–45.

[111] Quoted from the tenth edition of *The Visions of Dom Francisco de Quevedo Villegas: Made English by Sir Roger L'Estrange* (London: Richard Sare, 1708), p. 72.

[112] See "Dies Novissima," *The Works of the British Poets*, VI, 502–03; for Marshall Smith's epic, see the title referred to in n. 78.

[113] See *The World to Come: The Glories of Heaven and the Terrors of Hell, Lively Display'd* (London: John Gwillim, 1711).

[114] See pp. 31–32.

[115] See also Roscommon, "On the Day of Judgment," *The Works of the British Poets*, VI, 433; Young, *The Complete Works*, I, 279, ll. 1–28; *The Gentleman's Magazine Extraordinary*, pp. 397, 408, 410, 413, 421, 424, 428.

[116] Pomfret, *Poems upon Several Occasions*, p. 132; see also Daniel, "Sentence Pronounced upon Sinners," *Miscellaneous Poems and Translations*, ed. Pope, p. 280; *The Gentleman's Magazine Extraordinary*, pp. 398, 408, 414, 421, 424.

[117] "The Grounds of Criticism in Poetry" (1704), *The Critical Works of John Dennis*, ed. Edward Niles Hooker, 2 vols. (Baltimore, 1939–43), I, 356.

[118] Flatman, "A Dooms-Day Thought," *A Collection of English Poems*, p. 191; Roscommon, "On the Day of Judgment," *The Works of the British Poets*, VI, 433; Watts, "The Day of Judgment," *Early Eighteenth Century Poetry*, p. 26; *The Gentleman's Magazine Extraordinary*, pp. 399, 414.

[119] *Sacred Miscellanies*, p. 20; see also *The Gentleman's Magazine Extraordinary*, p. 401.

[120] For this and the following, see Hermann Josef Real, *Untersuchungen zur Lukrez-Übersetzung von Thomas Creech* (Bad Homburg v.d.H., 1970), particularly pp. 11–19, 75–99; Sabina Fleitmann, *Walter Charleton (1620–1707), "Virtuoso": Leben und Werk* (Frankfurt, 1986), pp. 212–39. There is a comprehensive bibliography in either work.

121 Rochester's translation of Lucretius, I, 57–62 (= II, 645–50), ed. Thomas Creech (Oxford: Abel Swall and Tim. Child, 1695); *The Complete Poems of John Wilmot, Earl of Rochester*, ed. David M. Vieth (New Haven, 1974 [1968]), p. 35.

122 See the succinct summary by G. Gawlick in *Historisches Wörterbuch der Philosophie*, II, s.v. "Deismus," and the more recent and detailed account in Karl-Josef Walber, *Charles Blount (1654–1693), Frühaufklärer: Leben und Werk* (Frankfurt, 1988), pp. 237–62.

123 See on this Kathleen Williams, *Jonathan Swift and the Age of Compromise* (Lawrence, 1968 [1958]), pp. 34–38; Phillip Harth, *Swift and Anglican Rationalism: The Religious Background of "A Tale of a Tub"* (Chicago, 1969 [1961]), pp. 20–22, 31–32, 47–48, 161–162; [*The Prose Writings of Jonathan Swift*], ed. Herbert Davis et al., 14 vols. (Oxford, 1939–68, various reimpressions, sometimes corrected, 1957–69), IX, 108–11; hereafter *Prose*.

124 *The Folly of Atheism, and (What is now Called) Deism*, The Works of Richard Bentley, ed. Alexander Dyce, 3 vols. (Hildesheim, 1971 [1838]), III, 4; see also pp. 6–7, and, in addition to the work by Walber referred to in n. 122, George Depue Hadzsits, *Lucretius and His Influence* (London, 1935), pp. 284–332.

125 Margaret C. Jacob, *The Radical Enlightenment* (London, 1981), p. 66; see also Fleitmann, *Walter Charleton*, pp. 240–59.

126 See p. 151 (stanzas 44–45).

127 See Fairchild, I, 119; *The Gentleman's Magazine Extraordinary*, p. 410.

128 See Part I, 11, ll. 199–204; see also Pomfret's attack on Lucretius in "On the General Conflagration," *The Works of the British Poets*, VI, 499.

129 John Irwin Fischer in the *Scriblerian*, 18 (1986), 197.

130 *Religio Laici: Written in a Letter to John Dryden* (London: R. Bentley and S. Magnes, 1683), p. 71.

131 See on the background of this idea, Swift, *The Battle of the Books*, ed. Hermann Josef Real (Berlin, 1978), pp. LVIII–LX.

132 *Prose*, IX, 78.

133 *Prose*, IX, 166, 161; introduction by Louis Landa, *Prose*, IX, 109; see also *Prose*, IX, 190.

134 Arno Löffler, *"The Rebel Muse": Studien zu Swifts kritischer Dichtung* (Tübingen, 1982), p. 33; see also pp. 61, 64, 71, 78, 83.

135 This procedure is no doubt generally true of Swift's verse and prose (see also Clive T. Probyn, *"Gulliver's Travels": A Critical Study* [Harmondsworth, Mddx., 1987], p. 108), even if it is not "mechanically" true; see the healthy warning by Charles Peake, "Swift's Birthday Verses to Stella," *Proceedings*, pp. 175–86.

136 Charles Peake, "Poetry, 1700–1740," pp. 140–41 in *Dryden to Johnson*, ed. Roger Lonsdale (New York, 1987 [1971]).

137 This argument is not original, of course, but it has not been substantiated in the detail that seems desirable; see particularly Rodino, "Varieties of Vexatious Experience," pp. 331–33; John Irwin Fischer, "The Dean *contra* Heathens: Swift's *The Day of Judgement*," *Revue des Langues Vivantes*, 43 (1977), 592–97; Irwin, "Swift the Verse Man," pp. 234–35; Arno Löffler, "Jupiter als Weltenrichter:

Swifts 'The Day of Judgement' und das Satire-Verständnis des englischen Klassizismus," *Von Herzen gern: Festschrift zum 240jährigen Bestehen des Gymnasium Fridericianum Erlangen* (Erlangen, 1985), pp. 75–77.

[138] I do not entirely agree with T. Henry Smith, who also sees a tripartite structure; see "Swift's *The Day of Judgement*," *Explicator*, 22 (1963), #6.

[139] See Rodino, "Varieties of Vexatious Experience," p. 332; A. B. England, "Byron, Swift, Butler, and Burlesque," *Byron's "Don Juan" and Eighteenth-Century Literature: A Study of Some Rhetorical Continuities and Discontinuities* (Lewisburg, 1975), p. 121.

[140] Peter J. Schakel, "Swift's Poetry Revisited," *Proceedings,* pp. 238–39.

[141] *The Poems of Alexander Pope*, ed. John Butt et al., 11 vols. (New Haven, 1939–69), II, 163, 53–54; hereafter *TE*.

[142] See Anton Ksoll, "Die französischen Lehn- und Fremdwörter in der englischen Sprache der Restaurationszeit," Diss. Breslau 1933, p. 92.

[143] Quoted from the edition by C. B. Macpherson (Harmondsworth, Mddx., 1986 [1968]), p. 411.

[144] Max Byrd, *Visits to Bedlam: Madness and Literature in the Eighteenth Century* (Columbia, SC, 1974), pp. 64–65.

[145] Irwin, "Swift the Verse Man," p. 234.

[146] See Jaffe, p. 27; *Swift: The Critical Heritage*, p. 197; Mayhew, pp. 218–19; Henry Craik, *The Life of Jonathan Swift*, 2nd ed., 2 vols. (London, 1894), II, 228; Philip Wolff-Windegg, *Swift* (Stuttgart, 1967), p. 280.

[147] See *Twelfth Night*, ed. J. M. Lothian and T. W. Craik, 2nd ed. (London, 1977 [1975]), pp. xxiii–xxiv. The italics are mine.

[148] This interpretation is corroborated by *Spectator* 558 and 559 as well as by W. B. Carnochan, "Swift's Poetic Gods: Jove, Apollo, Janus," *Proceedings*, pp. 15–17.

[149] This view that the poem is a "satire on all" is held, among others, by W. B. Carnochan; see his "The Occasion of Swift's 'Day of Judgement,' " pp. 518–20; "Swift's Poetic Gods," p. 17; see also Maurice Johnson, *The Sin of Wit: Jonathan Swift as a Poet*, (Syracuse, 1950), pp. 81–82; Basil Hall, " 'An Inverted Hypocrite': Swift the Churchman," *The World of Jonathan Swift: Essays for the Tercentenary*, ed. Brian Vickers (Oxford, 1968), pp. 50–51; Donald Greene, "Swift: Some Caveats," *Studies in the Eighteenth Century*, II, ed. R. F. Brissenden (Canberra, 1973), p. 342; Jaffe, pp. 29–30; Allan Ingram, *Intricate Laughter in the Satire of Swift and Pope* (London, 1986), pp. 163–64.

[150] James Hay, *Swift: The Mystery of His Life and Love* (London, 1891), p. 335.

[151] See Johnson, "Text and Possible Occasion for Swift's 'Day of Judgement,'" pp. 210–17; Gulick, "Jonathan Swift's 'The Day of Judgement,'" pp. 850–55; Peterson, "Jonathan Swift and a Prose 'Day of Judgement,' " pp. 401–06. There is a good summary of the critical history of the two positions in Fischer, "The Dean *contra* Heathens," pp. 592–94.

[152] For the definition of "intrinsic genre," see E. D. Hirsch, Jr., *Validity in Interpretation* (New Haven, 1967), pp. 78–89.

153 See *Prose*, IX, 190; *Prose*, XI (rev. ed., 1959) 267. According to the *OED*, *frailty* suggests not only "moral weakness" like fleshly vice but also "instability of mind."

154 *TE*, III. 1, 30, l. 123 and n. See also the *Gentleman's Magazine*, 4 (1734), 382, where the line from Pope is quoted, together with this comment: "*The impiety of putting ourselves in the place of God and judging of his dispensations.*"

155 (London: T. Newcomb for R. Boulter, 1679), p. 754. In the sale catalogue of Swift's library, the *Works* is lot 629 (Harold Williams, *Dean Swift's Library* [Cambridge, 1932]); Williams, *Jonathan Swift and the Age of Compromise*, pp. 34–38; Arthur Clayborough, *The Grotesque in English Literature* (Oxford, 1965), pp. 115–17.

156 *TE*, I, 285, ll. 396–97; see also "The Universal Prayer," *TE*, VI, 147, ll. 25–28; and Joseph Glanvill's *Vanity of Dogmatizing* (London: Henry Eversden, 1661), the second edition of which, under the title *Scepsis Scientifica* (London: Henry Eversden, 1665), Swift read and denounced in 1699 (see *Scepsis Scientifica*, pp. 168–70 and *Corresp.*, I, 30). These parallels invalidate Richard Rodino's "Robert Gould and Swift's 'The Day of Judgement,' " *Notes and Queries*, 224 (1979), 549.

157 See Charles R. Sleeth, "Swift's 'Day of Judgement,' " *PMLA*, 88 (1973), 144–45.

158 For an interpretation of this view, see, among others, F. M. Darnall, "Swift's Religion," *Journal of English and German Philology*, 30 (1931), 379–82, and "Swift's Belief in Immortality," *Modern Language Notes*, 47 (1932), 448–51; Louis A. Landa, "Swift, the Mysteries, and Deism," *Studies in English* (University of Texas), 24 (1944), 239–56; Harth, pp. 46–47.

159 See *Prose*, IX, 77, 162.

160 See p. 410 (my italics); compare *Prose*, IX, 162, 164. For a reassessment of Swift's attitude towards Hobbes, see Irvin Ehrenpreis, "The Doctrine of *A Tale of a Tub*," *Proceedings*, pp. 62 71.

161 *The Gentleman's Magazine Extraordinary*, pp. 425–26; see also *TE*, III, 1, 25–26, ll. 91–98.

162 See Hermann J. Real and Heinz J. Vienken, " 'Lost to All Shame': Swift's *A Satirical Elegy on the Death of a Late Famous General*," *Festschrift für Karl Schneider*, ed. Ernst S. Dick and Kurt R. Jankowsky (Amsterdam, 1982), pp. 471–72.

163 See *A New Canting Dictionary* (London: sold by the booksellers of London and Westminster, 1725); Donald T. Siebert, "*Bubbled*, *Bamboozled*, and *Bit*: 'Low Bad' Words in Johnson's *Dictionary*," *Studies in English Literature*, 26 (1986), 489–90.

164 *Spectator* 504; see also *Tatler* 12.

165 *Corresp.*, I, 40; Swift was fond of "a good bite," and the word often occurs in his works; see, for example, *Journal to Stella*, I, 125 and n., II, 467, 599, 652; *Poems*, I, 107, 208; II, 708, 710 and elsewhere.

166 Rodino, "Varieties of Vexatious Experience," p. 334.

167 See on Jove's language, Irwin, p. 235; Rodino, "Varieties of Vexatious Experience," pp. 333–34.

[168] See *Leviathan*, p. 120.

[169] *Corresp.*, III, 368.

[170] *Corresp.*, II, 406.

[171] See Jaffe, pp. 28–29; Robert C. Elliott, *The Literary Persona* (Chicago, 1982), pp. 142–43.

[172] See *The Advancement of Learning*, ed. Arthur Johnston (Oxford, 1974), pp. 40–41.

Marita Born, Margret Geiping, and Annegret Woestmann have all discussed the poem with me on various occasions, and I gratefully acknowledge the inspiration I have had from them. I am also deeply grateful to a number of friends who read the manuscript and who were liberal of time, and advice, and encouragement: Edgar Mertner, Barry Miller, Helgard Stöver-Leidig, Heinz-Dieter Leidig, and Theodor Dopheide. I am indebted to Heinz J. Vienken for some of the material used in this essay.

Charles H. Peake

Swift on Poets and Poetry

THE NOTION THAT SWIFT had a peculiarly anti-poetic, sceptical, even sardonic view of poets and poetry seems to have originated in (or, at least, derived authority from) Herbert Davis's pronouncement in 1931 that Swift was

the most extreme example that we have ever had in England of reaction against the heroic or romantic view of the poet's function and art,[1]

an account reinforced by such statements as Ricardo Quintana's (1936) that

Swift's uncompromisingly hostile view of the poetic imagination was something unique, and not, as many would have it, the characteristic attitude of his age.[2]

Not surprisingly, this notion colored the reading of Swift's poetry, at that time neglected, and, as late as 1984, *Essential Articles for the Study of Jonathan Swift's Poetry*[3] found it necessary to entitle its first section "Poetry and Anti-Poetry," including in that section, on the one hand, "The Anti-Poetry of Jonathan Swift" (1965) by E. San Juan, Jr.,[4] and, on the other, Robert W. Uphaus's "Swift's Poetry: The Making of Meaning" (1972),[5] which protested against the "anti-poetic" label. The dates of these articles are significant: the first indicates the persistence of Davis's account into the fifties and early sixties, when the voguishness of *anti-* as a critical prefix made it tempting to follow "the anti-novel" and "the anti-hero" with "the anti-poet"; the second is representative of the resurgence of interest in Swift's poetry in the sixties, which eventually produced a radical revaluation.[6] This new interest, properly, concentrated on Swift's poetic practice rather than his theory, but the vestigial influence of the old generalizations about his critical attitude can still be detected in a readiness to present him as uncommonly down-to-earth and matter-of-fact in his views of poets and poetry. I shall argue that, insofar as Swift's views were extreme, they were extreme in their loftiness and heroic assumptions.

There are some obvious difficulties to be found in any attempt to ascertain Swift's position, difficulties which certainly contributed to its misrepresentation: the shifting indirectness of a writer who specialized in complex irony; the problem of distinguishing between comments on those who claimed to be poets and comments on those whom Swift judged worthy of the title; and the variations of meaning, according to literary and social context, in such crucial terms as *genius*, *poet*, and *inspiration*.

Genius, for instance, as used by Swift, may refer to no more than a natural bent or minor talent, and can be used for compliment, as when applied to Delany's verse-writing,[7] or in belittling fashion, as when Swift told Steele

> Thy *Genius* has perhaps a knack
> At trudging in a beaten Track,[8]

or spoke of "the true Genius of Party."[9] But when he speaks of a man of genius, or a true, great, or sublime genius, Swift is moving to a different plane. Like Dr. Johnson, he seems to have believed that a true genius was "a mind of large general powers, accidentally determined to some particular direction":[10] Pope was "A Genius for all Stations fit"[11] and Bolingbroke a "superior universal Genius."[12] The belief that such genius, being bestowed by providence, was inseparably allied to virtue was a commonplace, of course, but it remained powerfully attractive to Swift throughout his career. In *The Battle of the Books* the Bee asserts, "*I am obliged to Heaven alone for my Flights and my Musick; and Providence would never have bestowed me two such Gifts, without designing them for the noblest Ends,*"[13] and in 1733 Swift agreed with Pope about "the morality of Poets":

I know not whither virtue can possibly find a corner to retire, except in the Hearts of men of Genius and Learning, and what you call their Levityes have not the least tinture of impiety, but directly otherwise, tend to drive vice out of the world.[14]

In his most sanguine estimate, Swift reckoned that such geniuses "are seldom above three or four Cotemporaries."[15]

At the lower level of genius, there existed the same bond with virtue, so that even a minor gift could not successfully be prostituted. Swift warned Delany that, if he planned to employ his muse in the service of faction, he would first have to become dull:

> If not, however seated high,
> Your Genius in your Face will fly

—this as a consequence of the fact that

> Wit, as the chief of Virtue's Friends,
> Disdains to serve ignoble Ends.
> . . . .
> For, though the Muse delights in Fiction,
> She ne'er inspires against Conviction.[16]

It was, no doubt, convenient for a controversialist like Swift to declare that his opponents, by attaching themselves to the wrong cause, had been deserted by any talents they might previously have possessed, but his conviction that genius, at either level, could not be divorced from virtue was part of his religious belief that all human gifts came from God, and were designed to serve the ends of Providence.[17] Short of seeing men of genius or poets as prophets or divine messengers, it would be difficult to frame a more exalted conception of their nature and function. What could be more "heroic" than the belief that such people, though so few in number, would, if united, "drive the world before them"?[18]

What was true of geniuses was equally true of the subgroup of true poets. Here, the opening lines of "On Poetry: A Rapsody" supply the most emphatic statement of Swift's position:

> Say *Britain*, cou'd you ever boast,
> Three *Poets* in an Age at most?
> Our chilling Climate hardly bears
> A *Sprig* of Bays in Fifty Years:
> While ev'ry Fool his Claim alledges,
> As if it grew in common Hedges.[19]

Such exclusivity would be rejected indignantly by the multitude of poets of that age or of this, and by most critics as well, but it is clearly a consequence, not of a low regard for poetry, but of an almost sublime vision of its supreme value, rarity, and difficulty. "On Poetry: A Rapsody" goes on in even more seemingly extravagant terms:

> Not *Empire* to the Rising-Sun,
> By Valour, Conduct, Fortune won;
> Nor highest *Wisdom* in Debates
> For framing Laws to govern States;
> Nor Skill in Sciences profound,
> So large to grasp the Circle round;
> Such heavenly Influence require,
> As how to strike the *Muses Lyre*.[20]

Taking into account what he said of men of genius, it is plain that Swift is not merely using a conventional figure in speaking of "heavenly Influence." There is no reason for supposing that he thought a true poet depended on the direct guidance of God, but he certainly believed the poet was bound to employ his gifts in accordance with some Providential design. And, like the genius, the poet paid a price in worldly terms for his gift. No one, however low in origin, was "so disqualified"

> To rise in *Church*, or *Law*, or *State*,
> As he, whom *Phebus* in his Ire
> Hath *blasted* with poetic Fire.[21]

His innate association with virtue made him unable to "bribe, betray, or plot,"[22] or even to flatter competently, and the productions of his muse were ignored or quickly dismissed. Swift's image of the poet, suffering for his gift, foreshadows the modern romantic myth of the artist with his incurable wound, presented by Edmund Wilson's *The Wound and the Bow*, and I suspect that very few critics of today would go as far as to assert that a true poet is inescapably a moral one.

Swift, like Horace, saw the distinction between true poets and mediocre poets as one not of degree but of kind: "Singers like their brothers the Poets must be very good, or they are good for Nothing."[23] When he was sent the works of John Hughes, to which both Pope and Orrery were subscribers, Swift wrote bluntly in his copy, "The Author is a mediocre [*sic*] Poeta,"[24] and informed both his friends of this assessment, adding for Orrery's benefit,

The Verses and prose are such as our Dublin third rate rimers might write just the same for nine hours a day till the coming of Antichrist.[25]

He was infuriated by laborious or supposedly inspired scribblers laying claim to the title of poet, an honor he did not claim for himself; the same lofty criteria that rendered him indifferent to the mediocre and contemptuous of the hacks made him describe himself as having been "only a Man of Rhimes."[26]

It is true that Swift, at times, modified his literary standards for the sake of friendship, though it was probably deliberately guarded praise to call Mrs. Barber "the best Poetess of both Kingdoms"[27] or William Dunkin "the best English as well as Latin Poet in this Kingdom"[28] (i.e., Ireland). In fact, his commendation of Mrs. Barber continues significantly, "If there be any others they are behind her, longo intervallo," and, in a private letter to Pope, he refers merely to her "knack of versifying."[29] Plainly his recommendation of deserving friends was a social rather than a critical act.

Perhaps the same may be said of his use of "inspires" when speaking of Delany's verse, though this is not the only occasion, by any means, on which he used the word and its cognate forms. But he rarely does so except where the context indicates that he is speaking figuratively or ironically. It may well be that the association with religious fanaticism made Swift somewhat uneasy about using the word: he had no wish to imply that a poet was the mouthpiece for "a divine breath"[30] (to use Sidney's phrase). But it would be foolish to conclude from this that he was unfamiliar with or did not recognize the phenomenon experienced by all writers—that at unpredictable times they compose with unaccustomed ease and with what seems like unpremeditated art, which, roughly speaking, is what most of us mean by "inspiration." When he learned that Pope had taken little pains and spent only two mornings over the "Imitation of the First Satire of the Second Book of Horace," Swift explained to Orrery the brilliance of the poem by saying that "this may happen when a Poet lights upon a fruitfull hint, and becomes fond of it," and later told Pope that his two mornings were "worth 2 years of any Poets life except yours."[31] At various times, in order to avoid the mystical connotations of "inspiration," Swift used such expressions as "when the humor sits" or when the "fitt" comes, or "a fruitful hint…owing as much to good Fortune as to Invention,"[32] but his distrust of the word cannot be interpreted as a distrust of poetic inspiration: he knew from his own experience how important an aspect of composition it was and was fully aware that no writer, however learned and industrious, would achieve much without it.

But, equally, he knew that a poet could not simply depend on his innate gift, his genius, his inspiration. The absurdity of the Moderns, represented by the Spider, was that they relied entirely on their *"native Stock, and great Genius,"* whereas the Bee produced sweetness and light by adding to its Providential gifts *"infinite Labor, and search."*[33] The *locus classicus* is provided by Horace:

> natura fieret laudabile carmen an arte
> quaesitum est: ego nec studium sine divite vena
> nec rude quid prosit video ingenium; alterius sic
> altera poscit opem res et coniurat amice,[34]

and echoed by Sir William Temple:

But tho' Invention be the Mother of Poetry, yet this child is like all others born naked, and must be Nourished with Care, Cloathed with Exactness and Elegance, Educated with Industry, Instructed with Art, Improved by Application, Corrected with Severity, and Accomplished with Labour and with Time, before it Arrives at any great Perfection or Growth.[35]

That is precisely Swift's position; he scorned those who, like Corusodes, had some erudition but were "utterly devoid of all *Taste, Judgment,* or *Genius,*"[36] and he was not impressed by the vogue for Stephen Duck, the thresher poet,[37] whose lack of learning was seen by some as a guarantee of his genius.

For Swift, the learning chiefly necessary to any writer was a familiarity with classical literature, although he urged Thomas Sheridan the younger "to lay aside some portion of time every day for the study of English,"[38] and he blamed on the neglect of such study "a flat Kind of Phraseology, often mingled with barbarous Terms and Expressions, peculiar to the Nation."[39] But, from the classics, the aspiring writer could derive not only general benefits—they would enlarge his mind, extend and refine his imagination, direct his judgment[40]—but the essentials of his art—the nature of the literary kinds and the methods and diction appropriate to each of them. All these were common recommendations of classical learning; what is especially characteristic of Swift is the argument that the writer should study the classics not just to imitate them but to perceive how they might be emulated or improved on:

If a Writer would know how to behave himself with relation to Posterity; let him consider in old Books, what he finds, that he is glad to know; and what Omissions he most laments.[41]

Talk of the supposed hostility of early eighteenth-century writers to originality, commonplace fifty years ago, is now infrequent, but it remains true that, more emphatically than most of his contemporaries, Swift dwelt on the importance of being original. No criticism of *A Tale of a Tub* seems to have angered him more than the suggestion that he had borrowed from other authors: "*I know nothing more contemptible in a Writer than the Character of a Plagiary.*"[42] Attacks on plagiarists and "plodding, servile, imitating Pedants"[43] are to be found in his early pindarics and recur throughout his work. Ironically he suggested, looking at the contemporary literary world, that success in poetry, as in robbery, was "attained by transferring of Propriety, and a confounding of *Meum* and *Tuum*,"[44] while the typical hack-poet was pictured

starving in a Garret,
Conning old Topics like a Parrot.[45]

Even friends whose work he greatly admired were liable to criticism for failing to pursue originality. When Gay declared his intention of writing more fables and another play, Swift urged him to "take some new scheme quite different from any thing you have already touched,"[46] and, after Gay's death, Swift remembered this advice and regretted that Gay had not followed it:

I have sometimes chid poor Mr Gay for dwelling too long upon a hint (as he did in the sequell of the Beggars opera, and this unlucky posthumous production [i.e., *Achilles*])…. I have been told that few Painters can copy their own originals to perfection, And I believe the first thoughts on a Subject, that occurs to a Poets imagination are usually the most natural[.][47]

This idea of what was most "natural" to a writer was an important element in Swift's concept of originality. An original stylist was not one who labored to write differently from everyone else but one who found a form of expression that was natural to him; "I would have every man write his own English," he told Mrs. Pilkington, and grew angry with her husband for failing to understand the distinction between "good English" and "his own English."[48]

In his *Letter to the Lord Treasurer*, Swift was explicit about the quality and character of originality in men of genius:

I do not mean by a true Genius, any bold Writer, who breaks through the Rules of Decency to distinguish himself by the Singularity of Opinions; but one, who upon a deserving Subject, is able to open new Scenes, and discover a Vein of true and noble Thinking, which never entered into any Imagination before: Every Stroke of whose Pen is worth all the Paper blotted by Hundreds of others in the Compass of their Lives.[49]

The most remarkable illustration of this devotion to the concept of the originality of true genius is that, when Pope's translations of Homer were being generally acclaimed as masterpieces, Swift saw them as distractions from Pope's real work in life:

I am exceedingly pleased that you have done with Translations[.] Lord Treasurer Oxford often lamented that a rascaly World should lay you under a Necessity of Misemploying your Genius for so long a time.

What Lord Oxford may have said to Swift we cannot know: what we do know is that it was Swift, writing to Oxford, who expressed the opinion that Pope's *Odyssey* would "bring more Profit than Reputation," and added, "I wish his Fortunes could afford him to employ his own Genius."[50] It was not that Swift despised translation, but, as he told William Diaper, he was "a little angry when those who have a genius lay it out in translations."[51]

Swift was not the only critic of his time to place originality high in the scale of literary values, but his insistence on that quality is a major characteristic of his critical position, and he might have forgiven certain misjudgments and errors in Dr. Johnson's life of Swift for its conclusion:

perhaps no writer can easily be found that has borrowed so little, or that in all his excellences and all his defects has so well maintained his claim to be considered as original.[52]

However, for Swift, the kind of authorial independence suggested by his demand that a true poet should write his own English and employ his own genius did not imply that there was no help to be derived from other people:

every one can best find hints for himself; though it is possible, that sometimes a friend may give you a lucky one just suited to your own imagination.[53]

He himself had a fertile imagination and gave "hints" to Pope, Gay, and Steele, as well as to such lesser writers as Mrs. Manley and Harrison. It is more remarkable to find a supposedly proud and irascible man so ready to spend time on minute criticism of the work of others, before it was published, and so welcoming of similar criticism of his own writings. He and his "little senate" corrected and improved the poems of Mrs. Barber, and he both offered, and apologized for offering, minor criticisms of Pope's work, "for since I have left off writing, I am sunk into a Critick."[54] He showed the same humility, though in a more didactic manner, to Thomas Beach, author of *Eugenio, or a Virtuous and Happy Life*:

You will do right to read over your poem carefully, and observe where there be any more oversights of the same kind with those I have noted, and to be corrected; which you can do better than any other person. A friend can only see what is amiss, but the writer can mend it more easily.[55]

Conversely, the story of his submission to Addison's corrections of "Baucis and Philemon" ("Mr *Addison* made him blot out fourscore [lines], add fourscore, and alter fourscore"[56]) is confirmed by numerous passages in his correspondence. He gave Pope permission to burn or correct his verses as he wished; he thanked the Rev. Philip Chamberlain for pointing out faults in his proposed Latin inscription for Schomberg's monument; he complained that, in Ford's absence in England, he lacked "somebody qualifyed to censure and correct what I write."[57] In the hours of mourning following Stella's death, he acknowledged his indebtedness to her outspoken criticism of his work:

Neither was it easy to find a more proper or impartial judge, whose advice an author might better rely on, if he intended to send a thing into the world, provided it was on a subject that came within the compass of her knowledge. Yet, perhaps, she was sometimes too severe, which is a safe and pardonable error.[58]

Swift's scorn for critics whom he believed were motivated by envy or faction cannot be attributed to the pride of an artist unwilling to listen to those he regarded as his inferiors: on the contrary, William King described him as "the most patient of criticism of all I ever knew,"[59] and, as the passage on Stella indicates, he preferred that such criticism should err on the side of severity rather than be restrained by friendship.

Clearly this readiness to submit to criticism relates to Swift's view that, to whatever gifts and learning he might possess, the poet needed to add application, industry, and time. He recognised that occasionally a genius like Pope might achieve in two mornings what would cost another poet two years, and had himself plenty of experience of rapid composition of what he regarded as trifles: he could dash off "5 or 6 Grubstreet papers" in a week, had dictated impromptu a *Tatler* essay for Harrison, and boasted with humorous exaggeration of having written, signed, and sealed a verse letter to Sheridan in five minutes and eleven seconds.[60] But, as a young man, he spoke of the labors of writing verse,[61] and he frequently returned to this theme, as, for instance, when he told Gay of his work on the "Verses on the Death of Dr. Swift": "I shall finish it soon, for I add two lines every week, and blott out four, and alter eight."[62] It was haste, he believed, that had made Dryden "so very uncorrect,"[63] and he advised Gay against it:

You are young enough to get some lucky hint, which must come by chance and it shall be a thing of importance, quod et hunc in annum vivat et plures and you shall not finish it in hast.[64]

As much as he honored genius and originality, they did not, for Swift, exempt the poet from what he called "the little mechanicall Parts of Poetry"[65]—proper management of versification and rhyme—and these required time and application. Notably he waged a campaign against what he considered to be the corruption of introducing triplets with closing alexandrines into poems written in couplets. He prided himself on having dealt a mortal blow, in "A Description of a City Shower" and by subsequent persuasion of Pope, Gay, and Young, to a practice which he regarded as "a vicious way of rhyming" due to "haste, idleness, and want of money." He blamed it on the example of Dryden, who was "in great haste to finish his plays, because by them he chiefly supported his family," and he regarded it as mere slovenly craftsmanship.[66] Presumably the reason why what seems a fairly harmless variation aroused Swift's intense and long-lasting aversion was that he felt that violent and unnecessary interruption of the couplets detracted from the subtle variations of pace, rhythm, and accent of which the regular couplet-form was capable. This would associate his aversion with Pope's dislike of the "needless Alexandrine," "That like a wounded Snake, drags its slow length along,"[67] and would suggest that Swift might have allowed the propriety of Pope's use of triplet with alexandrine when speaking of Dryden in "The First Epistle of the Second Book of Horace

Imitated."[68] But he may also have felt that the high dignity of the art of poetry demanded that its difficulties be faced and overcome, not evaded.

The same principle seems to have governed Swift's insistence on other aspects of "correct" versification, to be achieved without recourse to forced elisions, useless epithets, or mere expletives used to fill out the meter. Swift was (as "The Humble Petition of Frances Harris" and "Mary the Cook-Maid's Letter to Dr. Sheridan" demonstrate) a master of irregular versification and could, on occasion, make his verse hobble with the worst.[69] But such irregularities were deliberate and significant, not the result of incompetent or lazy craftsmanship. It was part of the poet's art to convert apparent defects into virtues, just as it was part of Pope's art as a gardener to overcome the problem of the road which separated his house from his garden by building a subterranean passage, "whereby you turned a blunder into a beauty which is a Piece of Ars Poetica."[70] For instance, in "A Description of a City Shower," there is a manifestly awkward enjambment, made even clumsier by an internal repetition of the rhyme-word:

> Such is that Sprinkling which some careless Quean
> Flirts on you from her Mop, but not so clean:
> You fly, invoke the Gods; then turning, stop
> To rail; she singing, still whirls on her Mop.[71]

The movement of the verse exactly expresses the situation of the careless, singing quean and the sudden and short flight of her victim—an effect which would hardly be noticeable in verse where the author ran over line-ends inconsequently.

Most modern readers will understand and share Swift's dislike of expletives, used "In gaping Lines to fill a Chink,"[72] whether they were merely empty or superfluous adjectives (in his correction of Beach's *Eugenio*, Swift pounced on "Cuzzoni fam'd" as "an expletive, not a proper epithet") or such standard line-fillers as *do* and *does* (he told Beach to avoid *does* "as a mere expletive"[73]). But his hostility towards elisions now seems based, at least in part, on a misunderstanding of how and why the English language was changing, and a prejudice in favor of the "harmony" of the languages derived from Latin. He blamed poets since the Restoration for what had happened:

These Gentlemen, although they could not be insensible how much our Language was already overstocked with Monosyllables, yet to save Time and Pains, introduced that barbarous Custom of abbreviating Words, to fit them to the Measure of their Verses; and this they have frequently done, so very injudiciously, as to form such harsh unharmonious Sounds, that none but a *Northern* Ear could endure. They have joined the most obdurate Consonants, without one intervening Vowel, only to shorten a Syllable: and their Taste in Time became so depraved, that what was at first a poetical Licence, not to be justified, they made their Choice; alledging, that the Words pronounced at length, sounded faint and languid.

He went on to complain that the same practice, having spread into prose, had produced such "Manglings" as *"Drudg'd, Disturb'd, Rebuk'd, Fledg'd,"*[74] none of which seems objectionable to a modern ear. The complaint against the abundance of monosyllables in English was a common enough one at the time (though Elizabeth Elstob had no difficulty in showing that on this, as on other linguistic matters, Swift was incompetent to pronounce[75]), and the idea that the change in English habits of speech and writing was a consequence of poets' attempts "to save Time and Pains" is naive. Swift himself seems to have believed that he was fighting a last-ditch battle, but the battle was long over and had been decided by factors far removed from the practice of poets. All that can be said in his favor is that his campaign was motivated by a desire to serve literature. He wanted to preserve what he believed to be the limited harmony of the language; he distrusted any developments which appeared to sacrifice correctness to ease of composition; and he feared the effect of rapid changes in language, caused, in his opinion, by laziness, affectation, or passing fashion:

> The Fame of our Writers is usually confined to these two Islands; and it is hard it should be limited in *Time* as much as *Place*, by the perpetual Variations of our Speech.[76]

A more interesting comment on versification is in the letter to Charles Wogan, where Swift reports that blank verse has fallen into the hands of *"Sholes* of Wretches who write for their Bread":

> One *Thomson*, a *Scots*-Man, hath succeeded the best in that Way, in four Poems he hath writ on the four Seasons: yet I am not over-fond of them, because they are all Description, and nothing is doing, whereas *Milton* engages me in Actions of the highest Importance, *modo me Romae, modo ponit Athenis.*[77]

The implication of this passage is not that Swift disliked descriptive poetry or blank verse, but that he believed that English blank verse was essentially an epic (or, at least, narrative) medium, an opinion very close to Dr. Johnson's:

> Contending angels may shake the regions of heaven in blank verse; but the flow of equal measures and the embellishment of rhyme must recommend to our attention the art of engrafting, and decide the merit of the "redstreak" and "Pearmain."[78]

The tastes of Swift and Johnson were similarly shaped by their sense of Milton's sublime energy, not by a narrow attachment to rhyme.

But exactness of rhyme was another of "the little mechanicall Parts of Poetry" on which Swift insisted. Though he was pleased with the first volume of Pope's *Iliad*, he wrote to the poet, "Yet I am angry at some bad Rhymes and Triplets, and pray in your next do not let me have so many unjustifiable Rhymes to *war* and *gods*."[79] It is easy to see why he regarded some of Pope's rhymes as "unjustifiable." His own practice is absolutely consistent, if somewhat lacking in variety: he rhymes *war* with *(a)far* (4 times), *scar(s)* (twice), *car*, *star*, and *tar*; and *god(s)* with *odd(s)* (9 times), *nod(s)* (7 times), *trod* (3 times), and *rod* (twice). But in the first two books of the *Iliad* alone, Pope uses, on the one hand, *spare, dare, care, prepare(s)*, and *fair* (besides the approved *far* and *car*), and, on the other, *bestowed, abode(s), owed, load* and *roads* (in addition to *nod*). Pope seems to have taken Swift's fault-finding in very good spirit and wrote, as late as 1733, that he would keep his new poems "till you come to carp at 'em, and alter rhymes, and grammar, and triplets, and cacophonies of all kinds."[80] However, an examination of later books of the *Iliad* provides no evidence that he mended his ways as a result of Swift's strictures. Swift told Beach, "I cannot suffer an ill rhyme,"[81] and Orrery reports,

SWIFT, who had the nicest ear, is remarkably chaste and delicate in his rhymes. A bad rhyme appeared to him one of the capital sins in poetry.[82]

"One of the capital sins in poetry" sounds like one of those overstatements to which critics and commentators on Swift seem inevitably drawn (he hardly seems to regard Pope's offence as "capital"), and "chaste and delicate" are an odd pair of adjectives to apply to the work of a writer who often took delight in forced and cumbersome rhymes. But, of course, in Swift's verse these are intentionally comic or serve some specific mimetic purpose, as in

> Pursue thy Trade of Scandall picking,
> Thy Hints that Stella is no Chickin.[83]

Swift would certainly not have objected to a half-rhyme or a near-rhyme that served a similar purpose. What angered him were such rhymes introduced for no better reason than that the poet or versifier could not be bothered to wrestle with the difficulties of his art and thus diminished it.

As for the other, non-mechanical, aspects of the art of poetry, Gulliver's account of the writings of the noble Houyhnhnms suggests the qualities Swift valued:

In *Poetry* they must be allowed to excel all other Mortals; wherein the Justness of their Similes, and the Minuteness, as well as Exactness of their Descriptions, are indeed inimitable. Their Verses abound very much in both of these.[84]

This cannot be read as an expression of Swift's ideal human poetry, but there is a clear implication that he considered just similes and minute and exact descriptions to be poetic virtues of the highest importance. In the latter respect, he differs from those eighteenth-century critics who preferred "general properties and large appearances,"[85] but his own poetic practice confirms his delight in the vivid and significant detail rather than more generalized presentation—none of which conflicts with his scorn for

> Descriptions tedious, flat and dry,
> And introduc'd the Lord knows why,[86]

or with his opinion that blank verse was not a suitable medium for long descriptive poems.

The praise of the Houyhnhnms' just similes is also significant, coming from a writer who so frequently complained of "Similes that nothing fit"[87] and who has often, during the eighteenth century and since, been said to be inordinately suspicious of figurative language and extremely reluctant to use it. Dr. Johnson, for instance, having exempted *A Tale of a Tub* from his judgment, declared:

That he has in his works no metaphor, as has been said, is not true; but his few metaphors seem to be received rather by necessity than choice.[88]

The truth of the matter was well summed up by William Monck Mason, who, having paraphrased Johnson's statement, added the following note:

Mr. Melmoth says that Swift has this peculiarity, not to have one metaphor in his works.—Fitzosborne's Letters, Vol. II.—Dr. Warton reports, that Dr. Johnson, speaking of the simplicity of Swift's style, said once to him, "the rogue never hazards a simile."—These remarks of those vastly learned persons shew that they had but very slight knowledge of Swift's works: the observation is indeed true when applied to particular pieces, but given in the general way which it is here stated, it is altogether a false position.

After giving a list of works "abounding in similies," Mason concluded by echoing in reverse Johnson's judgment: "when Swift rejected this sort of embellishment, it was through choice, not from necessity."[89]

What Swift required of similes, in his own or others' writings, was that they should be new, apt, and exact, not borrowed or idle embellishments, a point his friend, Lord Bathurst, realized when he ironically complained that Swift's works contained

None of those pretty similes wch some of our Modern Authors adorn their works with that are not only a little like the things they wou'd illustrate but are also like twenty other things.[90]

Similes and metaphors, above all other figures of speech, were seen to be the products of the imagination. They inscribed striking, surprising resemblances, but, like other products of the poet's imagination, they had to pass the scrutiny of his judgment. The imagination of a hack-poet was so unproductive that he was forced to rely on poetical stock, but, on the other hand, the imagination of a good poet might, like that of William Diaper, be "too fruitful as appears by the frequency of your similes." Swift told the poet that the translation of Oppian, on which Diaper was engaged, "may teach you to write more like a Mortal man, as Shakespeare expresseth it."[91]

Swift wanted poets to write like mortal men but acknowledged their gifts and powers to be above those of other men:

> True Poets can depress and raise;
> Are Lords of Infamy and Praise:
> They are not scurrilous in Satire,
> Nor will in Panegyrick flatter.
> Unjustly Poets we asperse;
> Truth shines the brighter, clad in Verse;
> And all the Fictions they pursue
> Do but insinuate what is true.[92]

It is impossible to interpret such an assertion as the work of a man with an anti-heroic view of the poet's nature and art. Even Shelley's famous declaration that "poets are the unacknowledged legislators of the world"[93] does not place a higher value on the poet's function. His field of activity was unlimited:

> The world is wider to a Poet than to any other Man, and new follyes and Vices will never be wanting any more than new fashions. Je donne au diable the wrong Notion that *Matter* is exhausted. For as Poets in their Greek Name are called Creators, so in one circumstance they resemble the great Creator by having an infinity of Space to work in.[94]

Finally, in the judgment of posterity, it was the poets themselves, rather than those they celebrated, who earned immortality of fame:

> Whatever the Poets pretend, it is plain they give Immortality to none but themselves: It is *Homer* and *Virgil* we reverence and admire, not *Achilles* or *Aeneas*.[95]

What this brief examination of Swift's remarks about poets and poetry shows is that to "reverence and admire" (i.e., wonder at) was precisely his response to both; that he held the poet's art to be something extremely rare, drawing on God-given talents, indissolubly linked with virtue, requiring the sacrifice of any hope of worldly preferment, dependent on inspiration and originality of mind, demanding prolonged study and application, and capable of being a powerful force for good on earth. This is almost to regard poets as literary saints, let alone heroes. Certainly, so far from being down-to-earth, his concept of the poet's function and art seems to have been singularly and characteristically exalted. The total misconception of his position was no doubt due in part to the fact that, in many of his writings, he endeavored to uphold and preserve the honor of true poets by scathing mockery of those who falsely pretended to the title; but I suspect that it was equally due to the long-established and grossly simplified fictional character of Dean Swift, the brilliant, hard-headed iconoclast, interested in the practicalities of living rather than in metaphysics, delighting in dispelling illusions, and deflating any notions that smacked of the sublime. The fiction helped determine the interpretation of Swift's critical position, and the interpretation reinforces the fiction. In his views on poetry and poets, at least, Swift seems to have combined the loftiest vision with scrupulous and meticulous attention to the details of craftsmanship, believing that such attention was part of the poet's duty in the pursuit of his lofty art.

[1] "Swift's View of Poetry," *Studies in English by Members of University College, Toronto* (Toronto, 1931), p. 9.

[2] *The Mind and Art of Jonathan Swift* (New York, 1936), p. 276. In a reissue of his book, Quintana made a partial withdrawal of this judgment, describing it as "not so much misleading as obscure" (London, 1953), pp. ix–x.

[3] Ed. David M. Vieth (Hamden, CT, 1984).

[4] First published *Philological Quarterly*, 44 (1965), 387–96.

[5] First published *Eighteenth-Century Studies*, 5 (1972), 569–86.

[6] For a brief account of this resurgence, see Peter J. Schakel, "Swift's Poetry Revisited: The Achievements of a Decade of Criticism," *Proceedings of the First Münster Symposium on Jonathan Swift*, ed. Hermann J. Real and Heinz J. Vienken (Munich, 1985), pp. 233–46.

[7] *The Poems of Jonathan Swift*, ed. Harold Williams, 2nd ed., 3 vols. (Oxford, 1958), II, 503, line 114. Hereafter cited as *Poems*.

[8] *Poems*, I, 183, lines 103–04.

[9] [*The Prose Writings of Jonathan Swift*], ed. Herbert Davis et al., 14 vols. (1939–68; various reimpressions, sometimes corrected, Oxford, 1957–69), XII, 160. Hereafter cited as *Prose*.

[10] *Lives of the English Poets*, ed. G. Birkbeck Hill, 3 vols. (Oxford, 1905), I, 2.

[11] *Poems*, II, 482, line 79.

[12] *The Correspondence of Jonathan Swift*, ed. Harold Williams, rev. David Woolley (Oxford, 1963–72), V, 119. Hereafter cited as *Corresp.*

13 *Prose*, I, 149.

14 *Corresp.*, IV, 134.

15 *Corresp.*, II, 465.

16 *Poems*, II, 503, lines 113–14, 99–100, 105–06.

17 See, for example, *Prose*, IX, 142.

18 *Corresp.*, II, 465.

19 *Poems*, II, 640, lines 5–10. "On Poetry: A Rapsody" has attracted a good deal of attention in the last ten years. See, among others, A. B. England, *Energy and Order in the Poetry of Swift* (Lewisburg, 1980), pp. 43–53; John Irwin Fischer, *On Swift's Poetry* (Gainesville, 1978), pp. 177–97; Nora Crow Jaffe, *The Poet Swift* (Hanover, 1977), pp. 44–51; Donald C. Mell, "Imagination and Satiric Mimesis in Swift's Poetry: An Exploratory Discussion," *Contemporary Studies of Swift's Poetry*, ed. John Irwin Fischer and Donald C. Mell (Newark, DE, 1981), pp. 123–34, and "Irony, Poetry, and Swift: Entrapment in 'On Poetry: A Rapsody,' "*Papers on Language and Literature*, 18 (1982), 310–24; Peter J. Schakel, *The Poetry of Jonathan Swift: Allusion and the Development of a Poetic Style* (Madison, 1978), pp. 150–56.

20 *Poems*, II, 641, lines 25–32.

21 *Poems*, II, 641, lines 40–42.

22 *Poems*, II, 641, line 48.

23 *Corresp.*, II, 339. See Horace, *Ars Poetica*, 372–73, "mediocribus esse poetis / non homines, non di, non concessere columnae." (*Opera*, ed. E. C. Wickham [1901; Oxford, 1984], p. 265. Hereafter cited as *Opera*.)

24 *Corresp.*, IV, 368, n. 1.

25 *Corresp.*, IV, 368.

26 *Corresp.*, IV, 52.

27 *Corresp.*, IV, 186.

28 *Corresp.*, V, 86.

29 *Corresp.*, III, 479.

30 *The Defence of Poesie* (London: William Ponsonby, 1595; rpt. Scolar Press, 1968), sig. C1^v.

31 *Corresp.*, IV, 124, 134.

32 *Corresp.*, I, 8; IV, 124.

33 *Prose*, I, 151.

34 *Ars Poetica*, 408–11, in *Opera*, p. 266.

35 "Of Poetry," reprinted in *Critical Essays of the Seventeenth Century*, ed. J. C. Spingarn, 3 vols. (Oxford, 1908), III, 80.

36 *Prose*, XII, 44.

37 *Poems*, II, 520–21.

38 *The Life of the Rev. Dr. Jonathan Swift* (London: C. Bathurst et al., 1784), p. 28.

39 *Prose*, IX, 65.

40 *Prose*, IX, 74.

41 *Prose*, I, 242.

42 *Prose*, I, 7.

43 *Prose*, IV, 19.

44 *Prose*, I, 38.

45 *Poems*, II, 728, lines 25–26.

46 *Corresp.*, IV, 39.

47 *Corresp.*, IV, 124.

48 *Memoirs of Mrs Letitia Pilkington, 1712–1750, Written by Herself*, ed. J. Isaacs (London, 1928), p. 80.

49 *Prose*, IV, 19.

50 *Corresp.*, III, 103, 41.

51 *Corresp.*, I, 346.

52 *Lives of the English Poets*, III, 66.

53 *Corresp.*, III, 495.

54 *Corresp.*, IV, 133.

55 *Corresp.*, IV, 322.

56 Patrick Delany, *Observations upon Lord Orrery's Remarks on the Life and Writings of Dr. Jonathan Swift* (London: sold by W. Reeve and A. Linde, 1754), p. 19.

57 *Corresp.*, III, 193, 468–69, 5.

58 *Prose*, V, 231.

59 *Corresp.*, V, 140.

60 *Journal to Stella*, ed. Harold Williams, 2 vols. (Oxford, 1948), II, 548; I, 216; *Poems*, III, 980.

61 *Corresp.*, I, 8.

62 *Corresp.*, III, 506.

63 *Corresp.*, IV, 321.

64 *Corresp.*, IV, 58. See Horace, Odes, I, xxxii, lines 2 3, *Opera*, p. 26.

65 *Corresp.*, III, 73.

66 *Corresp.*, IV, 321. See note to "A Description of a City Shower" in Faulkner's edition of Swift's works (1735), quoted in Swift, *The Complete Poems*, ed. Pat Rogers (Harmondsworth, Mddx., 1983), p. 642. Hereafter cited as Rogers.

67 *An Essay on Criticism*, line 356 (*The Poems of Alexander Pope*, ed. John Butt et al., 11 vols. [New Haven, 1939–69], I, 280. Hereafter cited as *TE*).

68 "First Epistle of the Second Book of Horace Imitated," *TE*, IV, 217, lines 267–69.

69 Rogers, p. 649.

70 *Corresp.*, III, 103.

71 *Poems*, I, 137, lines 19–22.

72 *Poems*, II, 645, line 168.

73 *Corresp.*, IV, 321.

74 *Prose*, IV, 11.

75 *An Apology for the Study of Northern Antiquities* (1715; Augustan Reprint Society, No. 61, 1956), pp. x–xxviii.

76 *Prose*, IV, 14.

[77] *Corresp.*, IV, 53. See Horace, *Epistles*, II, i. 213, in *Opera*, p. 244. For Horace's Athens, Swift substitutes Rome.

[78] *Lives of the English Poets*, I, 319–20. (Johnson was referring to John Philips's blank verse poem, *Cider.*)

[79] *Corresp.*, II, 176. There is some reason for supposing that Pope's pronunciation of *god* differed from Swift's; see J. H. Neumann, "Jonathan Swift and English Pronunciation," *Quarterly Journal of Speech*, 28 (1942), 198–201.

[80] *Corresp.*, IV, 148.

[81] *Corresp.*, IV, 321.

[82] *Remarks on the Life and Writings of Dr. Jonathan Swift*, 3rd ed., corr. (London: A. Millar, 1752), p. 68.

[83] *Poems*, II, 735, lines 41–42.

[84] *Prose*, XI (rev. ed.), 273.

[85] *Rasselas*, ch. 10: " 'The business of a poet,' said Imlac, 'is to examine, not the individual, but the species; to remark general properties and large appearances.' " (*Samuel Johnson: Selected Poetry and Prose*, ed. W. K. Wimsatt and Frank Brady [Berkeley, 1977], p. 90.)

[86] *Poems*, II, 645, lines 155–56.

[87] *Poems*, II, 645, line 153.

[88] *Lives of the English Poets*, III, 51.

[89] *The History and Antiquities of the Collegiate and Cathedral Church of St. Patrick, near Dublin* (Dublin, 1820), p. 432.

[90] *Corresp.*, III, 407.

[91] *Corresp.*, I, 346.

[92] *Poems*, II, 729, lines 53–60.

[93] *A Defence of Poetry* (1821), *Shelley's Critical Prose*, ed. Bruce R. McElderry, Jr. (Lincoln, 1967), p. 36.

[94] *Corresp.*, III, 360. Cf. the *persona* in *A Tale of a Tub*: "Besides, it is reckoned, that there is not at this present, a sufficient Quantity of new Matter left in Nature, to furnish and adorn any one particular Subject to the Extent of a Volume" (*Prose*, I, 92).

[95] *Prose*, I, 242.

James Woolley

Stella's Manuscript of
Swift's Poems

THE IDENTITY OF ESTHER JOHNSON—Stella—is for us constituted
almost entirely by the written words of Jonathan Swift, to her and about her.
In her own handwriting she carefully preserved some of these words—
poems addressed to her—along with other poems by Swift. Her manuscript
of Swift's poems is not, however, simply an artifact of their unconventional
and sometimes tortured friendship; it is, more particularly, a token of
Stella's homage to Swift as a poet, at a time when he was increasing his
poetic activity after a relatively fallow stretch. Perhaps not coincidentally,
about the time that she undertook her compilation (*c*.1719), some of his
poems began to be written *to* her as well as transcribed by her.

Tracing the manuscript's descent suggests a new parallel between Stella
and Anne Acheson, another subject of Swift's pen and a heretofore unsuspected amanuensis in the years following Stella's death. Comparing the
poems in Stella's transcript with others Swift is said to have written at that
time demonstrates the need to redate some poems and to reopen questions
of attribution. And reconsidering the transcript's contents, centered so often
on Stella herself, suggests that the copyist if not the author acknowledged
a public dimension in poems many have thought wholly private. In short,
the manuscript raises questions whose interest is not just editorial but potentially biographical and critical as well: When was the transcription done?
What poems does the transcript include and what does it omit, and why?
When and why did Stella cease adding to it? How accurate are its texts? Are
they taken from holograph or other authoritative sources; that is, should a
modern editor adopt Stella's texts as copy texts?[1] Here I will focus on one
of the questions most amenable to investigation, which is what the
manuscript can tell us about the chronology of Swift's poems, both those
included in the manuscript and those omitted. Since datings are murkier in
the early 1720s than some other periods of Swift's poetry, the transcript's
evidence is doubly welcome.

The manuscript has never been fully described in print; hence the information my analysis rests on has never been generally available. The volume
presumably was among "all the Papers I have," part of Stella's bequest to

Swift, and I will suggest that he gave it, fairly soon after her death in 1728, to his friends Sir Arthur and Lady Acheson.[2] In 1768 their son gave it to the fourth Duke of Bedford, who wrote a prefatory note in it: "This Manuscript was given me, by Sr Archibald Acheson at Bath 9.^{ber} 2.^{d} 1768. It was given to his Father, by the Dean of St Patrick, and is of the hand writing of Stella, Mrs Johnson. / B."

Since then it has remained the property of the Dukes of Bedford. So far as I can tell, only two scholars have ever examined Stella's transcript directly: John Forster in the 1850s and Harold Williams in 1929 and 1930.[3] According to current Bedford Estates policy, all its manuscripts listed by the Historical Manuscripts Commission are to be kept among the Bedford Estates Archives in Bloomsbury. This manuscript, though so listed, is presently (1983–88) mislaid—not to be found either in the Archives or in the library at Woburn Abbey.[4] Its whereabouts were last documented in 1930, when by arrangement between the Duke of Bedford and the Clarendon Press it was deposited temporarily at the Public Record Office in London so that Williams could examine it there.

Fortunately, then or later Williams ordered photostats, and these and his detailed notes, now among his papers in the Cambridge University Library, are the basis of my own observations.[5] Williams records that Stella's transcript is a bound blank book, a small quarto of 85 leaves, onto 40 of which she has copied nineteen of Swift's poems.[6] A twentieth poem follows, in a hand Williams (unlike Forster) realized was not Stella's.[7] Scrutiny of the volume's organization from this evidence permits new inferences about when Swift composed several poems.

We find that Stella succeeded reasonably well in putting her nineteen poems in chronological order, the arrangement Swift preferred for the 1711 *Miscellanies* and for Volume II of his *Works* published by Faulkner (1735) as well.[8] Like those two collections, hers dates the poems, emphasizing their occasionality. At the time Stella began her compilation, the 1711 *Miscellanies* was the only published collection of Swift's poems. She owned a copy of it,[9] but Swift had written a number of poems since 1711, and she was supplementing it, for her own use and perhaps also as the draft or model for a new published collection. Stella produced a neat, clear, fair transcript, and—this is a matter of unexpected significance—in the course of transcribing she regularly used catchwords from page to page.[10] Each of the poems begins at the top of a fresh page.[11] Occasionally, however, catchwords are missing between poems. Probably the eight such absences of catchwords mark interruptions in the process of adding to the volume. Observing these interruptions makes possible a conjectural division of the manuscript into eight datable stages of copying, as shown in the following table.

DESCRIPTION OF STELLA'S MANUSCRIPT OF SWIFT'S POEMS[12]

[Preliminary note by the fourth Duke of Bedford, 1768]

[Stage I]
The Fable of Midas. Written AD. 1711[/12]. [ff. 1^r–2^v]
Toland's Invitation to Dismal, to Dine / with the Calves-Head Club: / Imitated from Horace, Epist. 5, Li, 1. / Written A:D: 1712. [ff. 3^r–4^r]
Imitation of Horace / to Lord Oxford. A:D: 1713. [ff. 4^v–7^v]
Imitation of Horace. L. 2^d Sat. 6th / Written AD 1714. [ff. 8^r–10^v]
On Stella's Birth-day / Written AD. 1718[/19]. [f. 11^r; catchword "Mary's"]
[three blank pages, ff. 11^v–12^v][13]
The Progress of Beauty / Written AD: 1719 [ff. 13^r–16^v]
Phillis, / Or, the Progress of Love. / Written A.D. 1719. [ff. 17^r–19^v; no catchword on 19^v]

[Stage II]
The Bubble. / Printed in Ireland A:D: 1720. [ff. 20^r–27^r; no catchword on 27^r]

[Stage III]
The Run upon the Bankers. / Written A:D: 1720. [ff. 27^v–29^v; no catchword on 29^v]

[Stage IV]
Apollo to the Dean. / Written A.D. 1720[/21]. [ff. 30^r–32^r; no catchword on 32^r]
[one blank page, f. 32^v]

[Stage V]
Stella's Birth-day. / Written AD. 1720–21 [ff. 33^r 34^r; no catchword on 34^r]
[one blank page, f. 34^v]

[Stage VI]
Epilogue for the Weavers / Written A.D. 1721. [ff. 35^r 36^r]
Atlas. / To the Earl of Oxford. / Writ AD. 1712. [ff. 36^v–37^r; no catchword on 37^r]

[Stage VII]
A quiet Life, and a good Name / To &c – Writ AD. 1719 [ff. 37^v–38^v]
[Three untitled epigrams: "As Thomas was cudgelld," "When Margery chastises Ned," and "Joan cudgell's Ned"; f. 39^r; no catchword]
[one blank page, f. 39^v]

[Stage VIII]
To Stella on her Birth-day. / Written AD 1721–2. [f. 40^r; no catchword]

[Stage IX]
On the five Lady's at Sots-hole and the / Doctor at their head [ff. 40^v–41^v; in the handwriting of Lady Acheson]

The first stage comprised the first seven poems in chronological order, beginning with "The Fable of Midas" and running through "Phillis, or The Progress of Love" in 1719. This shows that Stella began to transcribe no earlier than 1719. The poem "On Stella's Birthday" (1718/19) ends with a catchword, "Mary's," followed by three blank pages. The poem intended for these pages was probably "Mary's Letter to Mr. Sheridan" or, as the title would have been adjusted after Sheridan got his DD, "Mary the Cook-Maid's Letter to Dr. Sheridan." Stella may have left room for the poem and then discovered that, because its lines are very long, she had not left enough.[14] Stages II through V are each composed of a single poem, and the four are in approximately chronological order.[15]

In the sixth stage comes the first clear effort to add a poem missed earlier, "Atlas," and it is evident that Stella added it about 1721. The seventh stage adds another poem missed earlier, "A Quiet Life." Because the three epigrams appear *before* Stella's last session of copying, the birthday verses for 1721/22, Williams appears to have misdated the epigrams in assigning them to "?1723." A dating supported by the manuscript would be 1719–22.

Stella's poem-book shares with only two other collections of Swift's poems—the 1711 *Miscellanies* and Faulkner's Volume II (1735)—the distinction of being reliable as to canonicity. No poem not by Swift appears in any of the three.[16] Stella's dating, especially for the poems written near the time of her compilation, rests on first-hand knowledge rather than the guesswork, poor memory, or carelessness frequently evident in the datings of the two published collections. To claim for Swift a poem written earlier than, yet absent from, any of these three sources, an editor must demonstrate its authenticity fully and attempt some explanation for its omission. And the editor who rejects Stella's dating and chronology must offer persuasive justification for doing so.

While not all the poems Swift wrote after the 1711 *Miscellanies* are included—testimony, perhaps, that even Swift himself did not possess copies of all his poems—I suggest that Stella was, within certain limits, *attempting* completeness. In many if not most cases, she was probably transcribing other copies in her possession. Some of these were apparently printed. Others, notably the birthday poems to her, surely must have been holograph fair copies. My assumption is that it gratified her to make a formal collection of Swift's poems, whether for anything other than her own private use or not. We may expect her to have been aiming at a particularly complete gathering of Swift's poems from the period of her compilation—from 1719 to early 1722. These expectations of completeness can be even more confident where poems addressed to Stella herself are concerned. One bit of supporting evidence is her inclusion of the birthday poem for 1721/22 even though it is weak, sour, and marred by clichés. This poem was sufficiently unattractive to have been omitted both from the 1727 *Miscellanies* and from Faulkner's editions, and indeed it was not printed until 1766, when Deane Swift first raked it up for the reprint of Hawkesworth's edition of the *Works*.[17]

Yet for the three-year period from early 1719 through early 1722, Stella omits twelve poems Williams credits to Swift.[18] I can offer some rationale for her exclusion of eight of the dozen:

1. "An Elegy on Demar": This was a group production. Stella herself wrote part of the poem, so she knew it did not belong in a collection of Swift's own work.[19]

2. "Part of the 9th Ode of the 4th Book of Horace": First collected by Faulkner in 1746. The case for the poem's authenticity is shaky—simply that Faulkner included it. Though Williams dates it "?1720," there is in fact little or no evidence as to its date or occasion.[20]

3. "The Description of an Irish-Feast": Good evidence exists that the translation was too late for inclusion. Faulkner dates it 1720 in his 1735 editions.[21] But in both his 1737 editions, he moves the poem from the 1720 section to the 1730 section. While accepting Faulkner's realization that the earlier date was incorrect, we cannot adopt the later one. As Andrew Carpenter and Alan Harrison have shown, the poem survives in a draft transcribed by Anthony Raymond in 1723 or 1724. Apparently the translation was made in collaboration with Raymond and finished "by about 1724 perhaps."[22]

4. "Apollo's Edict": Oliver Ferguson has convincingly removed it from the canon, showing that it was largely if not entirely the work of Mary Barber.[23]

5. "The Journal": Swift almost certainly regarded this verse epistle to Delany (see lines 4–6, 115) as a private *jeu d'esprit* like the other trifles he wrote while at Gaulstown in 1721. Despite the notoriety of "The Journal" once Delany leaked it into print, Swift did not authorize its publication until 1732, when he wanted it included in the abortive Pilkington-Bowyer project.[24] Shortly thereafter it was published, slightly expurgated, in the 1732 *Miscellanies*.[25]

6. "The Bank Thrown Down": This poem was first collected by Williams, on the weak arguments (not accepted by Foxon) that it was a poem published by Swift's printer expressing a viewpoint Swift is known to have shared, and that its "movement and style [unspecified] are reminiscent of his manner." Perhaps Stella knew Swift did not write it.[26]

7. "The Progress of Marriage": Swift's foul copy is clearly dated January 1721/22, but the poem remained unpublished until Deane Swift edited it *from this draft* in 1765. Probably Swift regarded the poem as unfinished and therefore never gave it to Stella.[27]

8. "To Stella, Visiting Me in My Sickness": With reason Williams considers "manifestly wrong" the unusually precise date of October 1727 offered in the *Miscellanies* and repeated by Faulkner. Less persuasively, Williams chooses 1720,

apparently so he can say Swift's muse did not neglect Stella in that year, and also out of an undue respect for a date John Lyon scribbled without any explanation or support.[28] But Herbert Davis has plausibly associated the poem with Swift's illness of late 1724, linking its "Indignation" against "Kings and Ministers of State" (61–63) with the Wood's halfpence controversy then raging. Irvin Ehrenpreis suggests 1723 on thematic grounds, yet these arguments seem to apply almost as well to 1724, and for 1723 there is, so far as I know, no evidence that Swift was ill. Certainly either year is far likelier than 1720 or 1727. I believe that Stella would have copied into her book a poem Swift wrote to her in 1720.[29]

Two of the four remaining poems that Stella seemingly overlooked are "An Excellent New Song on a Seditious Pamphlet" (1720) and "A Quibbling Elegy on the Worshipful Judge Boat" (late 1721). Both have been associated with the King's Bench trial of Swift's printer Edward Waters, in 1720, and both were first published by Faulkner in 1735. Faulkner's edition was the first occasion on which Swift permitted himself any published comment on Waters's trial, except for an oblique reference in *A Short View of the State of Ireland* (1728).[30] If we assume that Stella was gathering a collection of poems to be published, the omission of "An Excellent New Song" is understandable: as yet Swift had no designs of publishing it. It is less clear that the absence of "A Quibbling Elegy" is really to be explained by Boate's association with the Waters trial. Depending on one's tolerance for punning on names, the poem seems either exuberant or silly; Stella probably passed it over as a bagatelle. If the poem really had a serious point, I am not convinced either by F. Elrington Ball's explanation (Boate's kinship with the wife of Swift's friend Knightley Chetwode) or by Williams's (revenge for Boate's role, whatever it was, in Waters's trial).[31]

Another seemingly overlooked poem, "The Progress of Poetry," is dated "1720" in Faulkner's 1735 editions but "about 1720" in his 1737 octavo edition. Assuming that Faulkner found good reason to doubt 1720 as the date, a plausible inference is that the poem was composed *later*: 1722–23 or later—too late, that is, for Stella to include it. This speculation assumes, once again, that if Swift had finished a poem while the transcript was in progress, she would have known about it and included it. Less probably, this poem might have been written earlier than 1719 and so missed. Williams, following Faulkner's original guess, dates the poem "1720."[32]

The last of the dozen omitted poems is "To Stella, Who Collected and Transcribed His Poems," dated "1720" by Williams on no stated evidence. The poem makes clear that Swift composed it at a time when he believed her still to be adding to her book.[33] He proposed this poem as the "next" she would copy. In any case I agree with Herbert Davis's conjecture that

Stella ended her collection to avoid accepting this poem's dare that she transcribe its reproaches about her bad temper:

> Say, *Stella*, when you copy next,
> Will you keep strictly to the Text?
> Dare you let these Reproaches stand,
> And to your Failing set your Hand?
> Or if these Lines your Anger fire,
> Shall they in baser Flames expire?
> Whene'er they burn, if burn they must,
> They'll prove my Accusation just (137–44).

All of this implies a date for the poem soon after that of the last poem to be transcribed—that is, soon after March 1722. Thus I would place "To Stella, Who Collected and Transcribed His Poems" in 1722.[34]

I want to add a hypothesis which, if accepted, would confirm this last redating. Forster MS 526 is a scrap of eight holograph lines of verse, endorsed by Swift "Verses on I know / not what. / 1732."[35]

> My latest tribute here I send
> With this let your Collection end
> Thus I consign you down to Fame,
> A Character to praise and blame.
> And, if the whole may pass for true,
> Contented rest; you have your due
> Give future times the Satisfaction
> To leave one handle for Detraction.

Deane Swift first printed the lines as a poem with the tantalizing title "Verses on I Know Not What"—though certainly this was not intended to be a title—in his 1765 additions to Swift's *Works*.[36] In 1732 Swift was 65, of undependable memory, sorting through his papers in preparation for a new volume, or perhaps an entirely new edition, of his poems.[37] We can guess, then, that in 1732 Swift came across these eight lines on he knew not what, thought them worth saving, transcribed them,[38] and filed them among the papers which eventually passed via Mrs. Whiteway to Deane Swift and from Deane Swift's son and grandson to the publisher John Murray for Forster's use in his biography of Swift.[39]

My supposition is that this mysterious fragment actually concerns, and had been designed in 1722 to accompany, "To Stella, Who Collected and Transcribed His Poems." If we ask what collections of writings Swift had ever contributed to, we get a short list: John Dunton's *Athenian Gazette* (1692), Tonson's *Poetical Miscellanies* (1709), the *Tatler* (1709–11), Concanen's *Miscellaneous Poems* (1724), the Swift-Pope *Miscellanies*

(1727–32), Sheridan's never-to-be-published collection of bons mots and anecdotes, and Stella's collection of his own poems.[40] And if we ask which of these contained Swift's character of the collector, a "Character" of both "praise and blame" which constituted only Swift's "latest" tribute to the collector, the answer is None. But one of these compilations might have included such a character if the compiler had seen fit to include it. The compiler is Esther Johnson; the character is "To Stella, Who Collected and Transcribed His Poems."

As early as 1720, Williams's date for "To Stella, Who Collected," the collection was hardly large enough to be called a "Pile of scatter'd Rhymes," as Swift does (5), and it was hardly of sufficient bulk, either, to speak of ending it, as Swift does in "Verses on I Know Not What." These facts strengthen the case for the 1722 dating of "To Stella, Who Collected."

Yet why, even in 1722, should Swift envisage the ending of Stella's collection? One possibility among several is that he looked forward to publishing such a collection.[41] Ball expresses "surprise…that Swift could have borne the publication" of his poems to Stella in the 1727 *Miscellanies*, implying that the poems are too private and tender to be exposed to public view.[42] I offer a contrary hypothesis. It is that Stella desired and intended their publication, since in them she would appear not only as Swift's valued friend but as the model, shaped by him, to which intelligent women could turn for an alternative to traditional models of female behavior. The Stella of these poems could (in her words) help "redeem the women's ruined cause."[43] Her compilation, except (Ball would think) for the poems to her, excludes the private poems, as well as the bagatelles and the dangerous lampoons. It shows Swift as he presumably would have been willing to be known as a poet. If I am right about this, Esther Johnson early expected the Stella poems to be published.[44] That she was the compiler as well as the subject shows graphically that Swift's public role as poet was a matter in which she was interested (in all senses of that word). Nevertheless, although Stella sometimes served Swift as amanuensis, there is no evidence that she made this transcript at Swift's request or that he used it.[45] Collation suggests that it did not serve as the source for any later publication of the poems it contains.[46]

Someone else copied into Stella's book one of the first poems Swift wrote after her death, "On the Five Ladies at Sots-Hole." The poem was probably composed at Market Hill, the home of Sir Arthur and Lady Acheson, whom Swift visited for seven months beginning in June of 1728 (fig. 1).[47] It has not been noticed before that the same hand is also responsible for four other manuscript items associated with Swift. They are the Huntington

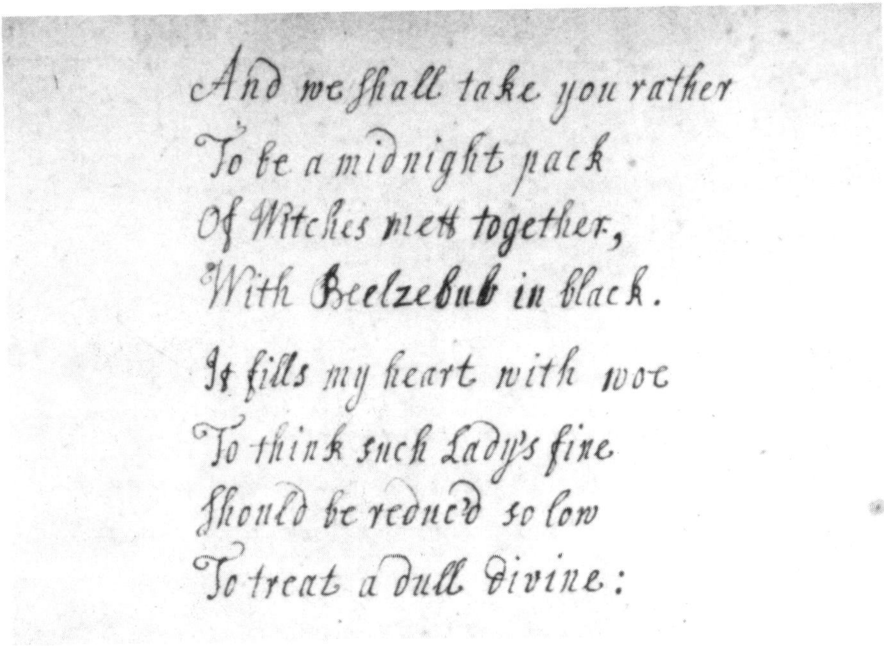

And we shall take you rather
To be a midnight pack
Of Witches mett together,
With Beelzebub in black.

It fills my heart with woe
To think such Lady's fine
Should be reduced so low
To treat a dull Divine:

FIG. 1

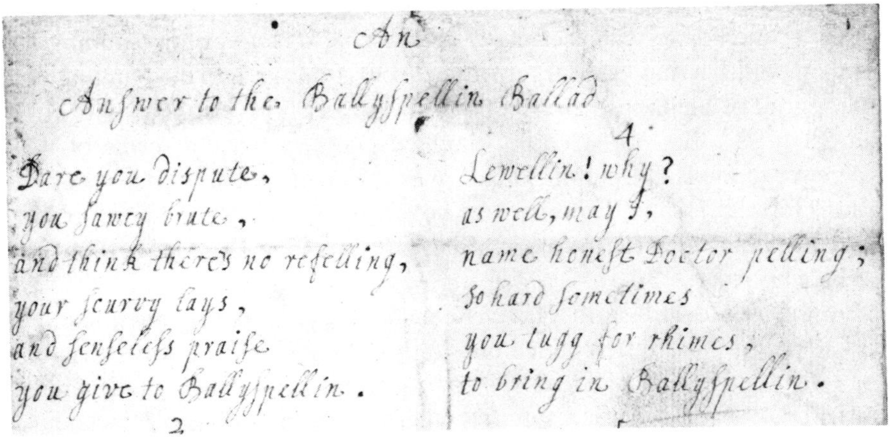

An

Answer to the Ballyspellin Ballad

Dare you dispute,
you sawcy brute,
and think there's no repelling,
your scurvy lays,
and senseless praise
you give to Ballyspellin.

2

Lewellin! why?
as well, may I,
name honest Doctor pelling;
so hard sometimes
you lugg for rhimes,
to bring in Ballyspellin.

FIG. 2

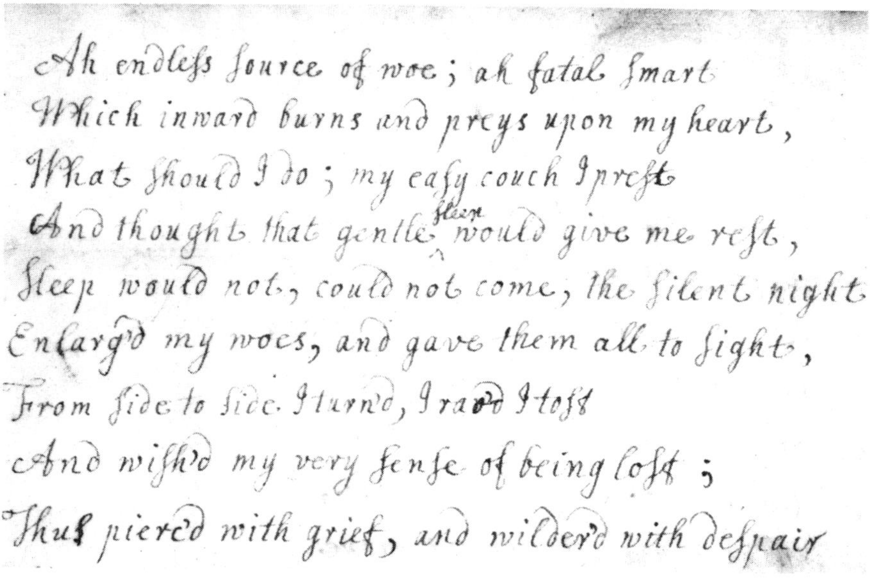

Ah endless source of woe; ah fatal smart
Which inward burns and preys upon my heart,
What should I do; my easy couch I prest
And thought that gentle sleep would give me rest,
Sleep would not, could not come, the silent night
Enlarg'd my woes, and gave them all to sight,
From side to side I turn'd, I rav'd I toss
And wish'd my very sense of being lost;
Thus pierc'd with grief, and wilder'd with despair

FIG. 3

Library manuscript of "An Answer to the Ballyspellin Ballad," a Market
Hill poem of 1728 (fig. 2);[48] the Huntington manuscript parodying a poem
by Dean Daniel, who was an object of scorn in the Market Hill circle in 1728
(fig. 3);[49] the Forster manuscript, "The D—s reasons / For not Building at
Draper's hill," written at Market Hill in 1730 (fig. 4);[50] and the Huntington
manuscript of Stella's poem "Stella to the Dean on his Birthday, Novem-
ber 30 1722" (fig. 5).[51] George Mayhew guessed that the scribe of the
"Answer to the Ballyspellin Ballad" was the dean's vicar at St. Patrick's,
John Worrall. This is disproved, however, by Worrall's signature in the
British Library manuscript of Sheridan's poem "The Humble Petition of
Stella's Friends."[52]

For the Market Hill scribe, Lady Acheson herself makes a much likelier
candidate. As Nora Jaffe pointed out, Lady Acheson in some ways became
for Swift what Stella had been.[53] It is highly probable that Swift gave Stella's
poem-book specifically and significantly to her, and not to her husband as
the 4th Duke of Bedford's note states. Documentary evidence that Lady
Acheson was indeed the Market Hill scribe comes in the form of Esther

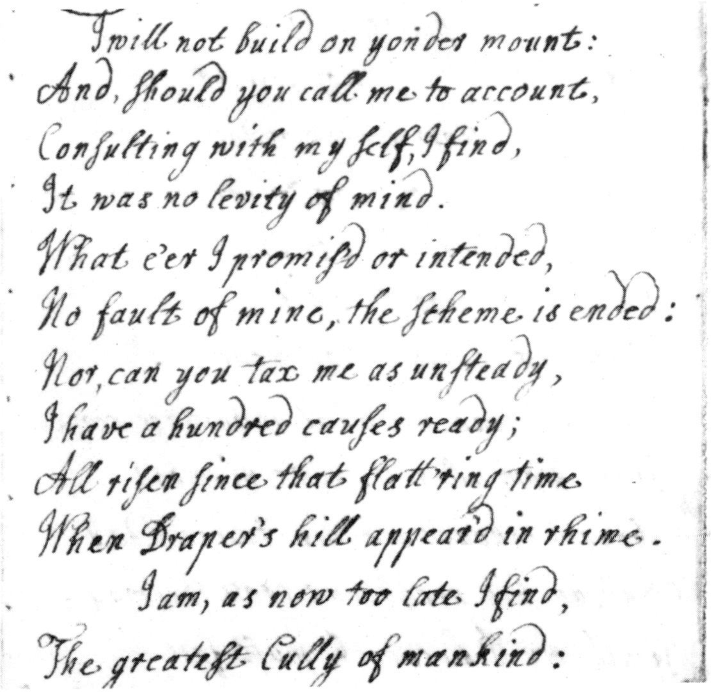

I will not build on yonder mount :
And, should you call me to account,
Consulting with my self, I find,
It was no levity of mind.
What e'er I promis'd or intended,
No fault of mine, the scheme is ended:
Nor, can you tax me as unsteady,
I have a hundred causes ready;
All risen since that flatt'ring time
When Draper's hill appear'd in rhime.
      I am, as now too late I find,
The greatest Cully of mankind:

FIG. 4

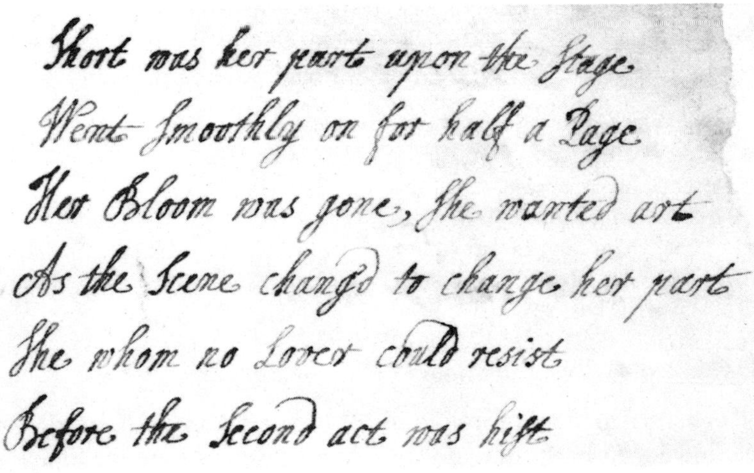

Short was her part upon the Stage
Went smoothly on for half a Page
Her Bloom was gone, she wanted art
As the Scene chang'd to change her part
She whom no Lover could resist
Before the Second act was hist

FIG. 5

Johnson's copy of *The Rape of the Lock*, a volume that passed to Lady
Acheson and that contains her signature as well, in the cursive hand of the
Market Hill scribe (fig. 6).[54] A similar cursive signature of hers appears on
the title-page of her copy of the Drapier's Letters (fig. 7).[55] Since very few
other authenticated samples of Lady Acheson's handwriting survive, and
since these are all in her printed rather than her cursive script, the survival
of these signatures is particularly satisfying in their confirmation (slight

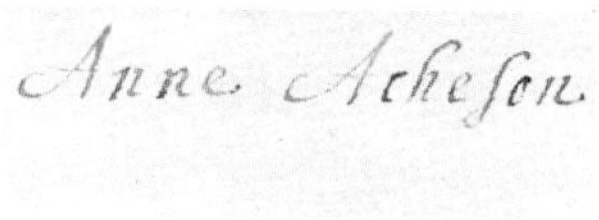

FIG. 6

FIG. 7

though it is) that it was she who wrote one poem into Stella's poem-book
and who served as Swift's amanuensis at Market Hill.[56] One might surmise
that she received the book as a gift shortly after Stella's death and that she
was therefore able to transcribe "On the Five Ladies" into it near the time
of the poem's composition.

The main interest of the book lies, however, not in its tie to Lady Acheson
but in its illumination of "Verses on I Know Not What" and its evidence
that the dating of that and several other poems should probably be revised:

"To Stella, Who Collected and Transcribed His Poems": from 1720 to 1722
"The Progress of Poetry": from 1720 to ?1722–27
"The Description of an Irish-Feast": from 1720 to 1724
"To Stella, Visiting Me in My Sickness": from 1720 to ?1724
"Stella to the Dean" (by Esther Johnson): from 1721 to 1722
"As Thomas was cudgelld": from 1723 to 1719–22
"When Margery chastises Ned": from 1723 to 1719–22
"Joan cudgell's Ned": from 1723 to 1719–22
"Verses on I know not what": from 1732 to 1722

As for textual matters, the reliability of Esther Johnson's transcripts would
appear to vary from poem to poem. The most reliable are the Stella poems
and others that would have been taken directly from Swift's holograph. But
since every poem transcribed must be collated against every other text of

that poem, full textual analysis must wait for another occasion. Perhaps the manuscript will yet surface. In the meantime, because of one of Swift's earliest collectors, Sir Harold Williams's papers have taken on an unexpected importance.

[1] In *The Poems of Jonathan Swift*, 2nd ed., 3 vols. (Oxford, 1958), Harold Williams sometimes adopted Stella's texts and sometimes did not. (His edition is hereafter referred to as *Poems*.)

[2] Esther Johnson's will was destroyed in the Four Courts fire of 1922, but a photograph of one page had been printed in a Dublin magazine, *The Lady of the House* (Christmas number, 1908); for a photocopy I am indebted to David Woolley. A transcript of the entire will may be read in W. R. Wilde, *The Closing Years of Dean Swift's Life* (Dublin, 1849), pp. 94–97.

[3] Deane Swift may also have had access to the volume; see note 46. See also Forster's *Life of Jonathan Swift* (London: Murray, 1875), p. viii; David Woolley, "Forster's *Swift*," *Dickensian*, 70 (1974), 194; *Poems*, I, l–li. In *The Poems of Jonathan Swift, D.D.* (London, 1910), William Ernst Browning used Forster's notes (Victoria and Albert Museum, uncatalogued Forster MSS, pressmark 47.C, Box 11), though not so thoroughly or carefully as Browning's preface (I, v) would lead one to believe. (For another instance of Browning's deceptive claims, see Arthur H. Scouten and Robert D. Hume, "Pope and Swift: Text and Interpretation of Swift's Verses on His Death," *Philological Quarterly*, 52 [1973], 210–11.) Pat Rogers refers to the manuscript in his edition of Swift's *Complete Poems* (Harmondsworth, Mddx., 1983; see p. 27 and notes to the individual poems), but he informs me that he used Williams's photostats at Cambridge, not the manuscript itself (letter of 1 July 1983). (Rogers's edition is hereafter cited as Rogers.)

[4] See Historical Manuscripts Commission 1, II. *Second Report* (1871; London, 1874), Appendix, p. 4. For their kind assistance I am indebted to Marie P. G. Draper, Bedford Estates archivist, and Lavinia Wellicome, curator at Woburn Abbey, as well as to Patricia Bell, Bedfordshire county archivist.

[5] R. W. Chapman, Secretary of the Clarendon Press, to the Duke of Bedford, 30 July 1930, in the Bedford Estates Archives; photostats in the Sir Harold Williams papers, Cambridge University Library MS Add. 7788, box 5; Williams's notes of collations made in 1929 (at Woburn Abbey) and again at the PRO in 1930, Cambridge University Library MS Add. 7788, box 10, envelope labeled "SWIFT'S VERSES (Transcripts of MS)"; the PRO's record of returning the manuscript to the Duke of Bedford. (For the latter information and for Chapman's letter I am indebted to Marie P. G. Draper; for permission to quote from Williams's papers I am grateful to the Cambridge University Library.)

[6] *Poems*, I, l–li, says 85 leaves, a count suggesting that something was excised or tipped in after binding. A fuller description, also reporting 85 leaves, appears in Williams's notes, "SWIFT'S VERSES (Transcripts of MS)."

[7] *Poems*, II, 425; Williams's notes on Forster's notes, Williams Papers, box 10: Notebook **, p. 67.

[8] Compare the haphazard arrangement of poems, mostly undated, in the so-called Last volume of the Swift-Pope *Miscellanies* (London: Motte, 1727).

[9] Harold Williams, *Dean Swift's Library* (Cambridge, 1932), p. 24.

[10] A photograph of two pages appears as the frontispiece in *Poems*, II.

[11] Except for the bottom two epigrams on a page of three.

[12] Foliation supplied; titles are transcribed exactly as they stand in the manuscript.

[13] The blank opening 11^v–12^r is not photostated but is recorded in Williams's notes, "SWIFT'S VERSES (Transcripts of MS)."

[14] Or perhaps she—or Swift—felt the poem too much a domestic trifle to appear in this collection. In any case, having been composed about Nov. 1718 (see *Poems*, III, 982), the poem would be slightly out of chronological order here, unless the verses on Stella's birthday in "1718" really were for 1717/18 and not 1718/19. The latter possibility seems less likely, since in other cases Stella usually uses old style. The fact that there is no catchword from the third blank page to "Phillis" may suggest that that poem was copied in a separate session.

[15] Williams was unaware of a contemporary Dublin printing of "The Run upon the Bankers," dated 1720 in an old manuscript annotation, but the dating may not be contemporary (D. F. Foxon, *English Verse, 1701–1750*, 2 vols. [London, 1975], S900); it may derive from a later owner's research in Faulkner, who dates the poem 1720. Regardless, if "The Run upon the Bankers" was written in 1720 as Stella says and as seems likely, it may well not have been written between "The Bubble" (probably Dec. 1720) and "Apollo to the Dean" (Jan. or Feb. 1720/21).

[16] Except those replies and translations specifically identified in Faulkner's edition as by others. I don't class the 1727 *Miscellanies* with the two editions mentioned, because the Swift-Pope production deliberately obscures responsibility for authorship and because the degree of Swift's responsibility for the final form of any given poem must remain doubtful. Swift's dissatisfaction with the Swift-Pope *Miscellanies* can be inferred from, among other sources, the annotations in his own copy; see *The Rothschild Library*, 2 vols. (Cambridge, 1954), I, 367–72.

[17] *Poems*, II, 739.

[18] I am disregarding, as she would, the bagatelles and the verse in private letters to Vanessa.

[19] *Poems*, I, 233.

[20] *Poems*, I, 242. Rogers dates the poem "1720 or 1721" (p. 702). Whether Faulkner's 1746 volume reprints the 1746 *Miscellanies* or vice versa is a question ripe for detailed study. If the former, then the authenticity of the 1746 *Miscellanies* volume requires much closer scrutiny than it has received.

[21] It seems not to have been noticed that Faulkner continues to revise the datings of his 1735 octavo edition in his 1735 duodecimo, 1737 octavo, and 1737 duodecimo editions.

[22] "Swift's 'O'Rourke's Feast' and Sheridan's 'Letter': Early Transcripts by Anthony Raymond," in *Proceedings of the First Münster Symposium on Jonathan*

Swift, ed. Hermann J. Real and Heinz J. Vienken (München, 1985), pp. 27–46. Williams's discussion is in *Poems*, I, 243–44.

23 "The Authorship of 'Apollo's Edict,' " *PMLA*, 70 (1955), 433–40. Ferguson believes that the poem dates from 1724 or later. Williams resists Ferguson's conclusions (*Poems*, I, 269–72 and 355–56), as does Rogers (p. 710). Herbert Davis excludes the poem from the Oxford Standard Authors *Poetical Works* (London, 1967), however, and D. F. Foxon (B75) accepts Ferguson's conclusions as to authorship.

24 Swift, *Correspondence*, ed. Harold Williams, rev. David Woolley, 5 vols. (Oxford, 1965–72), V, 256; hereafter cited as *Corresp.*

25 *Poems*, I, 276–83; compare *Corresp.*, IV, 26. For Swift's other Gaulstown poems, see *Poems*, III, 1020–24, 1026–27.

26 *Poems*, I, 286; Foxon B60. Rogers considers it "a possible rather than a probable attribution" to Swift (p. 717).

27 *Poems*, I, 289.

28 *Poems*, II, 723; Sir Harold Williams, *The Text of* Gulliver's Travels (Cambridge, 1952), p. 75; and Lyon's note in leaves at the end of Forster MS 579, Victoria and Albert Museum.

29 *Stella* (New York, 1942), pp. 91–92. Davis appears to have forgotten this good idea in his OSA edition of the *Poetical Works*, p. 180. I am less certain than he (*Stella*, p. 91) that Swift means the ladies have moved into the Deanery: "The Ladyes bear me company in my Illness, I can hear nothing but Trebbles. I have put Mrs Johnson into a Consumption by squalling to me...." (Swift to Ford, 27 Nov. 1724, *Corresp.*, III, 43.) Ehrenpreis, associating the poem with "A Letter to a Very Young Lady on Her Marriage," and without noting Davis's argument, suggests that the poem was written in 1723 (*Swift: The Man, His Works and the Age*, III [London, 1983], 413 n).

30 In Faulkner's edition were also first published two Drapier's Letters alluding to Waters's prosecution, "A Letter to the Lord Chancellor Middleton" and "An Humble Address to Both Houses of Parliament." See [*The Prose Writings of Jonathan Swift*], ed. Herbert Davis et al., 14 vols. (1939–68; various reimpressions, sometimes corrected, Oxford, 1957–69), X, 100–01 and 137, and XII, 8; hereafter cited as *Prose*.

31 Ball, *Swift's Verse: An Essay* (London, 1929), p. 164; *Poems*, I, 284.

32 *Poems*, I, 230. Stella's volume would cast doubt on Rogers's dating, much as on the Faulkner-Williams date. Rogers's remark is that "the poem is perhaps most naturally grouped with the earlier [*sic*] 'progress' poems of *c.* 1719" (p. 689). The latest date for the poem would be 1727, when the *Miscellanies* volume in which it appears was being assembled.

33 See line 83, "*Stella*, when you these Lines transcribe"; and line 137, "Say, *Stella*, when you copy next" (*Poems*, II, 730, 732). Williams was the first to observe that Stella's book did not include the poem (*Poems*, 1st ed. [Oxford, 1937], II, 732).

34 Davis suggests "1722 or 1723" in *Stella*, p. 63, but overlooks this suggestion in his OSA edition, p. 183. Rogers notes that the poem's apparent allusion to Curll's

4th ed. of *Miscellanies*, published in Dec. 1721, implies a date later than that for the poem (p. 694). Angus Ross and David Woolley place the poem in 1720 but say that "a later date (1723) is more apt." *Jonathan Swift*, The Oxford Authors (Oxford, 1984), pp. viii, 664.

[35] Victoria and Albert Museum Library.

[36] *Poems*, II, 608.

[37] In 1732 Swift wanted Matthew Pilkington to bring out a volume in London, but it was forestalled by the unsatisfactory "Third" volume of the *Miscellanies*, edited by Pope (*Corresp.*, V, 254–58); Faulkner's edition was already being advertised in Feb. 1732/33 (*Prose*, XIV, 42).

[38] Onto a piece of paper he had first begun to use for something else; see *Poems*, II, 608.

[39] David Woolley, "Forster's *Swift*," pp. 194–95.

[40] To the list of collections might be added that which Matthew Pilkington failed to publish in London in 1732 (*Corresp.*, V, 254–58) and possibly even Faulkner's own edition of Swift, which may have been being planned by late 1732. For Sheridan's collection, see James Woolley, "Thomas Sheridan and Swift," *Studies in Eighteenth-Century Culture*, 9 (1979), 103.

[41] Joseph Horrell, in his *Collected Poems of Jonathan Swift*, 2 vols. (London, 1958), proposes that Swift intended a new published collection (I, 393); Rogers makes a similar suggestion (p. 694). Horrell's view that Pope *used* Stella's transcript for the 1727 *Miscellanies* is not supported by my collations.

[42] P. 212. Williams, *Poems*, I, xxi, disagrees with Ball on grounds different from mine. See also Ehrenpreis, III, 740–41.

[43] In "Stella to the Dean" she looks to Swift for such redemption, but I am supposing that she accepted her role as the primary example through which Swift, in his various poems to her, could convey this guidance to the public. See *Poems*, II, 738. At the time Stella wrote, Swift's "Letter to a Young Lady on Her Marriage" (1723) was not yet in being.

[44] This expectation may have been complicated, and publication correspondingly delayed, by "Cadenus and Vanessa," which she may have discovered before Esther Vanhomrigh's death 2 June 1723 and which Dublin society discovered thereafter. *Cadenus and Vanessa* was first published in 1726. Davis also assumes a connection between "To Stella, Who Collected" and Stella's knowledge of Swift's relationship with Vanessa. See *Stella*, p. 63; *Poems*, II, 685; and Ehrenpreis, III, 415.

[45] On her work as amanuensis, see *The Rothschild Library*, II, 2264 and accompanying plate; a comment by Thomas Sheridan the younger, quoted in *Prose*, IX, 104–05; Irvin Ehrenpreis, ed., Swift's *An Enquiry into the Behavior of the Queen's Last Ministry* (Bloomington, 1956), pp. xxiv, xxix; A. C. Elias, Jr., "Stella's Writing Master," *Scriblerian*, 9 (1977), 134–39; Elias, *Swift at Moor Park* (Philadelphia, 1982), pp. 4, 35, 313.

[46] Exceptions would be the epigram "Joan cudgells Ned," first published by Browning from Forster's notes on Stella's book, and perhaps also "To Stella on

her Birth-day" (1721/22), first published by Deane Swift in 1766 (*Poems*, I, 327–28; II, 739). See also *Poems*, I, 197.

47 Ownership of the missing manuscript is claimed by the Bedford Estates, and accordingly I thank the Marquess of Tavistock and the Trustees of the Bedford Estates (to whom the 13th Duke has relinquished ownership of the Bedford Estates Archives) for permission to reproduce the photostats here.

48 Huntington Library MS HM 14340; *Poems*, II, 437–43. I am grateful to the Huntington Library for permission to reproduce the manuscripts shown here and below.

49 "A Paraphrase on the Seven Penitential Psalms, by the Reverend M^r R——d D——l, D. of A[;] or Strephon to Belinda," Huntington Library MS HM 14359. Whether the manuscript was owned by Swift is not clear; it is not docketed by him but was among the Theophilus Swift papers which presumably came from Swift via Mrs. Whiteway and Deane Swift. See George Mayhew, *Rage or Raillery* (San Marino, CA, 1967), p. 176. The manuscript is an accurate transcription of the printed halfsheet of the parody, which Foxon dates "?1727" (Foxon P60). For the contempt of the Acheson circle toward Daniel in 1728, see *Poems*, III, 858 and n.

50 Forster MS 524, Victoria and Albert Museum; *Poems*, III, 898. The title is in Swift's hand. I am grateful to the Victoria and Albert Museum for permission to reproduce the manuscript.

51 Huntington Library MS HM 14328; *Poems*, II, 736–38. Deane Swift published this manuscript after redating the poem "1721." Because the manuscript was his copy-text, and because the scribe's accuracy is independently verifiable (see n. 49), Deane Swift appears to err in redating the poem. He would have been attempting to make Stella's claim to be 36 (line 42) fit her age as Swift gives it in his birthday poem for 1721; see *Poems*, II, 735, line 18.

52 Mayhew, p. 11; BL MS Add. 5017(2), f. 75.

53 Nora Crow Jaffe, "Swift and the 'agreeable young Lady, but extremely lean,'" in John Irwin Fischer and Donald C. Mell, Jr., eds., *Contemporary Studies of Swift's Poetry* (Newark, 1981), pp. 149–58.

54 This volume is owned by R. G. Moore, Battle, East Sussex, to whom I am indebted for kind permission to reproduce the signature from the verso of the frontispiece. The volume has been described in Hermann J. Real and Heinz J. Vienken, "Books from Stella's Library," *Swift Studies*, 1 (1986), 71–72, though Real and Vienken do not mention Lady Acheson's signature on the verso of the frontispiece but only her title-page signature (dated "1729"), an example of her printed rather than cursive script.

55 *The Hibernian Patriot* (London: A. Moor, 1730), now Goldsmiths' 6798, University of London Library; reproduced by permission.

56 The printed handwriting may be seen in her annotations in her copy of *The Hibernian Patriot*, p. 264; title-pages of Faulkner's 8° Swift (1735), vols. I, III, and IV, now at the University of Pennsylvania (see plate facing p. 385 in H. Teerink, *A Bibliography of the Writings of Jonathan Swift*, 2nd ed., ed. Arthur H. Scouten [Philadelphia, 1963]); the title-page of a copy of Temple's *Introduction to the His-*

tory of England, 2nd ed. (London: Simpson, 1699), the gift of Swift and now Rothschild 2399, Trinity College, Cambridge; and the title-page of a copy of *Memoirs of Capt. John Creichton* (1731) now in the Huntington Library.

An earlier version of this essay was presented at the meeting of the American Society for Eighteenth-Century Studies in New York, April 1983. I am grateful to the Committee on Advanced Study and Research, Lafayette College, for supporting both research and photography.

Angus Ross

The Anatomy of Melancholy and Swift

IN THE DISCUSSION OF JONATHAN SWIFT, problematic modest proposer and wielder of Alecto's whip, there hovers intermittently at the reader's elbow the shade of a writer almost a century older, the comparably quizzical Democritus Junior, Robert Burton, anatomist of melancholy. Burton and Swift, particularly in *A Tale of a Tub*, have long been linked, though it is impossible to say how well Swift knew the *Anatomy*. Specific connection between *The Anatomy of Melancholy* and Swift's writing has therefore been more often suggested than fruitfully established, and has sometimes even been needlessly dismissed. Perhaps more important, however, at the present time is the fact that in both cases the text with its myriad voices is suitable for theoretical treatment but also stubbornly refuses to be dissociated from its author and his concerns.

Bergen Evans outlines as an "open career" the publishing history of the *Anatomy*, from its first appearance in 1621 through successively enlarged editions to the fifth of 1638 (just before the death of Burton in 1640) and the sixth of 1651–52 (the version with his last thoughts and corrections). There was a ninth in 1800 and forty-one editions (not including abridgments) in the nineteenth century. Evans also draws attention, however, to "a peculiar underground existence. Fletcher, Ford, and Milton were indebted to it, as was Addison, and possibly Swift."[1] Miriam Starkman, on the other hand, though finding "the digression developed to an extraordinary extent and ingenuousness" in Burton's *Anatomy*, concluded, "It appears very doubtful to me that Swift had Robert Burton particularly in mind when he wrote the *Tale*. Granted their digressions in common, there is very little other reason to suppose that Swift is satirizing Burton...."[2] It might indeed be thought difficult to "satirize" the *Anatomy*, in which three long digressions, on Air, Heroic Love, and Religious Melancholy, take up almost half the book. The question of Burton's "ingenuousness" is quite a Swiftian one. Interest and profit in juxtaposing Burton and Swift lie in more than indebtedness or simple target practice.

No record exists of a copy of *The Anatomy of Melancholy* owned by Swift, but it is difficult to believe that Sir William Temple's library at least did not hold a copy of such a famous and, in Sir William's youth, such a modish work. Although its publishing history suggests that the book had lost popularity after the eighth edition of 1676, there is clear, if limited, evidence that Swift had at least read in, and recollected, the *Anatomy*. In *A Tale of a Tub*, towards the end of the account of Jack's adventures in Section XI, the narrator asserts that "whoever desires to catch Mankind fast, must have Recourse to some other Methods. Now, he that will examine Human Nature with Circumspection enough, may discover several *Handles*, whereof the * *Six* Senses afford one apiece...."[3] Note * adds "*Including* Scaliger's," a reference to Julius Caesar Scaliger's [Five Books of Exoteric Exercises] *De Subtilitate* (first published in 1557). It is possible that Swift had looked into this work, a satirical attack on Jerome Cardan (Girolamo Cardano, 1501–76), the Italian mathematician, hermeticist, astrologer, and Paracelsan physician, ten volumes of whose works he later possessed.[4] It is, however, by the phrasing almost certain that he is recalling *The Anatomy of Melancholy*, where this work of Scaliger's is cited by title more than twenty-five times:

The *apprehensive* faculty [of the soul] is subdivided into two parts, *inward* or *outward*; *outward*, as the five senses, of *touching*, *hearing*, *seeing*, *smelling*, *tasting*, to which you may add *Scaliger's* sixth sense of *titillation*, if you please; or that of *speech*, which is the sixth external sense according to *Lullius*...(*AM*).[5]

There are also what seem to be several other reminiscences of Burton in the *Tale*'s dangerous joking on the soul. A good example is to be found by juxtaposing a passage on "philosophers" from Burton's subsection "Of the Soul and her Faculties" with a few lines near the beginning of Section VIII of the *Tale*, on the Aeolists.

According to *Aristotle*, the soul is defined to be *entelecheia*...the perfection or first act of an organical body, having power of life, which most Philosophers approve. But many doubts arise...about it.... Some therefore make one *soul*, divided into three principal faculties: others, three distinct *souls*: (which question of late hath been much controverted by *Picolomineus*, and *Zabarel*): *Paracelsus* will have four *souls*, adding to the three granted faculties a *spiritual soul* (*AM*).[6]

Man is in highest Perfection of all created Things, as having by the great Bounty of Philosophers, been endued with three distinct *Anima's* or *Winds*, to which the Sage *Aeolists*, with much Liberality, have added a fourth of equal Necessity, as well as Ornament with the other three; by this *quartum Principium*, taking in the four Corners of the World; which gave Occasion to that renowned *Cabbalist*[,] *Bumbastus* [Paracelsus], of placing the Body of Man, in due position to the four *Cardinal* Points (*Tale*).[7]

It might be added that Burton in a note to his citation of Paracelsus gives an unlocated quotation which reveals that the fourth spirit stays with the body for some months after death, recalling the passage in the *Battle of the Books*:

some Philosophers affirm, that a certain Spirit, which they call *Brutum hominis*, hovers over the Monument, till the Body is corrupted....[8]

Naturally, not too much can be made of such reminiscences of the *Anatomy* as unique sources of Swift's text. The phrase *brutum hominis* may come from Thomas Vaughan's *Anthroposophia Theomagica* (1650) or from Paracelsus.

Another interesting pair of parallel passages, though perhaps no more than commonplaces, concerns "our great Philosphers and Deists" in Burton's subsection on "Religious Melancholy in Defect" and the tailor-worshipers in the *Tale*, Section II:

Couzin-germans to these men [the ancient atheists and sceptics] are many of our great Philosophers and Deists...(accounting no man a good Scholar that is not an Atheist) *nimis altum sapiunt*, too much learning makes them mad...a peevish Generation of men.... They will acknowledge nature and fortune, yet not God.... To this purpose *Minucius in Octaviano*, and *Seneca* well discourseth with them...[:] *They do not understand what they say; what is Nature but God?... God is the fountain of all, the first Giver and Preserver...à quo et per quem omnia* [Augustine].
Nam quodcunque vides Deus est, quocunque moveris,
[Lucan, IX, 580; altered]
God is all in all, God is everywhere, in every place *(AM)*.[9]

Others of these Professors [the tailor-worshipers], though agreeing in the main System, were yet more refined upon certain Branches of it; and held that Man was an Animal compounded of two *Dresses*, the *Natural* and the *Celestial Suit*, which were the Body and the Soul: That the Soul was the outward, and the Body the inward Cloathing; that the latter was *ex traduce*; but the former of daily Creation and Circumfusion. This last they proved by *Scripture*, because, *in Them we Live, and Move, and have our Being*: As likewise by Philosophy, because they are *All in All, and All in every Part (Tale)*.[10]

A sentence in the *Anatomy* seems to be specifically echoed in a famous flourish in the *Tale*'s "Digression concerning Criticks," Section III:

Because [scholars] cannot ride an horse, which every clown can do; salute and court a gentlewoman, carve at table, cringe, and make congies, which every common swasher can do, *his populus ridet*, &c. they are laughed to scorn, and accounted silly fools by our gallants.... [Burton's note adds: "Pers(ius) Sat. 3.(86). They cannot fiddle; but as Themistocles said, he could make a small town become a great city."] *(AM)*[11]

Now, 'tis certain, the Institution of the *True Criticks*, was of absolute Necessity to the Commonwealth of Learning. For all Human Actions seem to be divided like *Themistocles* and his Company; One Man can *Fiddle*, and another can make *a small Town a great City...(Tale)*.[12]

The story comes from Plutarch's *Life of Themistocles* (II, 2): "When therefore, he was laughed at, long after, in company, where free scope was given to raillery...he was obliged to answer..., ''Tis true I never learned how to tune a harp, or play upon a lute, but I know how to raise a small and inconsiderable city [Athens] to glory and greatness....' "[13]

There are so many hundreds of stories in the *Anatomy*, and so many authors cited and quoted, that it would be surprising if there were not some echoes and parallels in Swift's writings. Gulliver's fire-fighting activity is perhaps foreshadowed in a sentence from Burton on the cure of melancholy by "Help from friends by Counsel, Comfort...witty Devices...etc.":

The pleasantest dotage that ever I read, saith *Laurentius* [Cap.8 *de mel(ancolia)*] was of a Gentleman at *Senes* in *Italy*, who was afraid to piss, lest all the Town should be drowned; the Physicians caused the bells to be rung backward, and told him the Town was on fire, whereupon he made water, and was immediately cured.[14]

Enough has probably been said to suggest Burton's book was a text which Swift probably knew and which is at least worth very serious consideration in reading Swift. Hunting for specific sources, however, is not the most profitable aspect of the comparison. In addition, the focus of interest in Swift's text is not only in the *Tale*, though here the *Anatomy* is instantly and obviously useful.

Both Burton and Swift habitually address the reader in a far from straightforward way, speaking behind masks, and so more speculative uses of the comparison might start with a brief biographical foray. At the very outset, in the first paragraph of his massive "Satyricall Preface," Burton appears as Democritus, declaring to the reader: "I would not willingly be known." Yet in Swiftian fashion, this is a transparent mask, though what is seen behind it is not straightforward either. Little is known of Burton's life, apart from the details he actually gives us in the *Anatomy*, where for instance he mentions his family, his father, mother, and brothers, and his experience of education:

Tyrannical, impatient, hare-brain Schoolmasters...as bad as hangmen and executioners, they make many children endure a martyrdom all the while they are at school, with bad diet, if they board in their houses, too much severity and ill usage, they quite pervert their temperature of body and mind: still chiding, railing, frowning, lashing, tasking, keeping...[children] moped many times, weary of their lives…and think no slavery in the world (as once I did myself) like to that of a Grammar Scholar….[15]

There is thus in the *Anatomy*, more than two generations earlier than Swift's writing career, the same complex mixture of a text that is clearly designed to be read according to sophisticated and (to us) partly unfamiliar rules, a public life of a writer framed in the politico-religious-economic structure of the Church of England, and what look like personal reports of the inner life of a kind apparently familiar and attractive to the modern reader. Just as Burton's single, though multifarious, text is contrasted with Swift's more varied and extensive writings, so the sparse biography of the reclusive Burton, a life-long bachelor Student (fellow) of Christ Church, Oxford, contrasts with a much fuller record of Swift in autobiography, professional writing, correspondence, recollection, contemporary accounts, and public action. The differences reflect much of the cultural history of the intervening century, but the resemblances between the two men are close enough to force us to consider Swift's at least plausibly one of a class of careers, rather than the solemnly unique profile it is sometimes represented as being.

Burton was born in 1577, the fourth of nine children, a younger son of a Northamptonshire gentleman, and thus of that English "Landed Interest, which is most to be depended upon in such a Nation as ours" and which on occasion Swift viewed with nostalgic affection.[16] Burton, like Swift, was a devoted Anglican, but though he held two cures of souls he spent his life in his college. His description of a country living is not idealistic:

Often it falls out, from a polite and terse Academick [a priest] must turn rustick, rude, melancholise alone, learn to forget; or else, as many do, become Maltsters, Graziers, Chapmen, &c. (now banished from the Academy, all commerce of the Muses, and confined to a country village, as *Ovid* was from *Rome* to *Pontus*,) and daily converse with a company of idiots and clowns.[17]

He records the kind of ecclesiastical career which Swift also had and which has given some trouble to unimaginative modern critics, for whom social bondage in this form seems unfamiliar and puzzling:

Had I done as others did, and put myself forward, I might have haply been as great a man as many of my equals (*AM*).[18]

I was once so mad to bustle abroad, and seek about for preferment, tire myself, and trouble all my friends, *sed nihil labor tantus profecit*…. [But all my labour was un-profitable; for, while death took off some of my friends, to others I was unknown; little liked by some, others made large promises; some pleaded strongly on my be-half, others fed me with vain hopes; while paying court to some, getting into favour with others, getting known to others, my best days were going, the years gliding by, my friends tired of my applications to them, and I myself the worse for wear; so now, sick of the world, and glutted with the falseness of human nature, I take things as they come.] (*AM*)[19]

In his already quoted subsection on "Love of Learning, or overmuch Study" (a Cause of Melancholy),[20] there is a Digression on the Miseries of Scholars, where Burton shows a not unexpected attitude, similar to Swift's in ambivalence, toward fellow clergy:

Divines [are] the most noble profession and worthy of double honour.... [The Priesthood is debased; and, since this is the case, I may venture to say so, and to give the low saying of a low person (St. Edmund Campion) about the Clergy, that they are a low lot, poor, ignorant, sordid, melancholy, wretched, despicable, and contemptible!][21]

The biographical details and asides which Burton offers have invited psychological theorizing of the sort familiar in discussions of Swift. Bergen Evans covers much of this ground, basing his diagnosis on meagre anecdotal material and biographical interpretation of the *Anatomy*:

That there was a neurotic strain in the family is suggested [by a story preserved of Burton's uncle, Anthony Faunt]. The assumption that [Burton's mother] was domineering and unaffectionate toward him—or at least that he thought she was—is supported by the intensity of feeling with which he so often alludes in the *Anatomy* to the cruelty and indifference of parents...(pp. 5–6).

...he does not list or describe one [symptom of melancholia] which he *demonstrates* on almost every page—namely, continual self-depreciation. [That it] does not represent a sincere and reasoned opinion of himself is shown in the ferocity with which, in hundreds of passages, he attacks all who disagree with him.... It is hard to accept his anonymity as a sincere and modest wish to remain unknown.... [In him one finds] pride disguised as humility, anonymity industriously providing a clew to its own identification.... Despite [his candid personal recollections and opinions], one lays down the book with a feeling that its author is elusive, noncommittal and evasive...(pp. 16–19).

His humour, for instance, perhaps the dominating feature of the book, is primarily aggressive.... Much of his aggression is directed against the reader...(p. 22).

Now all these characteristics—the resentments, the continual self-depreciation, the discontent, the aggressiveness, the mingled gaiety and depression—fit into a psychological pattern.... Denied love in his childhood, whether actually or in fantasy, he was ever after, in his own mind, rejected, discriminated against, and cut off from the opportunities and pleasures which were permitted to others.... But he felt that his fears, his feeling of insecurity in a loveless world, had forced him into a bad bargain. He could have been so much more than a college don if fate had not tricked him. And he never ceased to resent that fact, so that resentment became almost his dominant mood. He remained timid, and consequently his resentment does not dare to show itself too openly; it is cloaked in ambiguity, muffled in disarming absurdity, and strikes obliquely, anonymously, or under the protection of quotation…. It adds greatly to the pungency of his style, but it imposes certain limitations on his mind (p. 24).

The parallel with psychological criticism of Swift is significant in three ways, each suggestive, though contradictory if pushed too far. The quoted passages underline the generic nature of aspects of Swift's Anglican, post-Reformation, clerical circumstances; they show, given Evans's relatively naive expression of his ideas, the generic nature of much modern response to Burton as well as Swift; lastly, they draw attention to certain rhetorical or topical features which were common in the kinds of writing practiced by Burton and Swift and which may elicit such psychological criticism from modern readers.

A clear insight that comes from reading Swift in the light of Burton is the appreciation of how much of Swift's text is rooted, and how strongly, in the seventeenth century. There is indeed a considerable literature now which places aspects of *A Tale of a Tub* in particular in this historical context. As an example of Swift's satirical and tonal use of seventeenth-century "witty" prose, Kathleen Williams sets a passage from the *Anatomy*, the opening of the Digression on Air, beside a long, over-leaping sentence ostensibly mocking witty comparison from the *Tale*'s Section VIII on the learned Aeolists and their sect:[22]

As a long-winged Hawk, when he is first whistled off the fist, mounts aloft, and for his pleasure fetcheth many a circuit in the Air, still soaring higher and higher, till he be come to his full pitch, and in the end, when the game is sprung, comes down amain, and stoops upon a sudden: so will I, having now come at last into these ample fields of Air, wherein I may freely expatiate and exercise myself for my recreation, a while rove, wander round about the world, mount aloft to those ethereal orbs and celestial spheres, and so descend to my former elements again. In which progress I will first see whether that relation of the Friar of *Oxford* be true, concerning those Northern parts under the Pole, (if I meet *obitèr* with the Wandering *Jew, Elias Artifex*, or *Lucian's Icaromenippus*, they shall be my guides) …(*AM*).[23]

And, whereas the mind of Man, when he gives the Spur and Bridle to his Thoughts, doth never stop, but naturally sallies out into both extreams of High and Low, of Good and Evil; His first Flight of Fancy, commonly transports Him to Idea's of what is most Perfect, finished, and exalted; till having soared out of his own Reach and Sight, not well perceiving how near the Frontiers of Height and Depth, border upon each other; With the same Course and Wing, he falls down plum into the lowest Bottom of Things; like one who travels the *East* into the *West*; or like a strait Line drawn by its own Length into a Circle. Whether a Tincture of Malice in our Natures, makes us fond of furnishing every bright Idea with its Reverse; Or, whether Reason reflecting upon the Sum of Things, can, like the Sun, serve only to enlighten one half of the Globe, leaving the other half, by Necessity, under Shade and Darkness: Or, whether Fancy, flying up to the imagination of what is Highest and Best, becomes over-shot, and spent, and weary, and suddenly falls like a dead Bird of Paradise, to the Ground (*Tale*).[24]

Like the reversal of the soaring hawk to the falling Bird of Paradise, Swift's details of traveling from the East into the West, the sun causing light and darkness, may have some relation to the geographical and astronomical expatiation of Burton's following digression. The "witty comparison," as the energy of the passage suggests, is a send-up of antique *copia*. Another elaborate example, also with an antique ring to it, is to be found at the start of Jack's adventures (Section XI):

For in *Writing*, it is as in *Travelling*: If a Man is in haste to be at home [etc.]…On the other side, when a Traveller and his *Horse* are in Heart and Plight, when his Purse is full, and the Day before him [etc.]…[25]

The tone of a comparison in the *Anatomy*, however, at the start of a discussion of "how the Body works on the Mind," suggests caution in saying that Swift is "satirizing" old writers like Burton, who does not sound so "ingenuous" or unproblematic as he is often thought:

As a purly hunter, I have hitherto beaten about the circuit of the forest of this microcosm, and followed only those outward adventitious causes. I will now break into the inner rooms, and rip up the antecedent immediate causes which are there to be found…(*AM*).[26]

In Swift's ostensibly plain prose, an "insert" or passage that has the "witty," antique resonance to which the reader of Burton is alerted is to be found in the sentences borrowed from Samuel Sturmy's *Mariner's Magazine* (1669) which form the second paragraph of Gulliver's "Voyage to Brobdingnag."[27] The joke *is* about the density of the jargon, but there is force there too. Similarly, Swift's ambivalent attitude to the old proverbs in *Polite Conversation* and his delight in the *Journal to Stella*[28] in framing quasi-proverbs both indicate what Burton's varied registers of tone also suggest, that the imputation of "satirizing" is only a blunt description of what is happening in the use of "witty" prose.

The *Anatomy* is a useful repertory of the topics and ideas which Swift manipulates to assemble his mosiac of sometimes unsignaled allusions in the *Tale*, and which are likely to turn up in other writings too. A few lines from "Democritus to the Reader" will serve as an illustration:

'Tis most true, *tenet insanibile multos scribendi cacoethes* [Juv. VII, 51–52: many are possessed by the incurable itch to write], and *there is no end of writing of books* [Ecclesiastes 12:12], as the Wise-man found of old, in this scribbling age especial-ly, wherein *the number of books is without number* [Bishop King, *Preface to Jonah*].... [E]very man...will write no matter what, & scrape together it boots not whence.... They that are scarce auditors...must be masters & teachers, before they be capable & fit hearers. They will rush into all learning...divine, human authors, rake over all *Indexes* & Pamphlets for notes.... As Apothecaries we make new mix-tures every day, pour out of one vessel into another...; we skim off the cream of other men's wits, pick the choice flowers of their tilled gardens to set out our own sterile plots.... By which means it comes to pass, *that not only libraries & shops are full of our putid papers, but every close-stool and jakes, Scribunt carmina quae legunt cacantes* [Martial, xii.61.10: they write down poems which they have read in the jakes]; they serve to put under pies, to lap spice in, and keep roast-meat from burning.[29]

More intriguing than these parallels, suggesting literary commonplaces, are three substantial and related areas of complex speculation and controver-sy explored by Burton, and seized on by Swift in the *Tale*, but also else-where in his writing. These are the Renaissance concern with the relationship between the body, mind, and spirit; secondly, the characteris-tics, history, and effects of cultivated, personalized religious experience (particularly in its sixteenth- and seventeenth-century English forms herded under the term Puritanism); and thirdly, what Burton calls "heroical love," destructive forms of the sexual drive, which in the "scatological poems" Swift also satirizes in his attacks on corrupt male rhetoric which denies women's individuality. Each of these topics is too large for even a summary discussion here, but the *Anatomy* shows them placed together, just as they are in Swift's writing.

The first two areas may be taken together, and a brief comment could profitably start with the use J. R. Clark has made of Burton to construct "a typical 'anatomy' of the mind," a model that will show in simple form the functioning of memory as understood by Swift and his contemporary audience, and its absence in the moderns' madness delineated in the *Tale*.[30] Of great importance here are Burton's "Digression of Anatomy," his "Division of the Body, Humours, Spirits," and his Anatomy of the Soul.[31] As Clark correctly says, this Anatomy of the Mind (or Soul) is based on a traditional picture built up by Greek physicians and philosophers, medieval theologians, and Renaissance thinkers. But he is treading on dangerous ground when he calls Burton's work "that standard encyclopedia of sciences in the seventeenth century." As has been pointed out, "The *Anatomy* is a highly original work, not only because of the conscious literary art with which Burton joined his quotations together, but because of the metamorphoses which these quotations themselves had undergone in 'the deep well of unconscious cerebration.' "[32]

The meaning of the passages Burton cites or mentions, from Hippocrates and Galen, Aristotle, and many others like "T.W. Jesuit in his *Passions of the Mind*," was the subject of argument and commentary. Nevertheless, these passages are an important starting point for understanding the underlying play of ideas in, for example, Section VIII of the *Tale* on the Aeolists. A consideration of Burton, by directing attention to the presence of medical as well as philosophical, political, and theological argument, moves the reader out from thinking too closely in terms of the traditional "anatomy of the mind" into becoming aware of Swift's grasp of the Renaissance controversies about the relation of the body and the spirit, and the implications of the ferment of these ideas for political and religious life. Among the interests that Swift shares with Burton, which had a wider European importance, are Paracelsan chemical philosophy and related Hermetic doctrines like Rosicrucianism, millennialism, republicanism, despotism, Anabaptist views as well as the response of the Roman Catholic Church in the Council of Trent to revolutionary political and religious movements. In particular, from Burton or like Burton, Swift is attracted by the notion of enthusiasm, or "Puritan" individualism, or Atheism, or lawless intellectual speculation, as disorderly "religious melancholy," eccentric conditions with a physical side, or physical malfunctions with spiritual consequences. Like Burton, though with far more restrained reference in his text, he seeks similar or comparable conditions in the past or in other parts of the world away from Europe.

Michael Heyd has carefully explored with a wealth of detail

some of the ways by which the medical and philosophical tradition which linked enthusiasm with melancholy penetrated the vocabulary and contents of religious polemics in the seventeenth century, particularly in England.[33]

In this exploration, he finds Burton's *Anatomy* "a natural and convenient starting point," both because "he may have been—at least in England—the first to incorporate systematically the medical literature on melancholy for the purpose of religious polemics" and because of "his copious quotation from previous sources"(p. 18). In commentary on Swift, this had earlier been pointed out by Phillip Harth,[34] who drew attention to the conclusion that Puritans were sincere victims of Delusion, argued first in the *Anatomy* of Burton and then in the 1650s by writers such as Meric Casaubon, Henry More the Cambridge Platonist, and a couple of pamphleteers.[35] This commentary has been largely in terms of English religious controversy. Heyd, however, in his demonstration of Burton's use of "the themes of enthusiasm and religious melancholy" to combat the two enemies of Anglicanism—the radical sectarians on the one hand, the Catholic church on the other (Jack and Peter)—delves deeply into Burton's use of philosophical, medical, demonological, and theological sources. These include Plato, Bernard de Gordon[ius], Leonhard Fuchsius, Hercules Saxonia, Pieter von Foreest, Felix Platter, Elie de Montalto, Jerome Cardan, Caspar Peucer, Ludwig Lavater, and Johann Weyer.[36] Heyd not only shows that Burton uses his sources in true Swiftian fashion, polemically and creatively including "changes [that] never hurt the point that [he] was trying to make" (p. 31), but also gives some idea of the important historical and European context of the naturalizing and rationalizing of the discussion of psychic disturbance. This is in line with the realization that the appearance in Swift's *Tale* of Cabbalists, Rosicrucians, alchemists, and hermeticists—men such as Paracelsus, Boehme, and Thomas Vaughan—is not only satirical fooling with "dark authors" but shows an understanding on Swift's part of the outcome of the sixteenth- and seventeenth-century controversies over medicine and science as well as religion and politics.[37] Some very suggestive titles in the two book-lists of Swift's library, or mentioned by him in the *Tale* and elsewhere, appear as important sources in Burton's *Anatomy*; these include notably the works of Avicenna (cited and quoted by Burton more than 70 times), Jerome Cardan (140+), and Paracelsus (45+), as well as [*Regimen*] *Schola Salerna* (*Salernitana*, a widely reprinted book of practice by the doctors of Salerno in Latin rhyme).[38]

In handling the links between the body, the mind, and the soul, and in framing a polemic in the *Tale* against "errors" in religion and learning as madness on the part of leaders and delusion on the part of their followers, Swift clearly stands in some relationship with Burton, Henry More's *Enthusiasmus Triumphatus* lying between them. By his references More specifically acknowledges a debt to Burton. The complex question yet to be unraveled is to what extent Swift draws independently on any of the horde of authors cited by Burton (or others like them), to what extent on the *Anatomy* itself (Harth believes he probably consulted Burton[39]), to what extent on More. Perhaps all three possibilities have truth in them. Whatever the case, a careful study of Burton helps to confirm what has been suspected, the importance of the historical and European context of Swift's complex reaction to powerful currents of ideas flowing out of the Renaissance and eddying in the bitter seventeenth-century religious and political conflicts amid which he reached maturity.

Burton's influence, direct or indirect, on three stretches of Swift's writing on Enthusiasm is undisputed, namely Section VIII of the *Tale* on the "Learned Aeolists," Section IX: "A Digression on Madness," and the second and concluding piece that follows the *Tale* in its first (1704) and early editions, *A Discourse Concerning the Mechanical Operation of the Spirit: A Fragment*. It has been suggested that the *Fragment*, an important discussion of the cultivation of Enthusiasm, is in some way related to Jack's adventures in Section XI of the *Tale* itself.[40]

In his two long paragraphs "Of the species or kinds of Melancholy," Burton names one of the three kinds in "the most received division" as "*hypochondriacal or windy melancholy*," which "ariseth from the bowels, liver, spleen, or...*mesenterium*."[41] He also notes that "Some will reduce enthusaists, exstatical and demoniacal persons" to melancholics. Henry More improves this hint into "that *Spirit* then that wings the *Enthusiast*...is nothing else but that *Flatulency* which is in the Melancholy complexion...."[42] As Michael DePorte notes, in the Digression on Madness "Swift exploits most richly the belief of contemporary doctors that mental disturbance can be traced to physical causes."[43] The narrator of the Tale asserts in the "Digression":

Then it will follow, that as the Face of Nature never produces Rain, but when it is overcast and disturbed, so Human Understanding, seated in the Brain, must be troubled and overspread by Vapours, ascending from the lower Faculties, to water the Invention, and render it fruitful.[44]

Swift's sentences may be compared with Burton's on the "Distemperature" of the brain as a cause of melancholy:

The brain is still distempered by himself, or by consent: by himself or his proper affection, as *Faventinus* calls it, *or by vapours which arise from the other parts, and fume up in the head, altering the animal faculties.*[45]

In a note, Burton gives the Latin of the last clause apparently as a quotation from the *De Curanda Morbis* of Victorius Benedictus Faventinus (1481–1561), an important source in the *Anatomy*.

In the first lines of the Digression on Madness, Swift had modulated the cause of Enthusiasm from the Melancholy of Burton and More to "Madness or Phrenzy." The whole passage is of significance:

Nor shall it any ways detract from the just Reputation of this famous Sect [the Aeolists], that its Rise and Institution are owing to such an Author as I have described *Jack* to be; A Person whose Intellectuals were overturned, and his Brain shaken out of its Natural Position; which we commonly suppose to be a Distemper, and call by the Name of *Madness* or *Phrenzy*. For, if we take a Survey of the greatest Actions that have been performed in the World, under the Influence of Single Men; which are *The Establishment of New Empires by Conquest: The Advance and Progress of New Schemes in Philosophy; and the contriving, as well as the propagating of New Religions*: We shall find the Authors of them all, to have been Persons, whose natural Reason hath admitted great Revolutions from their Dyet, their Education, the Prevalency of some certain Temper, together with the particular Influence of Air and Climate.[46]

Burton, in his paragraphs on Diseases of the Mind, says that "*Madness, phrenzy*, and *melancholy*, are confounded by *Celsus* and many writers" but that he, in company with "our neotericks," prefers "to handle them apart."[47] He defines Madness

to be a vehement *dotage*, or raving without a fever, far more violent than *melancholy*, full of anger and clamour, horrible looks, actions, gestures.... Differing only in this from *phrenzy*, that it is without a fever, and their memory is most part better.

The cause, he says, is physiological, "choler adust, and blood incensed, brain inflamed, &c."

In opening his section on Religious Melancholy, Burton laments he has "no pattern to follow...no man to imitate. No Physician hath as yet distinctly written of it, as of [Love-Melancholy]; all acknowledge it a most notable symptom, some a cause, but few a species or kind."[48] Swift takes his cue from Burton's line of thought, and treats Enthusiasm as being in Burtonian terms a form of "non-natural [i.e., not hereditary] Melancholy, which produceth madness," a physical distemper of the humors caused by Burton's "six non-natural things so much spoken of amongst Physicians," i.e., "the six things necessary to health, but liable, by abuse or accident, to become the cause of disease, viz. air, meat and drink, sleep and waking, motion and rest, excretion and retention, the affections of the mind."[49] Swift further closely binds together religious Enthusiasts and heresiarchs with conquerors and political leaders, as well as system-building philosophers:

It will be a very delicate point, to cut the Feather, and divide the several Reasons to a Nice and Curious Reader, how this numerical Difference in the Brain, can produce Effects of so vast a Difference from the same *Vapour*, as to be the sole Point of Individuation between *Alexander the Great, Jack of Leyden*, and Monsieur *Des Cartes*.[50]

Even in this move, however, Burton still perhaps offers a model or parallel, but in another part of his book he works outside of Swift's earshot. One sprawling subsection of Part III is labeled

Causes of Religious Melancholy. From the Devil by miracles, apparitions, oracles. His instruments or factors, Politicians, Priests, Impostors, Heretics, blind guides. In them simplicity, fear, blind zeal, ignorance, solitariness, curiosity, pride, vainglory, presumption, &c. His engines, fasting, solitariness, hope, fear, &c.[51]

The Devil as visible proponent is too antique for Swift, as are citations from Wierus, *On Demonic Tricks*, or from Strozius Cicogna, *On Magic of All Kinds, Spirits and Incantations*. But there are Burtonian precedents for Swift's introduction into the *Tale* of Henri IV, with "the collected part of [his] *Semen*, raised and inflamed, becom[ing] adust, converted to Choler," making him a victim of disordered evacuation and retention;[52] or Alexander the Great:

Alexander after his victories in *India*, became so insolent, he would be adored for a god: and those Roman Emperors came to that height of madness they must have Temples built to them, sacrifices to their deities, *Divus Augustus, D. Claudius, D. Adrianus....* Our *Turks, China* Kings, great *Chams,* and *Mogors,* do little less, assuming divine and bombast titles to themselves; the meaner sort are too credulous, and led with blind zeal, blind obedience, to prosecute and maintain whatsoever their sottish leaders shall propose, what they in pride and singularity, revenge, vain glory, ambition, spleen, for gain, shall rashly maintain and broach, their disciples make a matter of conscience, of hell and damnation, if they do it not, and will rather forsake wives, children, house and home, land, goods, fortunes, life itself, than omit or abjure the least tittle of it, and to advance the common cause, undergo any miseries, turn traitors, assassinates, pseudo-martyrs, with full assurance and hope of reward in that other world...(*AM*).[53]

The anti-Catholic note in Burton's text is strong ("turn traitors, assassinates, pseudo-martyrs") and is echoed by a strain in Swift's *Tale* that is often discounted. Yet the *Anatomy* also contains far more reminiscences of scenes of violence than the *Tale*. Swift may have written in the shadow of the Civil War, Charles I's execution, and James II's war in Ireland. Burton, however, had lived almost in the smoke of burning churchmen. Cranmer, Latimer, and Ridley were burned in Oxford less than forty years before he went there as an undergraduate, Servetus (whose screams he mentions[54]) at Geneva in 1553, Giordano Bruno at Rome in 1600, and Vaninus at Toulouse in 1619 while the *Anatomy* was being written. Swift also makes the smooth steel mechanism of his satire more glittering by the appropriation as an Enthusiast of "Monsieur *Des Cartes*," placed alongside Alexander the Great and Jack of Leyden in that formidable move that has no model in the *Anatomy*'s blander "many of our great Philosophers and Deists."

A comment on the third area of "heroical love" might begin with a linguistic attitude which Burton and Swift held in common. At the start of his book, Burton declares that

it was not mine intent to prostitute my muse in *English*, or to divulge *secreta Minervae*, but to have exposed this more contract in *Latin*, if I could have got it printed. Any scurrile pamphlet is welcome to our mercenary Stationers in *English*, they print all,

> cuduntque libellos
> In quorum foliis vix simia nuda cacaret;
>
> [and beat out pamphlets, on the pages of which a poor monkey would scarcely shit]

but in *Latin* they will not deal; which is one of the reasons *Nicholas Car*, in his oration of the paucity of *English* writers, gives, that so many flourishing wits are smothered in oblivion, lie dead and buried in this our nation.[55]

In his *Proposal for Correcting. . .the English Tongue* (1712), Swift distantly echoes this despairing note: "The Fame of our Writers is usually confined to these two Islands."[56] Burton several times does refrain, however, from divulging the secrets of Minerva, leaving Latin quotations untranslated, as he wittily does in abusing the mercenary stationers above and also in four longer stretches of Latin. One of these has already been quoted from, the long passage in which he fraternally cloaks in the learned language abuse of his fellow clergy. Two others betray a certain worry about decorum of a kind relevant in reading Swift. The first is concerned with "medicaments to allay lust,"[57] and to the second, about strange couplings, Burton adds the comment:

[But I do not. . .make public, things which it is not proper for all to know, but only the learned for whose sake, like Rodericus (*On the Diseases of Women*), I would wish to have written; neither for light wits nor for depraved minds have I noted these filthy sins etc.; I am unwilling to inquire any longer into these nasty affairs.][58]

A fourth passage, in the subsection "Parents the Cause [of Melancholy] by Propagation," attracts the plea, "Good Master Schoolmaster, do not English this. . .; I spare to. . ."; it deals with intercourse with menstruating women which, it is alleged, begets "luckless ones. . .mad, doting, stupid, ailing, filthy, impotent, plague-ridden, of the lowest vitality."[59]

In the midst of the subsection on "Symptoms of Maids,' Nuns' and Widows' Melancholy," a sudden exclamation is addressed to the reader:

But where am I? Into what subject have I rushed? What have I to do with Nuns, Maids, Virgins, Widows? I am a Bachelor myself, and lead a Monastick life in a College, *nae ego sane ineptus qui haec dixerim* [I am indeed a very unskilled person to speak of these matters], I confess tis an *indecorum*; and as *Pallas*, a Virgin, blushed, when *Jupiter* by chance spake of Love matters in her presence, and turn'd away her face, *me reprimam* [I shall check myself]; though my subject necessarily require it, I will say no more.[60]

With these passages, and others on women, like the paragraph quoting Proverbs 5:4 and 7:27 on women causing madness,[61] we are in the same territory as Swift's so-called scatological poems and passages. Since they occur in a text less widely read, they have not attracted the same protesting comment, though tactics for dealing with them parallel the maneuvers of critics confronted with "A Beautiful Young Nymph" or "The Lady's Dressing Room." Floyd Dell and Paul Jordan-Smith, who in 1927 produced a handy edition of the *Anatomy* for the general reader, go down the biographical road:

Burton's large, genial, tolerant mind had its prejudices and its squeamishnesses. His chief prejudice was that against "Papists," his chief squeamishness was in regard to certain of the sexual aspects of Melancholia; and sometimes these traits are rather in conflict, for he does dearly love to relate scandal against the "Papists." Concerning all the pleasant, or odd and amusing, or impressively terrible, of "erotick" matters, he has a robust curiosity, which puts his discussion of "Heroical Love" among the most delightful things written on that subject in our language. But there were matters in connection with his theme which he found distasteful, and could not bring himself to deal with in English.... It is such traits that remind us that we are dealing with a "melancholy" bachelor whose acquaintance with the other sex was gained chiefly from his books.[62]

Bergen Evans, who, in addition to discussing *The Psychiatry of Robert Burton*, also as we have seen offers a brief psychoanalysis of him, goes further:

He delights to be amorous in a manly way.... He loves to pose as a connoisseur.... Yet among those dainty delights there are ugly smears of misogyny. This lusty smacking of the lips is interspersed with what comes suspiciously close to retchings. Women are "bad by nature and lightly given all."[63] Left to themselves "they think ill...for they have no other business to trouble their heads with."[64] To Jacobus de Voragine's "twelve motives to mitigate the miseries of marriage" he is quick to oppose a sneering "Antiparody."[65]

He dwells with morbid fascination upon the "dirtiness" of women, quoting with evident relish the more loathsome passages of the church fathers on the subject. The secret repulsiveness underlying their fair-seeming exteriors is ever in his mind. He can't leave it alone, but keeps coming back to it with insistent prurience, gloating over the details of certain physiological processes, which he seems to regard as infinitely more disgusting in women than in men.

His remedy for love [i.e., love melancholy] is to have the lover see his beloved as she really is....[66]

Evans then quotes a "dreadful passage" of bravura abuse from the subdivision of "Symptoms or signs of Love-Melancholy, in Body, Mind, good, bad, etc.," on the blindness of the followers of Love or Cupid.[67] He omits the start of the set of variations in a commonplace:

> Quisquis amat ranam, ranam putat esse Dianam.
> [Whosoever loves a frog thinks that frog Diana.]

Burton then rings the changes on "the frog": "ill-favoured, wrinkled, pimpled...clouds in her face...crooked, dry, bald...her dugs like two double jugs...her feet stink, she breeds lice...a fat fustilugs," and so on.

John F. Sena, noting that readers have found Swift's "scatological" poems disturbing, and that "even [his] most sympathetic critics have had difficulty in accepting the imagery and intensity" of these writings, seeks by using the *Anatomy* to place them in a normative medical context of curing "love-melancholy."[68] He observes that "[Burton] recommends all the known cures...from journeys to jocularity, from gentle persuasion to noisome drugs." If these fail, however, the last antidote is "metaphorical anatomization of the loved one." With detailed reference, Sena argues that this is in line with the medical writings, such as those of Laurentius, whose work, which includes a discussion of love-melancholy, is cited or quoted by Burton more than sixty times. Laurens advises that if the lover cannot be cured of his melancholy by enjoyment, then the physician may prescribe drugs or, more effectively, words which will make the patient hate what torments him.[69] Burton's subsection "[Cure of Love-Melancholy] By Counsel and Persuasion, foulness of the fact, men's, women's faults, miseries of marriage, events of lust, etc." is relevant here, particularly this passage, incompletely quoted by Sena:

To conclude with *Chrysostom, When thou seest a fair and beautiful person*, a brave *Bonaroba, a bella Donna, quae salivam moveat, lepidam puellam et quam tu facilè ames* [who would make your mouth water, a charming girl, with whom you would easily fall in love], *a comely woman, having bright eyes, a merry countenance, a shining lustre in her look, a pleasant grace, wringing thy soul, and increasing thy concupiscence, bethink with thyself that it is but earth thou lovest, a mere excrement, which so vexeth thee, which thou so admirest, and thy raging soul will be at rest* [in a note Burton gives a Latin version of Chrysostom's Greek text]. *Take her skin from her face, and thou shalt see all loathsomeness under it, that beauty is a superficial skin and bones, nerves, sinews: suppose her sick, now rivel'd, hoary-*

headed, hollow-cheeked, old: within she is full of filthy fleam, stinking, putrid, ex-cremental stuff: snot and snivel in her nostrils, spittle in her mouth, water in her eyes, what filth in her brains, &c. Or take her at best, and look narrowly upon her in the light, stand nearer her, nearer yet, thou shalt perceive almost as much, and love less, as *Cardan* well writes...though *Scaliger* deride him for it.... He shall find...crooked nose, bad eyes, prominent veins, concavities about the eyes, wrinkles, pimples,...scabredity, paleness, yellowness, and as many colours as are in a Turkey-cock's neck.... Examine all parts of body and mind, I advise thee to enquire of all. See her angry, merry, laugh, weep...dressed, undressed, in all attires, sites, gestures, passions.... Besides these outward neves, or open faults, errors, there be many inward infirmities, secret, some private (which I will omit) and some more common to the sex, sullen fits, evil qualities, filthy diseases, in this case fit to be considered... [Savanarola, Platina, Ludovicus Boncialus, Pet(er) Haedus, and Albertus are cited for details].[70]

This passage may be read with two particular passages in Swift's writing, as well as more generally "The Lady's Dressing Room" and "A Beautiful Young Nymph." First, in the *Tale*'s "Digression on Madness" are lodged the well-known sentences:

Last Week I saw a Woman *flay'd*, and you will hardly believe, how much it altered her Person for the worse. Yesterday I ordered the Carcass of a *Beau* to be stript in my Presence; when we were all amazed to find so many unsuspected Faults under one Suit of Cloaths: Then I laid open his *Brain*, his *Heart*, and his *Spleen*; But, I plainly perceived at every Operation, that the farther we proceeded, we found the Defects encrease upon us in Number and Bulk.[71]

Swift's satire is placed within the context of an "Anatomy Lesson," with Reason's "Tools for cutting and opening." But Burton's passage shows the actual change from the medieval *memento mori*, the icon of the corrupting body, to a use of scientific observation. After the presentation of Chrysostom's images, he invokes careful scrutiny—"look narrowly upon her in the light, stand nearer her"—and in a sentence not quoted in the above excerpt cites "the true rules of symmetry and proportion." For the latter, the reader is referred not only to Albrecht Dürer but also to Giovanni Paolo Lomazzo, the first volume of whose *Treatise on Painting* is on proportion.[72] Swift's "Anatomy" is paralleled by the equally "scientific" Renaissance rules of proportion and perspective.

Second, Swift's poem "The Progress of Beauty," assigned to 1719, contains a set of variations on themes deeply rooted in the *Anatomy of Melancholy*, not only the seventeenth-century manner of building up witty comparisons but, as in the Burton passage, the place of colors in apprehending the distinction between appearance and reality—

> Three Colours, Black, and Red, and White,
> So gracefull in their proper Place,
> Remove them to a diff'rent Light
> They form a frightfull hideous Face....

—and the grotesque details of personal appearance: "Crackt Lips, foul Teeth, and gummy Eyes."[73] The important antique details of astrological joking in the poem, it may be mentioned in parenthesis, underline the Burtonian resonance of this set of verses:

> ...all Astrologers maintain
> Each Night a Bit drops off her Face....

Both Burton and Swift inherited the unmanageable tradition in St. Paul and the Church Fathers of anti-women writing, but they both struggle to free themselves from it—it may be not with complete success—or to put it to better use. Careless reading of Burton's "railing" to press home an accusation of "misogyny" fails to direct attention to passages resisting such simple interpretation:

> ...But more herein to speak I am forbidden:
> Sometimes for speaking truth one may be chidden.
> [Ariosto, XXXIX.70]

I am not willing, you see, to prosecute the cause against [women], and therefore take heed you mistake me not, *matronam nullam ego tango* [Horace, *Sat.*, I.2.54], I honour the sex, with all good men, as I ought to do.... Let *Simonides, Mantuan, Platina, Pet. Aretine*, and such women-haters bear the blame, if aught be said amiss.... And that which I have said (to speak truth) no more concerns them than men, though women be more frequently named in this Tract; (to apologize once for all) I am neither partial against them, or therefore bitter: what is said of the one, *mutato nomine*, may most part be understood of the other.... If women in general be so bad (and men worse than they) what a hazard is it to marry![74]

The same argument of careless or incomplete reading is sometimes brought to the rescue of Swift in discussing the "scatological" poems as well as other difficult passages in his works. The difference is that in the *Anatomy* there is at least the more or less controlling framework of a "treatise," with its pattern of "causes," "symptoms and signs," and "cures" of the condition of "Melancholy," however complex this notion may be. The cast of probably about fifteen hundred writers, cited and quoted, also puts the attentive reader on guard and forces caution in outlining any single neat interpretation. Finally, a wide range of rhetorical forms *within the single work*, such as railing, historical and free narrative, direct address to the reader, parody, translation, and notably an insistent pattern of assertion followed by retraction,[75] is signaled by these specific quotations. This too reinforces caution. The reader of Swift's writings, however, tends traditionally to be confined in response to a single work (or group of works), *An Argument...against Abolishing Christianity* (or political pamphlets), "The Lady's Dressing Room" (or "scatological" poems), *A Modest Proposal* (or Irish writings), "Verses on the Death of Dr. Swift" (or occasional poems), or to the inchoate if useful notion of "Swift." Only *A Tale of a Tub* and its accompanying pieces, *The Battle of the Books* and *A Discourse concerning the Mechanical Operation of the Spirit*, may force the reader to treat the text in the same way as the assemblage in the *Anatomy* requires. Not that attention to individual works has not, in particular cases, produced good and persuasive readings.[76] But there seem to be two contradictory movements in response to Swift's works as a whole, the one reading each work independently or in the groups that his own division suggests, and the other prompting discussion of them as an ensemble like the *Anatomy*, but with the rhetorical signals, the signs of quotation, parody, structure, strangely blurred. The latter procedure causes mysterious but real offence to some readers, but the parallel with Burton's kaleidoscopic text reinforces its credibility and life.

The last, and most speculative, use of a comparison between the *Anatomy* and Swift's writing has often been made but is suggested with particular acuteness, though briefly, by Denis Donoghue.[77] This is to identify a kind of writing, associated with Democritus, Lucian, Rabelais, Sir Thomas More, Erasmus, and Montaigne, as well as Burton and Swift. Later exponents of the art might be (in a more romantic vein) Sterne, and notably James Joyce giving it modernist embodiment. Donoghue calls it a "plural form." It often relies on other texts and elaborated commentary on them; it "is propelled, however obliquely, by a paradoxical sense of life." It is not "linear," and conscious that "defeat is its own fate," sets out to "defeat [the] reader." The sense of life comes largely from the reader "wondering what can possibly come next." In this sense the *Tale* and *Gulliver's Travels* are strictly comparable. Both consist of a parable and digressions, of a text and commentary. The digression, the movement at the whim of "the author" is paramount, as it is in the *Anatomy*. As there is a movement in displayed or even vaunted "authorial" whim from earlier writers to Burton, there is a comparable and more subversive movement from Burton to Swift, and instructively from the *Tale* to the *Travels*.

The program of a "Treatise" cannot contain Burton's text. The scholastic arrangement of Parts, Members, Sections, and Subsections neither produces comprehensive presentation of the multiplicity of subjects nor advances an orderly argument. The myriad citations read like the last despairing attempt to organize a total coverage of the writing on a subject, yet in totality, if not intention, it is as wilful as the twists and turns of Burton's sentences. The attempt at inclusiveness is defeated (if it were ever seriously embarked on) by Burton's acknowledgment of the power, for good or ill, of advancing scientific thought, with its subsequent destruction of outmoded theoretical structures,[78] and by his response to the complexities of the inner life. Burton himself produces the real "unity" of the book. Swift lists "Treatises wrote by the same Author" at the start of *A Tale of a Tub*, and the text has a form of argument (parable and digressions), with citations and discussion, a form of mental ordering bred into Swift and Burton by their education and theological studies. In the *Tale*, however, the container is even less supportive than Burton's, and becomes itself anarchic, leaving the reader to cling to any detectable presence of the "real author" or to any suitable or cherished principles and theories of texts and reading. In *Gulliver*, the text, commentary, and all except very abrupt and idiosyncratic citation have become problematic. The presence of an apparently realistic report (intermittently introduced in the *Anatomy* and elusively there in the *Tale*) has been strengthened, giving a text that can be read convincingly in different ways, with minimal reliable signals to direct the reader along a particular path. In this, *Gulliver's Travels* is a modern book, but it is also comparable with the kind of writing of which Burton's *Anatomy* is a distinguished, powerful, and as yet partly unexplored exemplar known to Swift.

Taking Swift's writing as a whole, it becomes profitable to read it in the light of the *Anatomy*, of which there are limited but perceptible echoes in the later texts. Important specific areas of Swift's writing are illuminated by Burton's text. For example, Gulliver's account of "the several remote Nations of the World" is obviously related not only to Burton's *utopia* in his Preface[79] but also to the use of travel books, which is such a significant component of the *Anatomy*. Swift's "scatological" poems are related to Burton's massive digression in Part III on heroic love. Swift's preoccupation with individualistic, ecstatic religion is related to Burton's equally massive digression on religious melancholy in the same final part. More generally, and arguably, both Burton and Swift practice a similar kind of writing which, with its enjoyable problems for the reader, benefits from the wider comparative assessment.

¹ Bergen Evans in consultation with George J. Mohr, *The Psychiatry of Robert Burton* (New York, 1944), pp. 42–45.

² Miriam K. Starkman, *Swift's Satire on Learning in* A Tale of a Tub (Princeton, 1950; rpt. 1968), p. 107 and n. 2.

³ *A Tale of a Tub*, A. C. Guthkelch and D. Nichol Smith, eds., 2nd ed. with corrections (Oxford, 1973), p. 203. Page references to the *Tale, Battle of the Books*, and *Mechanical Operation of the Spirit* are to this edition, hereafter cited as *Tale*.

⁴ Details of Swift's library are taken from Harold Williams, *Dean Swift's Library* (Cambridge, 1932); and William LeFanu, *A Catalogue of Books Belonging to Dr Jonathan Swift* (Cambridge, 1988). Of Burton's sources Swift possessed in 1715 two folio volumes of Avicenna, *Libri in Re Medica Omnes* (Venice: Valgrisius, 1564); Cardan, *Opera Omnia* in 10 vols. folio (Leyden: Huguetan and Ravaud, 1630); Paracelsus, *Opera Omnia*, 3 vols. in 2 folio (Geneva: de Tournes, 1658; No. 596 in the sale catalogue [1746] of Swift's library); and [*Regimen*] *Medicina Salernitana* (Frankfurt: Saur, 1605; sale catalogue, No. 44). The appearance of the works of Girolamo Cardano in these circumstances invites investigation. Burton quotes from him far more often than he refers to Aristotle (100+), perhaps because two of his works, *De Subtilitate* (first published 1550) and *De Rerum Varietate* (first published 1557) are temptingly encyclopedic. J. M. Bamborough, "Burton and Cardan," in *English Renaissance Studies Presented to Dame Helen Gardner* (Oxford, 1980), a learned and wide-ranging essay, touches in a healthily unfamiliar context on some issues of Swiftian interest, such as "genitures" and horoscopes; the problems of identifying a writer's "character" or "autobiography" in texts constructed according to a contemporary code on a familiar contemporary theme; the difficulty of relying on incomplete or inaccurate (or altered) quotations; the hazards of judging the motives for writing behind a mask or *persona*; the "favourite Renaissance rhetorical gesture" of the "paradoxical encomium"; role playing; the status of Northrop Frye's remark in the *Anatomy of Criticism* that the *Anatomy of Melancholy* is "the greatest Menippean satire in English before Swift"; and the relationship between Burton's text and Erasmus, Montaigne, and Rabelais (pp. 180–93, esp. pp. 187–89). When the work being done at the University of Münster on Swift's library is published in detail, with adequate annotation of source citations, there will be an opportunity for following up this promising line of inquiry. The author wishes to thank Heinz J. Vienken for friendly assistance in the study of Burton's sources.

⁵ Robert Burton, *The Anatomy of Melancholy*, ed. A. R. Shilleto, 3 vols. (London, 1893; rpt. 1896, 1903, 1904, with the same pagination), I.I.II.6; I, 179f. References to the *Anatomy* will be to this edition (cited as *AM*), giving first the Part, Section, Member, and Subsection, and then the volume and page(s) in Shilleto's edition.

⁶ I.I.II.V; I, 176f.

⁷ Section VIII, pp. 151–52.

⁸ *Tale*, pp. 222–23.

⁹ III.IV.II.1; III, 440–41.

[10] Pp. 79–80.

[11] I.II.III.15; I, 352.

[12] P. 101.

[13] Text, *Plutarch's Lives* (Loeb Library, 1914–26; rpt. 1959), II, 4; translation, *Plutarch's Lives...Translated from the Original Greek...*by J. and W. Langhorne (1770; rpt. 1866), I, 130.

[14] *AM* II.II.VI.2; II, 132. This passage and other suggestive parallels between the *Anatomy* and *Gulliver's Travels* are neatly discussed in David Oakland, "Gulliver's Melancholy Dream of Power," *Transactions of the Samuel Johnson Society of the Northwest*, 13 (1982), 48–59.

[15] *AM* I.II.IV.2; I, 384.

[16] *The Public Spirit of the Whigs*, in [*The Prose Writings of Jonathan Swift*], ed. Herbert Davis et al., 14 vols. (1939–68; various reimpressions, sometimes corrected, Oxford, 1957–69), VIII, 481; hereafter cited as *Prose*. Cf. "In all free Nations, I take the proper Definition of *Law* to be the Will of *the Majority of those who have Property in land*," Drapier's Letter VII, *Prose*, X, 134; and "Thoughts on Various Subjects," *Prose*, IV, 245.

[17] *AM* I.II.III.15; I, 374.

[18] *AM* ibid., I, 369.

[19] *AM* II.III.VI; II, 217.

[20] *AM* I.II.III.15.

[21] *AM* I, 361 and 380; translated from Burton's Latin text.

[22] *Jonathan Swift and the Age of Compromise* (Lawrence, 1959), pp. 15f.

[23] II.II.III; II, 40.

[24] Pp. 157–58.

[25] *Tale*, pp. 188–89.

[26] *AM* I.II.V.1; I, 430. A *purly hunter* is one in an outlying part (purlieu) of an enclosed forest.

[27] *Prose*, XI (rev. ed., 1959), 84.

[28] Harold Williams, ed., *Journal to Stella*, 2 vols. (Oxford, 1948), I, 93, 140, 145, 171, 248, 272; II, 499.

[29] *AM* Pref.; I, 20. In the *Tale*, on *indexes* see pp. 145, 147; for a parallel with Burton's "cream of other men's wits" compare the Author's Preface to the *Battle of the Books*: "Wit, without knowledge, being a sort of *Cream*, gathers in a Night to the Top..." (*Tale*, p. 215); on the "ocular Conviction [of] a *Jakes*, or an *Oven*," see p. 36.

[30] John R. Clark, *Form and Frenzy in Swift's* Tale of a Tub (Ithaca, 1970), pp. 147–49.

[31] I.I.II.1–2, 5–11.

[32] David Renaker, "Robert Burton's Tricks of Memory," *PMLA*, 87 (1972), 391.

[33] Michael Heyd, "Robert Burton's Sources on Enthusiasm and Melancholy," *History of European Ideas*, 5 (1984), 18.

[34] *Swift and Anglican Rationalism: The Religious Background of* A Tale of a Tub (Chicago, 1961), pp. 71–72, 105–09, 112–17.

[35] Meric Casaubon, *A Treatise Concerning Enthusiasm as It Is an Effect of Nature: But Is Mistaken by Many for either Inspiration, or Diabolical Possession* (1655); significantly for Swift's reading, it was admired by Sir William Temple (see C. M. Webster, "Temple, Casaubon, and Swift," *Notes and Queries*, 160 [1931], 405). Henry More, *Enthusiasmus Triumphatus: or A Brief Discourse of the Nature, Causes, Kinds and Cure of Enthusiasm* ([London]: Flesher, 1656; also in *A Collection of Several Philosophical Writings by Dr. Henry More* [London: Flesher, 1662]) links zeal and ecstasy to sexual excitement. For other contemporary writers hostile to the Puritans see C. M. Webster's three papers containing useful information: "Swift's *Tale of a Tub* Compared with Earlier Satires of the Puritans," *PMLA*, 47 (1932), 171–78; "Swift and Some Earlier Satirists of Puritan Enthusiasm," *PMLA*, 48 (1933), 1141–53; "The Satiric Background of the Attack on the Puritans in Swift's *A Tale of a Tub*," *PMLA*, 50 (1935), 210–23 (contains a useful bibliography).

[36] Heyd, p. 18.

[37] Just as effective understanding of the *Tub* has broadened from narrow English literary criticism to include exploration of the contemporary religious and political situation in England and Ireland, so it is now showing signs of making a profitable move into the history of ideas in European terms. The puzzling but disturbing presence of Paracelsus in Swift's satire is only one area that might usefully attract attention. In his volume of *Renaissance Essays* (Chicago, 1985), pp. 149–99, Hugh Trevor-Roper shows in a brilliant piece on "The Paracelsian Movement" the ferment of religious, mystical, philosophical, scientific, medical, and political ideas in which lie the origins of the modern world that Swift clearly foresaw. I wish to thank Kenneth Craven for the opportunity of reading the manuscript of his forthcoming book on *A Tale of a Tub*, in which he opens up many of these fascinating questions.

[38] See n. 4 above.

[39] Harth, p. 113.

[40] Angus Ross and David Woolley, eds., *A Tale of a Tub and Other Works* (Oxford, 1986), pp. xvi f.

[41] *AM* I.I.III.4; I, 199f.

[42] Quoted by Michael V. DePorte, *Nightmares and Hobbyhorses: Swift, Sterne, and Augustan Ideas of Madness* (San Marino, CA., 1974), p. 38 and n. 87.

[43] DePorte, pp. 60–61.

[44] *Tale*, p. 163.

[45] *AM* I.II.V.2; I, 433.

[46] *Tale*, p. 162.

[47] *AM* I.I.I.4; I, 160.

[48] *AM* III.IV.I.1; III, 358.

[49] *AM* I.II.V.2; I, 434; see *OED*, s.v. *non-naturals*.

[50] *Tale*, pp. 169–70.

[51] *AM* III.IV.I.2; III, 373–97.

[52] *Tale*, pp. 164–65.

53 *AM* III.IV.I.2; III, 390–91.

54 *AM* II, 206.

55 *AM*, Pref.; I, 28f.

56 *Prose*, IV, 36.

57 *AM* III.II.V.1; III, 223f.

58 *AM* III.II.I.2; III, 55–57.

59 *AM* I.II.II.6; I, 244f.

60 *AM* I.III.II.4; I, 480.

61 *AM* I.II.III.14; I, 338.

62 2 vols. (New York, 1927; rpt. 1 vol. 1938, etc.), preface. This edition translates all Latin in Burton's text but omits his notes, so that it is sometimes difficult to say when Burton is quoting, or whom.

63 Burton is quoting Epistles ascribed to Hippocrates, "who had a smack of this disease [jealousy]"; *AM* III.III.I.2; III, 308f.

64 Burton is noting idleness as a cause of jealousy; "think ill" is Dell and Jordan-Smith's translation of a phrase quoted from Giovanni Nevisanni's witty book on marriage; and "'tis likely," Burton comments, "for the idle have no other business..."; *AM* ibid.; III, 305–06.

65 Burton says, "How easy a matter it is to answer these motives, and to make an *Antiparodia* quite opposite unto it? To exercise myself I will essay.... 'Tis a hazard both ways I confess, to live single, or to marry...it may bad, it may be good..." (*AM* III.II.V.5; III, 290–91). The whole passage is a good illustration of Burton's rhetoric of arguing on both sides of a question, which makes biographical criticism from quotation hazardous; cf. David Renaker, "Robert Burton's Palinodes," *Studies in Philology*, 76 (1979), 162–81.

66 Evans, pp. 20ff.

67 *AM* III.II.III.1; III, 178.

68 John F. Sena, "Swift as Moral Physician: Scatology and the Tradition of Love Melancholy," *Journal of English and Germanic Philology*, 76 (1977), 346–62.

69 André de Laurens (1558–1609), a Frenchman, was physician to Henri IV; his *Discourse* appeared in Paris in 1594, an English translation in 1599 (Shakespeare Association facsimile, Oxford, 1938: see esp. pp. 117–24).

70 *AM* III.II.V.3; III, 245ff.

71 *Tale*, Section IX, p. 173.

72 Lomazzo's Italian treatise was published in 1584 and translated into English in 1598.

73 *The Poems of Jonathan Swift*, ed. Harold Williams, 2nd ed., 3 vols. (Oxford, 1958), I, 226.

74 *AM* III.II.V.3; III, 248–49.

75 See Renaker.

76 See, for example, Charles Peake, "Swift's Birthday Verses to Stella," in Hermann J. Real and Heinz J. Vienken, eds., *Proceedings of the First Münster Symposium on Jonathan Swift* (Munich, 1985), pp. 175–97; or W. B. Carnochan, *Lemuel Gulliver's Mirror for Man* (Berkeley, 1968).

[77] Denis Donoghue, *Jonathan Swift: A Critical Introduction* (Cambridge, 1969), pp. 13, 18, and 161–62.

[78] On Burton's grappling with the new writing on astronomy, for example, see Robert M. Browne, "Robert Burton and the New Cosmology," *Modern Language Quarterly*, 13 (1952), 131–48; corrected by Richard G. Barlow, "Infinite Worlds: Robert Burton's Cosmic Voyage," *Journal of the History of Ideas*, 34 (1973), 291–302.

[79] "I will yet, to satisfy and please myself, make a *Utopia* of mine own, a new *Atlantis*, a poetical Commonwealth of mine own, in which I will freely domineer, build cities, make laws, statutes, as I list myself..." (*AM*, I, 109–22): see J. C. Davis, "Robert Burton and the Anatomy of Utopia," ch. 4 of *Utopia and the Ideal Society: A Study of English Writing, 1516–1700* (Cambridge, 1981); and Hugh Trevor-Roper, "Robert Burton and *The Anatomy of Melancholy*," in *Renaissance Essays*, esp. pp. 250–51.

C. P. Daw

"A Tast of Wit": Laud, Swift, and *A Tale of a Tub*

DESPITE THE AUTHOR'S INDIGNANT ASSERTION in the Apology prefixed to the fifth edition of *A Tale of a Tub* (1710) that "through the whole Book he has not borrowed one single Hint from any Writer in the World,"[1] the response of readers both then and now has been to regard that disclaimer as a challenge to discover precisely which writers did furnish Swift with grist for his satirical mill. The notable succession of editions, the perennial books of criticism, and the welter of articles and notes offer abundant testimony that the search for Swift's sources has been constant, though not always fruitful. Numerous intriguing puzzles remain. In what follows I hope to present hitherto unnoticed evidence regarding a possible inspiration for the religious allegory of Swift's first masterpiece.

It might well seem that a ponderous book like William Laud's *Conference with Fisher* (1639)[2] has little in common with a sprightly work like Swift's *Tale*, and it is important not to minimize the differences in tone, scope, and method between these two examples of Anglican apologetics.[3] Most of the Archbishop's work is a heavily documented refutation of the Jesuit John Fisher's account of their debate before the Countess of Buckingham.[4] But scattered among the dull expanses of erudite controversy glisten small nuggets of pithy and cogent writing, such as the following rebuttal to Fisher's insinuation that the dictum "no salvation outside the Church" means no salvation apart from the Roman Catholic Church:

Why but the *Romane Church* and the *Church of England* are but two distinct members of that *Catholike Church* which is spread over the face of the earth. Therefore *Rome* is not the House where the *Church* dwels, but *Rome* it selfe, as well as other Particular Churches, dwels in this great *Universall House*.... *Rome* and other *Nationall Churches* are in this Universall Catholike House as so *many Daughters*, to whom (under Christ) the care of the Houshold is committed by God the *Father*, and the Catholike Church the *Mother* of all Christians. *Rome*, as an *Elder Sister*, but not the *Eldest* neither, had a great Care committed unto her, in, and from the prime times of the Church, and to her *Bishop* in Her: but at this time (to let passe many brawles that have formerly beene in the House) *England* and some other *Sisters* of hers are fallen out in the *Family*. What then? Will the *Father*, and the *Mother*, God, and the Church, cast one Child out, because another is angry with it?

Or when did Christ give that power to an Elder Sister, that She, and her *Steward*, the *Bishop* there, should thrust out what Child shee pleased? Especially when shee her selfe is justly accused to have given the Offence that is taken in the House? Or will not both *Father*, and *Mother* be sharper to Her for this unjust and unnaturall usage of her younger *Sisters*, but their deare Children? Nay, is it not the next way to make them turne her out of doores, that is so unnaturall to the rest? It is well for all Christian men and Churches, that the *Father* and *Mother* of them are not so curst as some would have them. And Salvation need not bee feared of any dutifull Child, nor Outing from the Church, because this *Elder Sisters* faults are discovered in the House, and shee growne froward for it against them that complained (pp. 311–13).

Such a passage in a book Swift is known to have owned and read would be worth noting in any case, even when allowance is made for differences between Laud's vignette and comparable episodes in Swift's narrative of the three brothers.[5] And the possiblility that this book may have played a part in the formation of his allegory seems to be strengthened by an earlier discussion of the relative merits of scripture and tradition as rules of faith:

For we deny any Testament of Christ, but that which is written.... Nothing is more plaine in these two Fathers *Optatus* and *S. Augustine*, then that both of them appeale to the *Wrrtten* [sic] Will, and make that the *Judge* without any Exception, when a matter of Faith comes in Question. In *Optat.* the words are *Habemus in Evangelio*, we have it in the Gospell. And *in Evangelio inquiratur*, Let it be inquired in the Gospell: And Christ put it *in tabulas diu duraturas* into Written and lasting Instruments. In *S. Augustine* the words are: *Our Father did not dye intestate*; &c. And *Tabula aperiantur*, Let his Will, his written Instruments be opened. And *Legantur Verba mortui* let the words of him that dyed, be read. And againe *Aperi, Legamus*, Open the Will, and let us reade. And *Legamus, quid litigamus*? Why do we strive? Let's read the Will. And againe, *Aperi Testamentum, lege*, Open the Will, read. All which Passages are most expresse and full for his *Written* Will, and not for any *Nuncupative* Wil, as *Baldwin* would put upon us (p. 194).[6]

Before proceeding to identify other aspects of Laud's work that show an affinity with *A Tale of a Tub*, it would perhaps be best to pause here to consider some of the objective data which reinforce the likelihood that Swift would have been acquainted with this book. The demonstration of this connection is made immeasurably more convincing by the survival of Swift's own copy of Laud, now in a private collection.[7] Swift's signature appears both on the flyleaf and the title-page of this folio volume. Beneath the flyleaf signature are four graduated lines whose original letters are obscured by circular overwriting. Careful inspection reveals, however, that these lines read: "Ex dono Excellent^{mi} | D D Will Temple | April 16° | 1692"; a flourish beneath the four lines completes the inverted triangular pattern (fig. 1).[8]

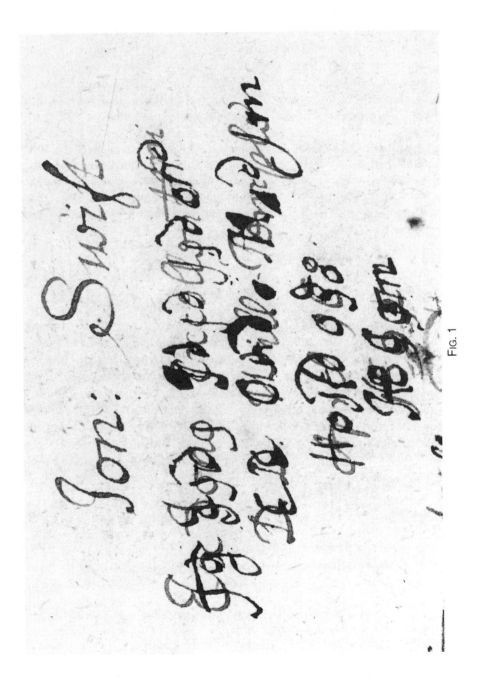

F IG. 1

Like the copy of Thomas White's *Institutionum Ethicarum sive Staterae Morum* (1660) also given to him by Temple on the same day,[9] this may have been a token of encouragement towards the MA Swift would receive from Oxford a few months later.[10] But of these two volumes of religious controversy, only the Laud remained in Swift's library until his death.[11] Nor did this leatherbound folio simply gather dust on the Dean's shelves, as indicated by his autograph evaluation on the flyleaf:[12]

This Book is not ill writt, but in some parts too Theologically nice for me. It excuseth him entirely from being Popishly inclined, and equally excuseth his Master. Yet they both lost their Heads as Favorites of Popery; I mean on that Pretence; for the Murderers knew that they both were innocent on that Article. The Author seemes also to have a Tast of Wit, and was surely well skilld in the Controversy he handles.

> May.15.th 1735.
> Jonath Swift

Knowing that Swift was reading this volume with such care so long after receiving it adds yet another consideration to the delicate task of discerning which marginalia and underscoring were his and which were those of others. After some study, it becomes evident that the marginalia can be classified into four principal groups: a dark brown ink, a light brown ink, a gray pencil, and a reddish-brown pencil. The dark brown ink includes some remarks demonstrably in Swift's hand as well as a number of minor corrections of typographical errors and occasional refinements of style. From what is known of Swift's reading habits as recorded in other books he owned, the marginal crossmarks and pointing hands made with the gray pencil may also be his.[13] The light brown ink associated with a flowing cursive hand seems to belong to a previous owner of the book.[14] The reddish-brown pencil has been used for occasional underscoring of the text and for small marginal marks which do not offer much suggestion about the identity of the person who made them.

There are only three marginal remarks which it seems reasonable to assign to Swift himself. The first appears in the prefatory letter to Charles I, where Laud declares:

'Tis true, the *Inward Worship* of the Heart, is the *Great Service of God*, and no Service acceptable without it: But the *Externall worship of God* in his Church is the *Great Witnesse* to the World, that Our heart stands right in that *Service of God*.... These *Thoughts* are they, and no other, which have made me labour so much, as I have done, for *Decency* and an Orderly settlement of the *Externall Worship of God in the Church* (pp. [xix-xx]).

In the margin beside the latter sentence Swift has written: "For which he sufferd much Obloquy."[15] No further remarks occur in Swift's hand until the latter half of the book in a section on church councils. Laud affirms that it is reasonable to trust in the assistance of the Holy Ghost and "that a Councell hath it" (p. 230). In the left-hand margin there is a crossmark and a terse comment, "this may be disputed." The only other annotation clearly attributable to Swift occurs in the Index, where the following entry is added at the appropriate alphabetical point: "Private Spirit, p. 137." The pertinent passage on that page reads as follows:

'Tis one thing for a private man, *Judicium suum praeferre*, to preferre, and so follow his private Judgement, before the *Whole Congregation*, which is indeed, *Lepra proprii Consilii* (as S. *Bernard* there cals it) the proud Leprosie of the Private Spirit. And quite another thing for an Intelligent man...modestly to propose his doubts even to the *Catholike Church*.

Also in the dark brown ink associated with Swift's remarks are a number of marginal crossmarks and pointing hands which it seems reasonable to assign to him. The first such hand appears in the margin beside the final sentence of Laud's metaphorical passage concerning people who are misled in their religious opinions:

They are *Bells* of passing good mettle and tuneable enough of themselves, and in their owne disposition; and a world of pity it is, that they are *Rung* so miserably out of *Tune*, as they are, by them which have gotten power in and over their Consciences. And for this there is yet *Remedy* enough; but how long there will bee, I know not (pp. [xvi–xvii]).

The only other pointing hand in this same ink appears in the margin opposite a remark particularly pertinent to the allegory of the *Tale*:

That the *Jesuite* in the Church of *Rome*, and the *Precise party* in the *Reformed Churches* agree in many things, though they would seeme most to differ (p. 100).[16]

This passage comes shortly after the only sentence in the book that seems to be underscored in the dark brown ink: "Every *Heretick* will shelter himselfe and his *Vanities* under this Colour of *Infallible Verities*" (p. 97). The remainder of the markings in dark brown ink are incidental corrections of style or spelling, as follows:[17]

p. 16 [Following passages from Eusebius in Latin and Greek concerning "Heretici alii":] Now th<is *Blastus*> **these both** taught that God was the Author of sin.[18]
p. 46 M *Rogers his exposition* <*of*> **or** *Notes upon the Articles*...
p. 90 I cannot finde, that the *Tradition* of the *present* Church...may reach to Infallibility, <much lesse> **much less** to a *Divine Infallibility*.
p. 119 we settle for our *Direction*, <but> **yet** not upon the first opening of the *morn-*

ing Light, but upon the *Sun* it selfe. Nor will I make needlesse enquiry, how farre, and in what manner a *Praecognitum*, or Supposed *Principle* in any *Science*, may be proved in a *Higher*, to which that is subordinate; or accepted <in> **for** a *Prime*.
p. 128   Con<d>ditions[19]
p. 161   But if he meane, that the whole Church cannot Erre in any one Point of *Divine Truth in generall*, which though by sundry Consequences deduced from the *Principles*, is yet **made** a *Point of Faith*....
p. 164   this...is spoken either of *S. Peters* person only, or *of him*, and his *Successors*, <or> *both*.
p. 165   And Christ who promised the Spirit should *lead*, hath no where promised that it shall *follow* its [the Church's] Leader *into all Truth*, and at least **not** *Infallibly*....
p. 371   For though the *Foundation* be one and the same, & sufficiently knowne by *Scripture* and the *Creeds*; Yet for the building upon the *Foundation*, the *adding* to it; the *Detracting* from it; the *Joyning* other things with it; The *grating* upon it: <And e>Each of these may bee *damnable* to some, and not to others....

The only other group of marginalia that may be tentatively regarded as Swift's are the pencil marks appearing primarily in the prefatory letter to Charles I. Most of the penciled marginalia are simple crossmarks, but there is a very interesting cluster of pointing hands around a passage with (superficial) overtones of *The Battle of the Books* rather than the *Tale* itself:

The *Church of Christ* upon Earth may bee compared to a *Hive of Bees*, and that can bee no where so steddily placed in this world, but it will be in some danger. And men that care neither for the *Hive*, nor the *Bees*, have yet a great minde to the *Honey*.... For we see it in daily and common use, that the *Honey* is not taken from the *Bees*, but they are destroyed first. Now in this great and Busie Worke, the *King* and the *Priest* must not feare to put their hands to the *Hive*, though they are sure to be *stung*.... It was *King Davids* Case (God grant it be never *Yours*.) *They came about mee* (saith the *Psal. 118*) *like Bees*.... But when it comes to the *Priest*, the Case is alter'd, They come about him like *Waspes*, or like Hornets rather; all *sting* and no *Honey* there (pp. [xiii–xiv]).[20]

The first group of penciled crossmarks occurs in connection with a passage discussing the condition of the Church of England with regard to what Laud calls the "Romanists" and the "Separatists":

The plaine truth is, She is between these two Factions, as betweene two *Milstones*.... And 'tis very Remarkeable, that while both these presse hard upon the *Church of England*, both of them Crye out upon *Persecution*, like froward Children, which *scratch*, and *kicke*, and *bite*, and yet crye out all the while, as if themselves were killed.... And there is no *Greater Absurdity* stirring this day in *Christendome*, then that the *Reformation of an Old Corrupted Church*, will we, nill wee, must be taken for the *Building of a New*.... One *in Substance*, but not one in

Condition of state and purity; Their part of the same Church remaining *in Corruption*: and Our part of the same Church under *Reformation* (pp. [xv–xvi]).[21]

Another crossmark lies alongside a strong simile for the empty jargon of religious controversy: "Both *Lips* and *Penns* open for all the World like a *Purse without money*: Nothing comes out of this, and that which is worth nothing out of them" (p. [xvii]). Another group of crossmarks appears in conjunction with a section that sounds as if it could be a summary of part of the *Tale*'s narrative:

Whereas according to *Christs Institution*, The *Scripture*, where 'tis plaine, should guide the *Church*: And the *Church*, where there's Doubt or Difficulty, should expound the *Scripture*; Yet so, as neither the *Scripture* should be forced, nor the Church so bound up, as that upon Just and farther Evidence, Shee may not revise that which in any Case hath slipt by Her.... And though I cannot *Prophesie*, yet I fear That *Atheisme*, and *Irreligion* gather strength, while the *Truth* is thus weakened by *an Unworthy way* of Contending for it. And while they thus Contend, neither part Consider, that they are in a way, to induce upon themselves, and others, that *Contrary Extreame*, which they seeme most both to *feare*, and *oppose. Besides*: This I have ever Observed, That many *Rigid Professors* have turn'd *Roman Catholikes*, and in that Turne have beene *more Jesuited* then any other: And such *Romanists* as have chang'd from them, have for the most part quite leaped over the *Meane*, and beene as *Rigid* the other way, as *Extremity* it selfe.... For a Man is apt to think he can never runne farre enough from that, which he once begins to hate; And doth not Consider therewhile, That where *Religion Corrupted* is the thing he hates, a *Fallacy* may easily be put upon him. For he ought to hate the *Corruption* which depraves *Religion*, and to runne from it: but from *no part of Religion* it selfe (pp. [xvii–xix]).[22]

Given the frequency of pencil markings in the prefatory letter, it is noteworthy that such markings occur at only three places in the work proper. The first of these is of some interest because it deals with Peter: "The *Fathers* I deny not, ascribe very much to S. *Peter*: But 'tis to S. *Peter* in his owne person" (p. 185). A second marginal crossmark in pencil offers some corroboration for the inference that Swift may have been the reader who left these marks, seeing that the mark appears opposite the line mentioning Ireland: "S. *Gregory the great*...in the beginning of the *seventh hundred* yeare sent such Letters to...other *Bishops in Ireland*" (p. 200). A third and final mark of this sort comes shortly thereafter in conjunction with a passage regarding the relative power of the Pope and the Emperor:

[Augustine's interpretation of the Church as Moon and Christ as Sun is applied so that] The *Pope* must be the *Sun*, and the *Emperor* but the *Moone*. And least Innocents owne power should not be able to make good his *Decretall: Gasper Schioppius* doth not only avow the *Allusion* or *Interpretation*, but is pleased to expresse many Circumstances, in which hee would faine make the world believe the *Resemblance* holds (p. 204).[23]

In addition to the passages that have already been cited for their themes and images related to the allegory of the *Tale* or for their connection with Swift's marginalia, there are a variety of phrases, sentences, and even longer sections of Laud's work worth noting for their possible influence in the development of Swift's narrative. His prefatory explanation that this work is being sent forth like a tub to protect the ship of state from "*Hobs*'s *Leviathan*, which tosses and plays with all other Schemes of Religion and Government," gives only a political meaning for the threatened vessel.[24] But the ship was also a well-known image for the Church; and, as Laud laments, "that poore *Ship* hath her ribs dashed by the waves of Contention" (p. 228). It may even be pertinent that the large factotum initial T at the beginning of Laud's dedicatory letter to Charles I depicts a vivid nautical scene including a ship (with what looks very like the flag of St. George flying atop its mast) preceded by a Triton. Such hints would not have been required by an inventive and informed writer like Swift, but their presence in Laud's book is worth noting for their possible catalytic effect in the formation of Swift's satire.[25]

The most significant parallels between Laud's *Conference with Fisher* and Swift's allegory occur in a matrix of other passages that may well have contributed to his story of the three brothers. The events of the first installment of the allegory (Section II), for example, might well be glossed by various remarks in Laud:

…for he [Christ] hath left an *Infallible Rule* the *Scripture*. And *that* by the manifest Places in it (which need no Dispute, no Externall Judg) is able to settle *Unity* and *Certainty* of *Beliefe* in *Necessaries* to *Salvation*; And in *Non necessariis*, in and about things *not necessarie*, there ought not to bee a Contention to a *Separation* (pp. 196–97).[26]

For the power of adding any thing contrary, and of detracting any thing necessary, are alike forbidden (p. 32).[27]

That there are many *unwritten words of God*, which were never delivered over to the Church, is manifest…. If neither Hee [Christ], nor *His Apostles*, or *Evangelists* have delivered them to the Church, the Church ought not to deliver them to her Children. Or if she doe *tradere non traditum*, make a *Tradition* of that, which was not delivered to her, and by some of Them, then She is unfaithful to God, and doth not *servare depositum*, faithfully keepe that which is committed to her *Trust*. I *Tim*. 6. And her Sonnes, which come to know it, are not bound to obey her *Tradition* against the *Word* of their *Father*…. So, there were many *unwritten Words of God*, which were never delivered over to the *Church*; and therefore never made *Tradi-*

tion. And there are many *Traditions*, which cannot be said to be the *unwritten word of God* (p. 68).[28]

Too many Over-burden the *Service of God*; And *too* few leave it naked (p. [xx]).[29]

[Can the Church err?] In *Absolute Foundations* she cannot; in *Deductions* and *Superstructures* she may (p. 165).[30]

As might be expected, there are numerous parallels between Laud's extended and detailed discussions of the errors of the Roman Catholic Church and Swift's narrative treatment of Peter's excesses in Section IV of the *Tale.* The two Anglican clerics share the assumption that the Reformation was both necessary and commendable because the Church during the centuries of Roman domination had fallen away from the integrity of the Primitive Church. Swift's lively caricature of Peter's behavior provides ample parabolic demonstration of Laud's assertion that the Roman Church "is exceeding corrupt, both in *Manners* and *Doctrine*" (p. 128). Consequently Laud's polemic (like Swift's satire) adamantly denies that the Reformers were guilty of either schism or separation from the True Church:

There may be therefore a necessary separation, which yet incurres not the blame of Schisme; And that is, when Doctrines are taught contrary to the Catholike Faith.... The *Protestants* did not get that Name by *Protesting against the Church of Rome*, but by *Protesting* (and that when nothing else would serve) against her *Errours, & Superstitions.* ...they have made no *separation* from the *Generall Church* properly so called...but their Separation is only from the *Church of Rome*, and such other *Churches*, as by adhering to her, have hazarded themselves, and do now miscall themselves, the *Whole Catholike Church.* Nay even here the *Protestants* have not left the *Church of Rome* in her *Essence*, but in her *Errours*; not in the Things which *Constitute* a Church, but only in such *Abuses* and *Corruptions*, as work toward the *Dissolution* of a Church (pp. 133–35, 192).[31]

And not only is the Roman Church in error, but it also is unwilling to admit error, even to the point of condemning those who refuse to accept the approved teaching:

But the Church of Rome hath solemnly decreed her *Errours*: And erring, hath yet decreed withall, *That she cannot erre.* And imposed upon Learned men, disputed and improbable Opinions, *Transubstantiation, Purgatorie*, and *Forbearance of the Cup* in the blessed Eucharist, even against the expresse Command of our Saviour, and that for *Articles of Faith*: And to keepe off *Disobedience*, whatever the Corruption be, she hath bound up her *Decrees* upon paine of *Excommunication*, and all that followes upon it (pp. 297–98).[32]

Laud continues with a familiar catalogue of abuses (including the veneration of images, the invocation of saints, and papal infallibility), all of which are incorporated into Swift's satire at some point.[33] It should also be noted that another recurring object of Laud's criticism, the calling of Councils that are not truly General Councils of the Church, is implied in Peter's failures to consult with his brothers and in his fondness for his own ideas.[34]

In the context of religious controversy, it was important to discredit the authority claimed by one's opponents. Laud does it primarily by appeals to Church Fathers and to the commonly accepted Councils of the early Church, with special attention to the ways in which the later and disputed Councils have not lived up to precedent. Swift similarly undermines Peter's authority by depicting him as doubly culpable: first, by failing to keep his father's injunctions, and second, by failing to maintain harmony with his brothers.[35] Such a failure in charity on Peter's part carries with it an inherent exoneration of the other two brothers, who are more sinned against than sinning. In both Laud's strategy and Swift's, the mantle of authority is denied to those who most vocally claim it by showing them as unfit to wear it, even by the criteria they present in their own favor.[36] At the same time, the alleged offenders (the Reformers, Martin and Jack) are portrayed as being forced to act against their will. As Laud so succinctly puts it: "The *Protestants* did not *depart*: For departure is *voluntary*, so was not *theirs*" (p. 135).[37]

In good Anglican fashion Swift depicts his hero of the *via media* as resisting the dangers of fanaticism as resolutely as he did those of popery. In moving on to explore this intra-Reformation struggle, Swift is dealing with a controversy which necessarily receives little attention in Laud's anti-Roman polemic. In view of Swift's clothes allegory, however, it is worth noting that Laud frequently refers to the Reformation as resulting in a "*miserable Rent* in the Church of Christ."[38] And Laud does clearly identify the dangers of an intemperate approach to matters of faith when he considers what it means to hold the faith inviolate:

I take the *true and first meaning* of *Inviolate*...not to be the holding of the *true sense*, but not to offer *violence*, or a *forced sense* or *meaning* upon the *Creed*.... For not to believe the *true sense* of the *Creed*, is one thing. But 'tis quite another, to force a *wrong sense* upon it.... Nor do we believe any one *Article of Faith* by our own *fancy*, or by *fallible Authority* of humane deductions; but next to the *Infallible Authority* of *God's Word*, we are guided by his *Church* (pp. 342–45).[39]

Such willingness to be guided by the deliberate and careful determinations of the Church is what differentiates Martin from Jack, for it is reliance on the community of faith rather than one's own views that makes a person (in a phrase Laud quotes from his opponent) "more Christian and less brainsicke" (p. 386).[40]

Although the *Conference with Fisher* deals primarily with only one threat to the Anglican *via media*, Laud was no less aware of the dangers of Puritanism than he was of those of Roman Catholicism. In the prefatory letter to Charles I, he notes the similarities between those at each extreme of the religious spectrum in a manner that anticipates the later chapters of Swift's allegory of the three brothers.[41] It is also worth remarking that Laud recognizes the dangers of "a Whirlewind of a Private Spirit, to ruffle the Church"—a repeated phrase that could possibly have played some part in Swift's eventual burlesque of Enthusiasm in the sketch of the Aeolists.[42]

A survey of the possible influence of Laud's *Conference with Fisher* on the formation of *A Tale of a Tub* also needs to take into account a highly popular and influential work of religious controversy that derived from Laud's book: Edward Stillingfleet's *A Rational Account of the Grounds of Protestant Religion*.[43] The connection here becomes more obvious with the subtitle of Stillingfleet's book: *Being a Vindication of the Lord Archbishop of Canterbury's Relation of a Conference, &c. From the Pretended Answer by T. C.* Swift left behind a copy of this book at Kilroot in 1696 and encouraged his successor, the Rev. John Winder, to keep it, as it "might have been usefull to You."[44] Although it was apparently a widely-read book, Stillingfleet's *Grounds* is not an especially well-written or engaging work. It is a largely derivative piece of religious polemic, but scattered among its rather tedious invective are a few passages which might have caught Swift's imagination. For example, the section on the pope's titles:

And whatever you stile the *Pope*, Whether *the Deputy*, or *Vicar General of Christ*, or *Servus servorum*, or what you will; it is all one to us as long as we know his meaning, whatever fair words you give him. As though men would take it one jot the better to have one usurp and *Tyrannize* over them, because he doth not call himself *King* or *Prince*, but *their humble servant*. Is it not by so much the greater *Tyranny*? to have such kind of *Ecclesiastical Saturnalia*, when the *servus servorum* must, under that name, *tyrannize* over the whole world (p. 471)?[45]

Similarly the section on biblical manuscripts is more vividly written than many other parts:

[We do not] pretend the *Apostles Autographa* are still extant for us to compare our *Copies* with (although some of your side tell us among other rarities of the *Vatican*, that the true ancient *Greek* text is there extant, which the *Pope* would do well to oblige the world with) but we whose eyes are not *blest* with such noble *sights* as are there *lockt* up from all such who have not a good *dose* of implicite Faith about them, pretend to no such thing…(p. 215).[46]

And it is intriguing to consider whether a passage like the following could have influenced Swift in the development of his parable of the coats:

Supposing all men were agreed, that some particular *habit* should be worn all over the world, will you say, That any number of men who found this habit extremely inconvenient for them, and therefore should disuse it, did on that account separate from humane nature, and ceased to be men by it? Such is the case of any particular *Churches* laying aside some customes or ceremonies, which in some one age of the *Church*, or more, the greatest part of *Christian Churches* were agreed in the practice of…(p. 358).[47]

To paraphrase Ecclesiastes, of the uncovering of possible sources there is no end. And even if the borrowing seems obvious, it would not be wise to assume that Swift's borrowing was intentional or conscious. This was, after all, a man who said, "If another man's reason fully convinceth me, it becomes my own reason."[48] Even his conscious borrowing was often forgotten, and his intention to quote from other writers was often thwarted by an imperfect memory.[49] Yet beyond this journeyman sort of recollection, Swift had an uncanny gift for drawing on a remarkable reservoir of materials that would seem unlikely sources of inspiration to a twentieth-century mind.

It is doubtful that we shall ever fully appreciate the creative and imaginative transformations that Swift wrought on the works he read, nor is it likely that we shall ever identify all his sources. But the more we read and appreciate books that we know he owned or read, the more we gain insight into the particular qualities of his genius and come to appreciate his own unequaled "Tast of Wit."

[1] Jonathan Swift, *A Tale of a Tub*, ed. A. C. Guthkelch and D. Nichol Smith, 2nd ed. (Oxford, 1958), p. 13; hereafter cited as *Tale*.

[2] The full title reads as follows: *A Relation of the Conference betweene William Lawd, Then, Lrd. Bishop of St. Davids; Now, Lord Arch-Bishop of Canterbury: And Mr. Fisher the Jesuite, by the Command of King James of Ever Blessed Memorie. With an Answer to Such Exceptions as A. C. Takes against It. By the Sayd Most Reverend Father in God, William, Lord Arch-Bishop of Canterbury* (London: Badger, 1639).

[3] For a cogent discussion of Swift's place in the tradition of Anglican apologetics, see Phillip Harth, *Swift and Anglican Rationalism* (Chicago, 1961).

[4] Fisher, whose real surname was Percy, published an account of the debate under the initials "A. C." (for "A Catholic"?).

[5] Cf. especially *Tale*, pp. 73–74, 105–22. Given that Laud's work so greatly antedates John Sharp's sermon (delivered 1686; printed 1735) which has been proposed as source for Swift's allegory, it seems more reasonable to regard Laud as their common progenitor. See *Tale*, pp. xxxi–xxxvi.

⁶ Cf. *Tale*, pp. 83 ff. The passage from Optatus is from the fifth book of his *De Chismate Donatistarum* and has been reprinted in full in *Tale*, pp. xl–xli, having been proposed as long ago as 1863 as a possible source of inspiration for Swift's more complex version. The quotations from Augustine are from his commentary on Psalm 21 in *Enarrationes in Psalmos* (*Patrologia Latina*, XXXVI, 179). Although Swift approved of "Quotations of antient Fathers...to confirm some Opinion controverted by those who differ from us," he owned few works of this sort. See [*The Prose Writings of Jonathan Swift*], ed. Herbert Davis et al., 14 vols. (1939–68; various reimpressions, sometimes corrected, Oxford, 1957–69), IX, 75 (hereafter cited as *Prose*); T. P. LeFanu, "Catalogue of Dean Swift's Library in 1715, with an Inventory of His Personal Property in 1742," *Proceedings of the Royal Irish Academy*, 37, sec. C (1927), 263–75; and Harold Williams, *Dean Swift's Library* (Cambridge, 1932). Swift did make abstracts of Cyprian, Irenaeus, and Epiphanius (*Tale*, pp. lv–lvi), but he showed little interest in works of the Fathers not directly concerned with controversy. Given his reading habits, Swift is much more likely to have encountered these passages from Optatus and Augustine in Laud than in their own works.

⁷ Annotations in Swift's copy of Laud are quoted and reproduced by kind permission of Lord Caledon. A microfilm copy of this volume is available for inspection in the Trinity College Library, Dublin.

⁸ For examples of comparable inscriptions (often similarly obscured) see A. C. Elias, Jr., *Swift at Moor Park: Problems in Biography and Criticism* (Philadelphia, 1982), pp. 108–10. I am grateful for the advice of William LeFanu (via David Woolley) that "D.D." here does not mean *Doctor Divinitatis* but probably *Domini Domini*, so that the sense of the inscription is "The gift of the Distinguished Gentleman (Domini), Sir (Domini) William Temple."

⁹ See Elias, p. 109; more information about the White volume can be found in Figgis Rare Books catalogue 31, item 491.

¹⁰ On 3 May 1692 Swift wrote to his cousin Thomas (who was also preparing to take an MA from Oxford): "I have gott up my Lattin, pretty well, and am getting up my Greek, but to enter upon causes of Philosophy is what I protest I will rather dy in a ditch than go about." See Irvin Ehrenpreis, *Swift: The Man, His Works, and the Age*, 3 vols. (London, 1962–83), I, 108; and *The Correspondence of Jonathan Swift*, ed. Harold Williams, rev. David Woolley, 5 vols. (Oxford, 1963–72), I, 11 (hereafter cited as *Corresp.*).

¹¹ See LeFanu, "Catalogue," p. 270, and Williams (catalogue No. 377). The White volume may have been among those left behind in Kilroot which Swift told his successor, the Rev. John Winder, "were not worth the Carriage" of being sent to him at Moor Park (*Corresp.*, I, 29).

¹² Swift wrote the first six words of this evaluation immediately below and somewhat to the left of the bottom line of the obliterated inscription of donation, then drew a single line through them. He began again by drawing a line lower on the page, following a two-line memorandum made by a former reader, then resumed writing his comment. He had apparently realized that the inch or so of clear space

above the old memorandum would not permit him room enough for what he wished to write.

[13] See the discussion of Swift's marginalia in *Prose*, V, xxx–xl and XIV, xiii; and in David Woolley, "Swift's Copy of *Gulliver's Travels*: The Armagh *Gulliver*, Hyde's Edition, and Swift's Earliest Corrections," in *The Art of Jonathan Swift*, ed. Clive T. Probyn (London, 1978), pp. 131–78.

[14] This interpretation is consistent with the memoranda on the flyleaf (cf. note 12) and with the position of Swift's signature on the title-page. His, "Jon: Swift." is written a bit below and to the right of the larger signature of "W. Longeville." Both the position of the title-page signature and its redundancy with the larger and more formal flyleaf inscription suggest that Swift was not the first owner of the book (which was already more than half a century old when it was given to him).

[15] Swift seems originally to have written the last word as "Oblloquy," then to have altered it to "Obloquy." In addition to this comment in Swift's handwriting, there is a crossmark in pencil beside the same passage (perhaps made by Swift at a different reading).

[16] Cf. *Tale*, pp. 198–200; Laud makes the same observation in another passage (quoted below) beside which are penciled crossmarks that may have been made by Swift.

[17] In the transcriptions which follow, deleted material appears between angle brackets <like this>, and manuscript additions appear in **boldface**. I have tried to quote enough of the context to indicate the nature of Swift's change, i.e., whether he was attempting to improve style or correct spelling. In at least one instance (p. 90), Swift apparently realized after marking through the printed phrase that it was the correct construction after all.

[18] Because this emendation occurs in one of the printed marginal glosses, it is very difficult to decipher. "These both" apparently refers to Florinus and Blastus, who are discussed in the adjacent section of text proper. In Swift's copy of Laud, page 16 is misnumbered as 4.

[19] Swift was here simply using his pen to augment a poorly inked piece of type.

[20] Cf. *Tale*, pp. 228–33.

[21] The four crossmarks appear in the margin next to each of the four sentences quoted. The fourth crossmark could also be construed as referring to the sentence following the last one quoted here: "The same *Namaan*, and he a *Syrian* still, but *Leprous* with them, and *Cleansed* with us; The same man still." The passage "but…us" is underscored in the light brown ink associated with the former owner; cf. note 14.

[22] The opening remark in this quotation is a central issue in Swift's allegory (see *Tale*, pp. 73–74, 81). Both Peter and Jack are guilty, in their respective ways, of forcing Scripture (*Tale*, pp. 83–91, 190–91), in contrast to the judicious Martin (*Tale*, pp. 136–37). For passages related to the latter part of this quotation see *Tale*, pp. 198–200.

[23] Cf. Swift's allusion to this issue in *Tale*, pp. 90–91.

[24] *Tale*, p. 40.

25 In this connection, it is pertinent to note that Swift was of the (erroneous) opinion that *swift* had once been a word for "dolphin" (see *Prose*, V, 188); such a usage is not supported by either Johnson's *Dictionary* or the *OED*. If Swift communicated this misconception to the designer of the artwork added to the fifth edition of the *Tale*, there may have been a cryptic allusion to his otherwise concealed authorship in the clearly dolphin-like "whale" of the frontispiece. It is more likely, however, that this was merely a conventional sea monster.

26 Cf. *Tale*, pp. 73–74, 81, 121, 139.

27 Cf. *Tale*, p. 81; Laud cites Deuteronomy 4:2; the (unauthorized) 1734 ed. of *Tale* was the first to introduce a reference to Revelation 22:18–19.

28 Cf. *Tale*, pp. 85–86. Laud devotes considerable energy to rejecting Bellarmine's treatise *De verbo Dei non scripto* (pp. 67 ff.).

29 Cf. *Tale*, pp. 85–90, 135.

30 Although Swift does not mark this passage, he had made emendations on this page and the preceding one.

31 In the Apology Swift carefully indicates that his satire is directed at "Corruptions in Religion" and "Abuses in Religion" rather than at religion itself (*Tale*, pp. 4–5).

32 Cf. *Tale*, p. 121.

33 Cf. *Tale*, pp. 83–91, 106–22.

34 Cf. *Tale*, p. 105. Laud devotes special energy to rejecting the determinations of the Fourth Lateran Council (1215) regarding transubstantiation, those of the Council of Constance (1414–18) permitting the administration of Communion in one kind, and those of the Council of Trent (1545–63) concerning the invocation of saints and the adoration of images (pp. 275–80).

35 Laud several times excoriates the failure of the popes to keep Christian love and harmony as their principal concern. Though he seldom lapses into sarcasm about his opponents in this debate, he is most likely to do so on this issue. For example, concerning the Council of Trent: "And the *Pope* himself, to shew his charity, had declared, and pronounced the *Appellants*, *Hereticks*, before they were condemned by the *Councell*" (p. 214); and concerning the Roman claim that there is no salvation in Protestant churches: "This denyall of Salvation is grounded upon Charity, as were the like threats of Christ, and the Holy Fathers.... Therefore...'tis more Charity to forewarne us of the danger, by these threats, then to let us runne into it, through a false security. For he thunders out all these threats and denyall of salvation, because we joyne not with the *Roman Church*, in all things; as if her Corruptions were part of the Catholike Faith of Christ" (pp. 283–85).

36 Most of Laud's debate with Fisher centers on this technique of discrediting the applicability of the precedents in the Fathers and the early Councils claimed by his opponent. In many ways, the effect of this show of superior wisdom and patience is to reduce the adversary to relative insignificance.

37 Cf. *Tale*, p. 122. The Protestants' defense on this issue is consistently to depict themselves as forced out of the Roman Church. As Laud puts it: "The Cause of the *Schisme* is yours; for you thrust us from you; because we called for *Truth*, and

Redresse of Abuses. For a *Schisme* must needs be *theirs*, whose the *Cause* of it is" (p. 133).

[38] This particular phrase comes from p. 125, but it is a locution that Laud uses from the prefatory letter to the end of the book.

[39] Cf. *Tale*, pp. 138–41.

[40] Cf. *Tale*, p. 141. Juxtaposition of the spiritual and mental dangers of rampant individualism is also at work in Swift's arrangement of Sections VIII (on the Aeolists) and IX ("A Digression concerning…Madness") of the *Tale*.

[41] See the passages quoted earlier.

[42] Laud, p. 245; cf. *Tale*, pp. 150–61.

[43] (London: White, 1665). It is pertinent here to note that the old memorandum on the flyleaf which made it necessary for Swift to begin again on his evaluation of Laud's book is a citation of Stillingfleet's continuation of the debate; interestingly enough, the memorandum cites Stillingfleet's book by its subtitle rather than by its title.

[44] *Corresp.*, I, 29. Because Swift refers only to "Stillingfleet's Grounds," some readers might be tempted to identify the work in question with the volume which remained in his library till his death, Stillingfleet's *Origines Sacrae, a Rational Account of the Grounds of Christian Faith, as to the Truth and Divine Authority of the Scriptures*, 4th ed. (London: by R. W. for Henry Mortlock, 1675). I think it unlikely that this was the book involved here, however. On the title-page of the work I discuss, "THE GROUNDS" appears in large Roman capitals as the fourth line of the title, making it natural for Swift to refer to it as he does in the letter to Winder. Furthermore, Swift's own holograph list of his books refers to the other work as "Stillinglt Orig. Sacrae," which seems to be the title universally used for it.

[45] Cf. *Tale*, pp. 105, 113–15.

[46] Cf. *Tale*, pp. 89–90, 121.

[47] Cf. *Tale*, pp. 76–81 and throughout.

[48] *Prose*, IX, 261.

[49] See, e.g., Swift's errors at *Tale*, pp. 51 and 142.

Michael Treadwell

Swift and *A Short History of the Kings of England*

SWIFT LIVED, READ, AND WROTE in the brazen age of the pamphlet, and he took ironic measures to ward off "the Danger hourly increasing, by new Levies of Wits all appointed (as there is Reason to fear) with Pen, Ink, and Paper which may at an hours Warning be drawn out into Pamphlets."[1] Students of Swift's reading and, in particular, of Swift's library, will, however, find that in the surviving lists of Swift's books, pamphlets are either omitted completely or lumped anonymously together as "Collection of Pamphlets London, 1681 &c" or "Pamphlets London 1701."[2] We would give a good deal to know which were those pamphlets from 1681 or 1701 or other years which Swift thought worth preserving in his library, but our curiosity seems unlikely to be satisfied, particularly since Swift signed or annotated only a small fraction of the works he owned or read. This being so, the discovery of a pamphlet bearing both Swift's signature and his annotations is of considerable interest, an interest which is enhanced by the fact that Swift also precisely dates his signing of the work.[3] But if the date is precise and the handwriting unambiguously Swift's, the pamphlet is still beset with problems concerning its authorship, publication, and provenance, some of which I have been unable to resolve. What I have been able to determine is set out below; those problems which still remain are also outlined here in the hope that from the information provided, other scholars may be able to piece out the solutions which have so far eluded me.

The pamphlet of which I have been speaking is *A Short History of the Kings of England. Shewing What Right Every King Had to the Crown, and the Manner of Their Wearing of It, Especially from William the Conqueror, to James the Second, That Abdicated His Three Kingdoms*, a small quarto described on its title-page as "Written by the Attorney General of England" and bearing the unusual imprint "London: Printed for R. Baldwin, and Sold by M. Gunne at the Bible and Crown at Essex-Gate, 1715. Price 13d."[4] It collates A^1 B–I⁴ [\$2 signed $(- A^1)$]; 33 leaves, pp. *i–ii, 1* 2–63 *64*, and consists of a title-page with its verso blank (apart from an inscription to which we will return), sixty-three pages of text, and a final blank. In spite of the single title on its title-page, the pamphlet consists in fact of two quite distinct sections, each bearing its own sub-title, neither of which corresponds exactly to that on the title-page. The first section, which is headed "The True Portraiture of the Kings of England, drawn from their Titles, Successions, Reigns and Ends, &c.," covers the first forty-eight pages; the second, headed "A Political Catechism: Serving to instruct those that have made the Protestation concerning the Power and Priviledges of Parliament; taken out of his Majesties Answer to the Nineteen Propositions," covers pages 49 to 63.

These internal headings are important, for it is they rather than the cover title which enable us to identify the whole as being not a single work by "the Attorney General of England," but in fact two quite separate works originally published over sixty years previously by the parliamentarian pamphleteer and political theorist Henry Parker (1604–52). *A Political Catechism* (Wing P416),[5] which is described in the best modern study of Parker's life and thought as "a careful analysis of the relations of the king and Parliament" embodying Parker's "theory of parliamentary sovereignty," was first published in 1643.[6] *The True Portraiture of the Kings of England* (Wing P429) appeared seven years later in 1650 after the execution of the King and is described on its title-page as "a short and exact historical description of every king, with the right they have had to the crown, and the manner of their wearing of it...wherein is demonstrated, that there hath been no direct succession in the line to create an hereditary right, for six or seven hundred years." Both works seem to have enjoyed some popularity in their own time, but Parker's early death and the subsequent restoration of the monarchy worked against their republication. In extreme Whig and republican circles, however, they were obviously not forgotten, for in the radically altered circumstances of the Revolution of 1688, both were immediately reprinted, *A Political Catechism* as one in the great Whig folio volume of *State Tracts* (1689; Wing S5329) and *The True Portraiture* (1688; Wing P430) as a separate publication (updated to include lengthy summaries of the reigns of Charles II and James II and the "happy Deliverance from Popery and Slavery" wrought by "his Highness the Prince of *Orange*") in which *A Political Catechism* was again reprinted as a sort of appendix.

Four years later, in 1692, the unsold sheets of this latter edition of the two works together were reissued with a new title-page and new title, *A Short History of the Kings of England*, but without the two-page preface "To the Reader" signed "H.P.,"[7] with the result that Wing failed to identify the reissue as Parker's work and gave it a separate entry under its title as S3601. The 1688 edition of *The True Portraiture* bore the anonymous imprint

"London, Printed in the year 1688," but the 1692 retitled reissue announced itself as "London, Printed for R. Baldwin."[8] Since the Dublin edition of Parker's two works annotated by Swift carries both the new title *A Short History* and the imprint "London: Printed for R. Baldwin, and Sold by M. Gunne at the Bible and Crown at Essex-Gate, 1715," it is clear that the Dublin title-page was set up not from the 1688 but from the 1692 London title-page,[9] presumably right after the latter had been torn off the pamphlet concerned since, incredible though it seems, the 1715 Dublin "edition" is once again nothing more than the unsold sheets of the 1688 London edition with yet another cancel title-page. The work upon which Swift left his signature and annotations is thus not one work but two, originally published in London in 1643 and 1650, and read by Swift not in an edition printed in Dublin in 1715 as at first appears, but in an edition printed in London in 1688, reissued in London in 1692, and then finally reissued again in Dublin twenty-seven years after the sheets were printed off. Why a Dublin bookseller might, in 1715, have possessed an unsold stock of a mildly seditious London pamphlet a generation old, how he might have come by this stock, and why he might have decided to reissue it in the first year of the new Hanoverian dynasty I am at a loss to explain.[10]

Turning now from what it was that Swift read and annotated to the nature of his annotations, I must begin by confessing that they are disappointingly sparse and consist for the most part of crosses and other similar marks in the margins of the work. The one major exception is Swift's initial note (fig. 1), which is written in ink on the otherwise blank verso of the title-page and which reads

> This would be a most excellent
> Discourse if the Author had not been
> swayd by his Partiality in favor
> of Kings.
> Decemb^r 28.th 1736.
> Jonath: Swift.

Coming as it does at the head of a text which describes the kings of England (in circumstantial detail) as the most pernicious race of little odious vermin ever suffered to rule, and which adds, on the subject of their various rights to the throne, that even "granting Succession in itself to be a good Title...no Title was ever more broken and unjust than of our Kings" (p. 10), Swift's comment shows that even in his seventieth year he had not lost his ironic sense of humor.

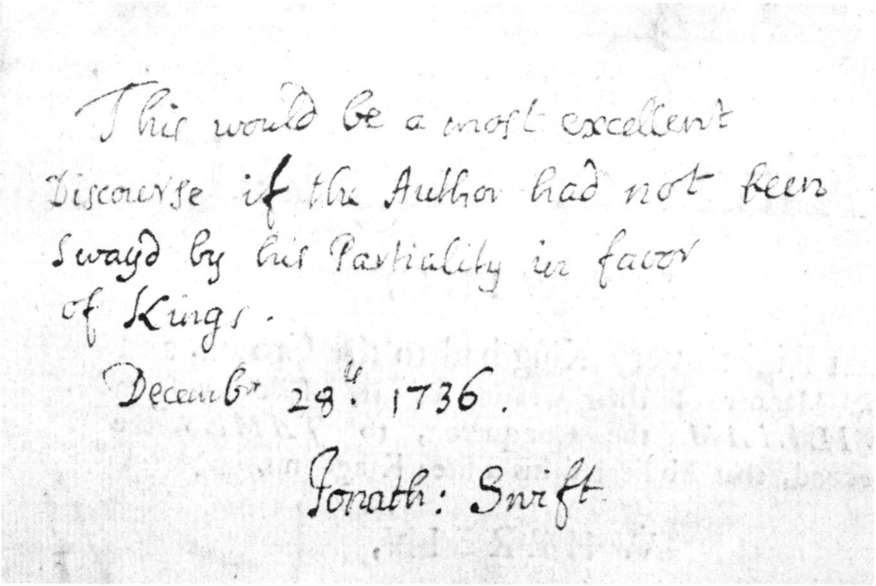

FIG. 1

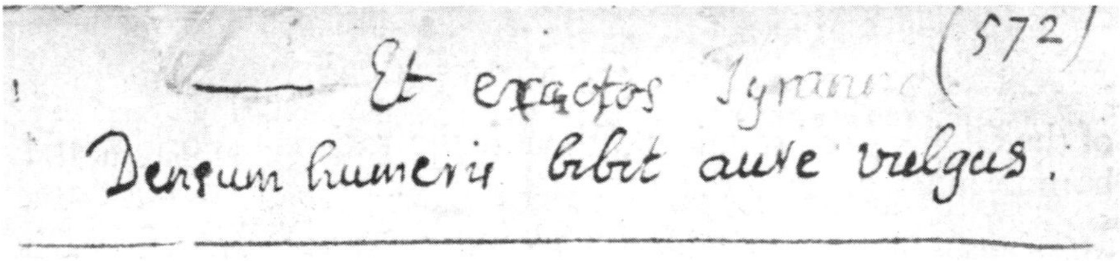

FIG. 2

Across from this, in a blank space above the first page of the text proper, Swift has written the following line and a half of Latin verse (fig. 2):

—— Et exactos Tyrannos
Densum humeris bibit aure vulgus.

This passage from Horace's *Odes* (II.xiii.31–32) describes the imagined effect in the crowded underworld of the recitals of the poets Sappho and, in particular, Alcaeus, and may be roughly translated "[when they speak of battles] and the driving out of tyrants, the crowd, packed shoulder to shoulder, drink it in with their ears."[11] The overthrow of a tyrant is a noble thing, but *tyrannos* in this context presumably stands for kings, and given Swift's well-known antipathy for the mob—both word and thing—he may well have intended this passage too as an ironic comment on the readiness of the *mobile vulgus* to be swayed by political rhetoric.

The remaining annotations consist entirely of dates, crosses, lines, a pointing hand, and two single words, one of which, "ever" (p. 26.11),[12] is merely Swift's marginal correction of the misprint "over" in the text. The first six annotations are the dates "1066" (p. 11.29), "1087" (p. 12.29), "1100"

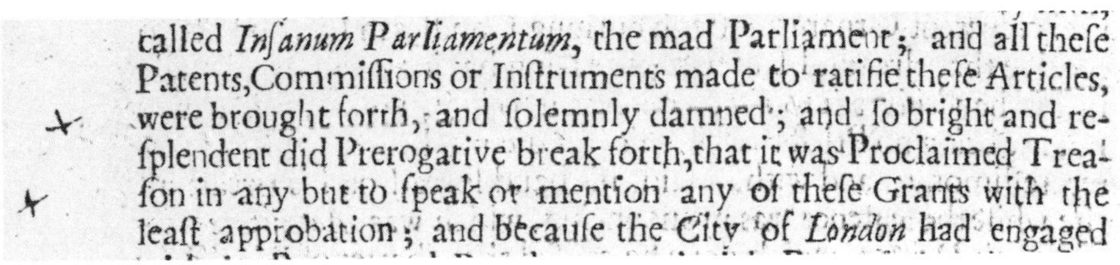

called *Infanum Parliamentum*, the mad Parliament; and all thefe Patents, Commiffions or Inftruments made to ratifie thefe Articles, were brought forth, and folemnly damned; and fo bright and re-fplendent did Prerogative break forth, that it was Proclaimed Trea-fon in any but to fpeak or mention any of thefe Grants with the leaft approbation; and becaufe the City of *London* had engaged

FIG. 3

(p. 12.34), "1135" (p. 13.15), "1154" (p. 13.19), and "1189" (p. 13.22), which Swift has simply added in the margin opposite the events to which each refers, the accessions of "*William* the *Norman*," William Rufus, Henry I, Stephen, Henry II, and Richard I respectively, none of which is dated in the text. Following the accession of Richard, Swift seems to have lost interest in his dating and shifts instead to marginal crosses, of which there are twenty-eight in all, placed for the most part not opposite the accessions of subsequent monarchs, but rather next to some fact or judgment which Swift seems to have wished to retain.[13] One example from the reign of Henry III, though involving two crosses placed close together (p. 26.29 and 31), must suffice for all:

...and all these Patents, Commissions or Instruments made to ratifie these Articles, were brought forth, and solemnly damned; and so bright and resplendent did Prerogative break forth, that it was Proclaimed Treason in any but to speak or mention any of these Grants with the least approbation...(fig. 3).

Apart from dates and crosses there are only two marks in the margins of the text: a set of light and not very straight lines beside a passage (p. 48.1–5) concerning James II and his attempt "to pretend an Heir of the Queens Body...by a borrow'd Impostor," and a typical Swiftian pointing hand (p. 25.22) opposite the following passage, which again refers to the prerogative in the reign of Henry III, the monarch to whom Parker devotes more space than to any other:

The People knowing that no civil Promises, or verbal Professions would hold in Kings raptured by Prerogative and devoted to Perjury to maintain their Tyranny, take a more Ecclesiastical and divine way of obligation, swearing to excommunicate all that should be found infringers of that Charter...(fig. 4).

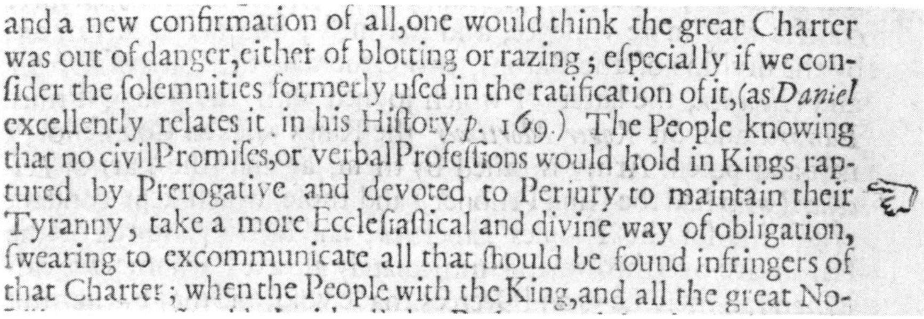

and a new confirmation of all, one would think the great Charter was out of danger, either of blotting or razing ; especially if we consider the solemnities formerly used in the ratification of it, (as *Daniel* excellently relates it in his History *p.* 169.) The People knowing that no civil Promises, or verbal Professions would hold in Kings raptured by Prerogative and devoted to Perjury to maintain their Tyranny, take a more Ecclesiastical and divine way of obligation, swearing to excommunicate all that should be found infringers of that Charter ; when the People with the King, and all the great No-

FIG. 4

This then is the sum total of Swift's annotations to the *Short History*, but there remains a single word, the second of the two to which I referred above, which constitutes Swift's only annotation to the *Political Catechism*. This word occurs in the margin of the section of observations following the question "What kind of Government then is that of the State of England?" and the answer "Regulated Monarchy." The particular observation to which the word refers is the second: "It needs not be accounted a Solecism (as some would perswade us) to speak of free Subjects in a Monarchy, such a Monarchy as ours is," and it refers in particular to the oxymoron "free Subjects" which Swift has underlined in the text. Beside this in the margin he has written simply "Hobbes" (p. 50.13).[14]

It is disappointing that Swift's annotations to Parker's two works are so few and so very limited, particularly in the case of *A Political Catechism*, a work which might well have sparked Swift to some very interesting observations of his own had he read it at a time when he was himself preoccupied with the question of the kinds of civil government, for example at the time of his composing of the *Contests and Dissensions*. However, if these annotations leave much to be desired in the way of intrinsic interest, they nevertheless provide additional evidence of Swift's habits of annotation. Swift's most important set of annotations, those made in his own copy of his greatest work, is the subject of David Woolley's classic paper on "Swift's Copy of *Gulliver's Travels*." It contains not only a description of that copy but also an important catalogue of the variety of Swift's marginal markings (with attention to the crucial distinction between those in ink and those in pencil), together with the best account we have of Swift's handwriting.[15] It was Woolley's account and invaluable list of examples which enabled me to confirm that the two lengthy notes in the *Short History* were written in Swift's "fair" hand and that the bulk of the annotations were in the form of what Woolley calls a saltire cross, a mark also used by Swift (though much less frequently) in annotating *Gulliver*. I must follow Woolley's excellent example in recording the fact that the six saltire crosses on pages 15, 16, and 17 are the only annotations in the pamphlet to have been made in pencil instead of ink, although in the present case the distinction serves only to demonstrate that Swift's reading of the *Short History* must have been interrupted on at least two separate occasions.

I come finally to the vexed question of provenance, of how this obscure pamphlet came to be where it is now and what its origins can tell us about the circumstances in which it may have been read and annotated by Jonathan Swift. The simple answer to the question of the work's provenance is that we know nothing whatsoever about it. It is one of a volume of thirty-one items printed between 1620 and 1722, bound in early nineteenth-century embossed calf and labeled on the spine "Tracts," which currently resides in the Westcountry Studies Library in Exeter (pressmark s080).[16] And, in the words of the former Westcountry Studies Librarian, Ian Maxted, "The volume was probably received by Exeter City Library during an appeal for books after the Blitz, when full records of accessions were not maintained." Much research has ended with just such an uncompromising fact as this, but in the present case we are fortunate that the volume contains just enough internal evidence to enable us to pursue the matter further.

To begin with, it carries on the front pastedown the armorial bookplate of one Henry William Stephens,[17] whose signature also appears on the verso of the front flyleaf and who, judging by the handwriting, seems also to have been responsible for the manuscript list of contents which is at present loose in the volume but which was probably originally tipped in at the front. Maxted has dated the bookplate on stylistic grounds as "1840 plus or minus 20 years," which, given that the binding is of roughly the same date, makes it likely that it was Henry William Stephens who had the volume bound in the early nineteenth century and who prepared the manuscript table of contents for it at that time. Henry William Stephens, however, was apparently not the person who brought together this particular collection of tracts, for no fewer than twenty-six of the thirty-one bear the signature of

"D Stephens" in what appears to be an eighteenth-century hand and which almost certainly predates the putting together of the volume, since two of the signatures (those on Nos. 29 and 30) have been cropped in the act of binding. Of the five tracts which do not bear the "D Stephens" signature on their title-pages, one (No. 13) has lost its title-page, and another (No. 4) has a large piece missing from its title-page, suggesting that both may originally have bccn signed.[18] Of the other three, two (Nos. 2 and 3) show no evidence of ever having had title-pages and may possibly be unsigned for this reason. The fifth and last of the unsigned tracts (No. 22) is *A Short History of the Kings of England*, and I am at a loss to say why it should not have been signed—unless it was because "D Stephens" did not in fact own it. Possibly it was lent to Stephens and for some reason not returned.

It seems not too much to assume that "D Stephens" was an ancestor of Henry William Stephens, and given the uniformity of his signature on the twenty-six signed tracts, it also seems possible that the tracts either came into his possession as a group or that he acquired them over a relatively short period of time. There is no direct evidence of where or when this may have been, but I will venture the hypothesis that it may have been in Dublin in the 1720s or 1730s. The reason for this is the curious composition of the collection, which, leaving aside one item (No. 2) of uncertain date and place of origin, is made up of twenty-six items published between 1620 and 1689, twenty-four in London, one in Rotterdam, and one in The Hague, and four dating from 1709, 1715, 1720, and 1722, all published in Dublin. There exist a limitless number of explanations of how such a collection of pamphlets might have been assembled, but very few that plausibly explain how a collection in which all the most recent items have a Dublin origin could have been assembled anywhere but Ireland.

Unfortunately the subject matter of the items which make up the collection offers almost no clue to the reason for which they were acquired. The London-published items may be divided into two main chronological groups, fifteen published between 1640 and 1655 and nine published between 1673 and 1689, each group being loosely representative of its time. The Civil War and Interregnum items, for example, include three sermons (Nos. 5, 9, 28), *A Tract against...Usurie* (No. 29), a defense of episcopacy (No. 6), and three pamphlets concerning tithes (Nos. 7, 21, 23), while those from the 1670s and 1680s include accounts of a fire (No. 12), a flood (No. 15), and an earthquake (No. 18), two political pamphlets by L'Estrange (Nos. 14, 30), and Bathsua Makin's celebrated *Essay* on the education of gentlewomen (No. 11). The one curious similarity between the two groups arises from the fact that the latest in date of each group is a pamphlet related to Ireland, Vincent Gookin's *The Great Case of Transplantation in Ireland Discussed*, 1655 (No. 8),[19] and George Philips's *The Interest of England in the Preservation of Ireland*, 1689 (No. 4). These are, however, the only items with an Irish connection except for the four Dublin-published pamphlets, which, apart from their common place of origin, show the same random variety of subject matter as the others.

These Dublin pamphlets are the controversial work *A Collection of Mr. J. Boyse's Several Scurrilous and Abusive Reflections on…the Church as by Law Established* (Dublin, 1709) (No. 26) by the Rev. Matthew French, junior fellow of Trinity College and curate of St. Werburgh's; the equally disputatious *A Stroke at the Foundation of Quakerism* (Dublin: S. Powell, 1722) (No. 24); the *Short History of the Kings of England* (No. 22) discussed above; and finally a poem, the only one in the entire collection, which lacks title-page, author's name, and date and place of publication, but which turns out on examination to be a copy (and only the second copy known) of the 1720 Dublin printing of Swift's satire *The Run upon the Bankers* (No. 3).[20]

The existence in the collection of a Swift poem as well as of a pamphlet bearing Swift's annotations suggests that "D Stephens" may have had some connection with Swift himself, but obvious sources like Ehrenpreis's life or Swift's own prose works, poetry, correspondence, or account books and their editors' annotations offer no evidence of any such acquaintance. Instead, the clue lies in an obscure nineteenth-century parish history, B. W. Adams's *History and Description of Santry and Cloghran Parishes, County Dublin* (London, 1883), which, in a list of the rectors and curates of the parish of Cloghran, identifies a David Stephens, AB, as curate of the parish in 1733–35. This is presumably the David Stephens who graduated from Trinity College Dublin in 1720.[21] And the vestry book of Cloghran which survives in the Church of Ireland Archives in the Representative Church Body Library in Dublin contains examples of the signature of "D Stephens Min.r" which leave no doubt that it was the curate of Cloghran who signed the pamphlets in the Exeter volume.[22] As for the Swift connection, it perhaps lies in the fact that the rector of the parish of Cloghran (and thus David Stephens's employer) at this time and for many years both before and after was the Rev. John Wynne, DD, prebendary of Swords and subsequently of St. Audoen's in the Cathedral chapter, from 1730 Precentor of the Cathedral and Librarian of Marsh's Library, and from April 1739 Sub-Dean of St. Patrick's, appointed to that post by the Dean himself, who was "not able by reason of Sickness to be present and personally to preside in the Chapter of our said Cathedrall Church."[23]

John Wynne, one of the three witnesses to Swift's will in May 1740, was undoubtedly close to the Dean during his later years. Thus he might easily have been the channel through whom a pamphlet with Swift's annotations passed from the Dean's library to a more distant admirer, or, to reverse the process, through whom a young admirer might have submitted a curious pamphlet to the Dean for his comments, even though by the 28 December 1736 date of Swift's signing of the *Short History*, David Stephens had left the curacy of Cloghran for that of Derralossory in the neighboring diocese of Glendalough, where he seems to have remained until his death in 1765. Or perhaps the annotated *Short History* came into his hands much later, and by some means about which we can now only speculate.

But speculation is the permanent business of scholarship, that constant reordering of the factual pieces of the puzzle which it is the original business of scholarship to discover, identify, and add to the common store. To that store may now be added the title *A Short History of the Kings of England*, the name of the Reverend David Stephens, and the date Tuesday, 28 December 1736, three more pieces of the sad puzzle of Swift's last years which some future scholar may better see how to fit together.

---

[1] Jonathan Swift, Preface to *A Tale of a Tub*, in [*The Prose Writings of Jonathan Swift*], ed. Herbert Davis et al., 14 vols. (1939–1968; various reimpressions, sometimes corrected, Oxford, 1957–69), I, 24; hereafter cited as *Prose*.

[2] There are three surviving lists of Swift's library: (1) a catalogue in Swift's hand made in 1715, now in the library of King's College, Cambridge, and printed inaccurately by T. P. LeFanu, "Catalogue of Dean Swift's Library in 1715," *Proceedings of the Royal Irish Academy*, 37, sec. C (1927), 263–75; (2) an inventory in the hand of the Rev. John Lyon, now in Sir Walter Scott's library at Abbotsford; (3) the sale catalogue compiled after Swift's death, printed by George Faulkner in 1745, and reprinted in Harold Williams, *Dean Swift's Library* (Cambridge, 1932), pp. 97 ff. "Collection of Pamphlets London, 1681 &c" occurs in the 1742 list only and "Pamphlets London 1701" ("Pamphlets. 1701." in the printed version, p. 273) in the 1715 list only, but I suspect that both in fact recur in the 1745 sale catalogue, the former as item 514, "L'Estrange's Dissenters Sayings and other Pamphlets Lond. 1681, &c." and the latter as item 288, "Dr. Davenant's true Picture of a modern Whig; with other Tracts Lond. 1701." Neither the L'Estrange nor the Davenant pamphlet is present in the volume discussed below.

[3] The discovery is not mine but that of Ian Maxted, County Local Studies Librarian, Devon, who found the pamphlet among the holdings of the Westcountry Studies Library in Exeter while recataloguing them for the ESTC. Knowing me as

a fellow book-trade historian who also had a special interest in Swift, Maxted very kindly called my attention to the pamphlet and suggested that I work on it further, offering his own bibliographic help at every stage. I should say at once that I have not myself been able to examine the pamphlet or the volume in which it appears and have worked from the xeroxes and the expert bibliographical descriptions provided by Maxted. My debt to him is thus immense, but any errors of interpretation in the account that follows are entirely my own.

⁴ The imprint is unusual because of its inherent contradictions both of place and date. The place is given as "London," and "R. Baldwin" was a London trade publisher, but "M. Gunne" was a Dublin bookseller with a Dublin address, and the price of "13d." is also characteristically Irish. Moreover, the date "1715" is a date at which Matthew Gunne was at the Bible and Crown at Essex Gate, while Richard Baldwin, for whom the work was supposedly printed, had died in 1698. A more usual imprint in such cases would be "London: Printed…; Dublin: Reprinted…," which may have been avoided because the pamphlet was not, in fact, "reprinted." See below.

⁵ Donald Wing, *Short-Title Catalogue…1641–1700* (New York, 1945–51). All future references to "Wing" will be to the revised editions of vols. 1 and 2 (New York, 1972 and 1982) and the original edition of vol. 3. The Bodleian Library contains two separate editions of *A Political Catechism*, Pamph. D 57 (62) and G. Pamph. 636 (9), either of which could be Wing P416, "*For Samuel Gellibrand, 1643*," but neither of which could be P417, "[*London?* 1643?]," since both are printed for Gellibrand and both clearly dated 1643.

⁶ W. K. Jordan, *Men of Substance. A Study of the Thought of Two English Revolutionaries, Henry Parker and Henry Robinson* (Chicago, 1942), p. 144. Jordan discusses doubts concerning Parker's authorship only to dismiss them, p. 144, n. 6.

⁷ In the original 1650 edition the preface had been signed "Henry Parker," which had been shortened to "H.P." in 1688.

⁸ The folio volume of *State Tracts* (1689; Wing S5329) mentioned above which in 1689 bore the imprint "London: Printed in the Year, 1689," was also reissued in 1693, also bearing the imprint of Richard Baldwin.

⁹ In addition to the changes in the imprint, the 1715 title-page also added the false claim "With the Glorious Reign and Memory of King William the IIId" and the entirely mysterious attribution "Written by the Attorney General of England," neither of which had appeared on the 1692 title-page.

¹⁰ Mary Paul Pollard has called my attention to the fact that Matthew Gunne (or perhaps a like-named predecessor) bought "the remaining books… (for about *an Hundred Pound*)" following John Dunton's final Dublin auction sale in 1698 and that remaindered copies of the *Short History* may have been among them. See John Dunton, *The Dublin Scuffle* (London, 1699), p. 70.

¹¹ I am grateful to Bertrand Goldgar for help in identifying the passage. The text as Swift quotes it is virtually identical to that found in an edition of Horace that he owned, the Elzevir Leyden edition of 1629 (p. 43).

12 I.e., opposite line 11 on page 26. One of the twenty-eight crosses itemized in note 13 below occurs opposite this same line and may only be meant to indicate this same misprint.

13 The twenty-eight are at p. 15.7, 11 and 18, p. 16.15, p. 17.14 and 37–38, p. 26.11, 29 and 31, p. 27.1 and 7, p. 28.4, p. 30.11, 24, 33 and 38, p. 31.9 and 32, p. 32.10, p. 33.33, p. 34.30, p. 38.29 and 32, p. 39.6, 9, 13 and 19, and p. 46.1. Readers who wish to match the crosses to a text are reminded that although the 1715 Dublin issue is extremely rare if not unique, copies of Wing P430 and S3601, which are in fact earlier issues of the same edition, are much more easily available.

14 John Fischer has suggested that Swift may have had in mind *Leviathan*, ch. 21, "Of the Liberty of Subjects," in which Hobbes argues that it is quite consistent to speak of subjects as free whose very lives depend upon the unlimited power of the sovereign. This seems likely, but if so, Swift, who could scarcely have known that the work he was reading actually predated the publication of *Leviathan* by eight years, has been misled by a superficial resemblance in language, since it would be hard to imagine arguments of a more different tendency than Parker's and Hobbes's.

15 David Woolley, "Swift's Copy of *Gulliver's Travels*: The Armagh *Gulliver*, Hyde's Edition, and Swift's Earliest Corrections," in Clive Probyn, ed., *The Art of Jonathan Swift* (London, 1978), pp. 131–78.

16 To list all thirty-one items in detail would take more space than is available, so that I have adopted the expedient of reference by STC or Wing number to those seventeenth-century English items which appear *from an examination of xeroxes of their title-pages only* to have one. The four eighteenth-century Dublin items are all described later in the text and are therefore mentioned here with the note "see below." The thirty-one, in the order in which they are bound, are 1. P1749 (this item bears on its title-page the MS date [not in Swift's hand] "August ye 15th 1727," the significance of which is uncertain); 2. *Plain Directions to Church-Wardens and Constables* (n.p., n.d.); 3. see below; 4. P2027; 5. W1093; 6. C6039; 7. a variant of S3205; 8. G1273 with a variant title-page bound in; 9. W1419; 10. STC 20866; 11. M309; 12. P987; 13. S3163 but lacking first two leaves; 14. L1248; 15. a variant of E2999; 16. R1075; 17. S4033; 18. T2454; 19. A3209; 20. Bernhardus Comenius, *Prodromus exequiarum...* (Rotterdam, 1639); 21. G1627; 22. *A Short History of the Kings of England* (see below); 23. a variant of E1201, but "for John Wright...1644"; 24. see below; 25. W1705; 26. see below; 27. STC 10272; 28. V557 but lacking first two leaves; 29. C7552; 30. L1307A; 31. N1495. Future reference to these items in the text will be by their order of binding, for example, "No. 31."

17 Maxted describes the arms as: "Per chevron azure and argent, in the first two eagles volant. Crest: on a wreath of the colours an eagle volant, on the breast a mullet for difference." They are similar to the arms borne by several branches of the Stephens family in the nineteenth century, but in spite of that neither Maxted nor I have succeeded in identifying a Henry William Stephens.

[18] No. 28, however, has also lost its title-page but is nevertheless signed on its first remaining page, B1^r.

[19] No. 8, Wing G1273, is unique in having bound in immediately before it the variant title-page of Wing G1274, which also carries, in addition to D. Stephens's signature and the MS pagination carried by every item, the following annotations in a variety of hands: Top: "Miscellany [pamp]hlets A.A. Febr. 2. 1634 [indecipherable symbols] 27"; Bottom (above imprint): "This was written as I take it by Vincent Gookin Esqr that was Surveyor Generall of Ireland."

[20] I am grateful to Thomas V. Lange of the Huntington Library for confirming that the Exeter copy is identical to the Huntington copy, Teerink's 611A.

[21] *Alumni Dublinenses*, ed. G. D. Burtchaell and T. U. Sadleir (London, 1924).

[22] I am grateful to Raymond Refaussé, Librarian of the Representative Church Body Library, Dublin, for providing me with xeroxes of the relevant page of the Cloghran vestry book (RCB Library, Church of Ireland Archives, P. 242/3/1) as well as of J. B. Leslie's clerical succession lists for the parishes of Cloghran (MS 64/2/4/1) and Derralossory (MS 61/2/6), from which I take the information on David Stephens in the following paragraph.

[23] *Prose*, XIII, 195.

Henry L. Snyder

How Augustan Historians
Viewed the Later Stuarts:
The Contemporaries of Swift

NO SCHOLAR has yet attempted a detailed study of historical writing in the first half of the eighteenth century. F. Smith Fussner and specialists under the editorship of Levi Fox have treated historians working in the late sixteenth and early seventeenth centuries; Royce MacGillivray has dealt with the Restoration; Thomas P. Peardon and Herbert Butterfield with the reign of George III.[1] But what of the period that lies in between? Only the medievalists and antiquaries, essentially clerics, have received anything like their due, thanks to the contribution of D. C. Douglas[2] and a series of biographers dealing with the Augustan bench of bishops.[3] The period passed over begins with the publication of the Earl of Clarendon's *History of the Rebellion and Civil Wars in England* (1702–04) and ends with David Hume's *History of Great Britain* (1754–62). Hume's stylistic superiority, his moderate and dispassionate perspective, and his recognition of social and economic change mark a new turn in historical writing devoted to England's past.[4]

To some extent the historical writing of the Augustans is distinctive for its format. The three stately folios of Clarendon seem to have established a model that was hard to resist. Weighty tomes may have had a symbolic importance, for nearly all longer surveys of English history that emerged in the next four decades bore that format. The march of these formidable volumes from the presses was accompanied by a similar series of original documents in folio, notably John Rushworth's *Historical Collections of Private Passages of State*, Thomas Rymer's *Foedera*, and Thomas Birch's *Collection of State Papers of John Thurloe*.[5] The folio histories all aimed at filling what seemed to be commonly recognized as a glaring gap in English literature. In the preface to his *Introduction to the History of England*, Jonathan Swift's patron Sir William Temple criticized the absence of "one good or approved general History of *England*."[6] But Temple's own abortive effort to create such a work was only a scissors-and-paste project, a projected abridgment of a series of earlier writers. Rather it was the *General History of England* by James Tyrrell which became the first work of this kind to be published.[7] But his three folio volumes, issued between 1696 and 1704, ended with the death of Richard II and remained incomplete. Swift was tempted to write such a history as Temple envisaged, or at least a continuation of Temple's *Introduction*.[8] Yet his only completed historical work was concentrated on the last four years of Anne's reign and was not published until after his death.

A distinguishing feature of much of Augustan historical writing was its polemical inspiration and focus. This was true even of the medievalists and the ecclesiastical historians discussed by Douglas: among the more prominent, William Wake, White Kennett, Francis Atterbury, and Edmund Gibson. Embroiled in the Convocation controversy, the dispute over ecclesiastical authority and its lay basis was complementary to and intertwined with the larger Whig-Tory, Country-Court debate. (The parallel of the moderating influence of the Whig-dominated House of Lords in Parliament and the Latitudinarian, Whig-dominated House of Bishops in Convocation is just one example.) Grounded in the Revolution of 1688, the dispute reached its height in the reign of the last Stuart sovereign.[9]

The Augustan historians of the later Stuarts not only chronicled the period but also were themselves combatants in the wars provoked by the party factions that dominated the era. The first salvo was fired by one of the most prominent politicians of the period, Laurence Hyde, Earl of Rochester, an elder statesman of the Tory-Church party. The work itself was not, in fact, on the later Stuarts at all. Rather it was the *History of the Rebellion*, written by his father, Clarendon, as an instruction for the young Charles II. Its publication by Rochester in 1702 was a deliberately provocative act.[10] The Tory peer wrote a pompous introduction with an oblique warning to his niece and Clarendon's granddaughter, the newly crowned Anne, not to repeat the mistakes of her grandfather or countenance apostasy and dissent. It may not have had the desired effect upon the Queen, but it was clearly fuel for party fire and was still inspiring rebuttals and defenses three decades later. The Tories found it a work of great strength and satisfaction, a powerful statement which gave voice to both their principles and their fears for the future. Thus John Evelyn could write Samuel Pepys, another staunch advocate and intimate of the royal brothers, Charles II and James II, "I acknowledge my selfe...transported with all the parts of this excellent History."[11] The Whigs regarded it as too self-serving, though Bishop Burnet found Clarendon's account "a faithful representation of the beginnings of the troubles, though writ in favour of the court, and full of the best excuses that such ill things were capable of."[12] Inevitably the work produced and continued to produce a strong partisan reaction, some of which will be noted later.

Shortly after the final volume of Clarendon's *History* was published in 1704, another massive three-volume compilation appeared. This was *A Complete History of England...to the death of...William III.*[13] The first two volumes, compiled anonymously by the minor poet John Hughes, were no more than "a collection of the best writers, of the lives and reigns of our several English princes."[14] The third volume, which treated the seventeenth century, was a different matter. Though "new writ by a learned and impartial hand,"[15] its Whiggish tone and criticism of Charles II and James II and their ministers made it appear as a deliberate answer to Clarendon. This was, however, not the intent. Though the success of Clarendon's *History* may have been an incentive to the publishers of the new work, it was rather the delayed composite work first proposed by Temple. The Jacobite recluse Thomas Hearne considered it "full of Whiggism, trifling, Grub-Street matter, & base reflections out of his way."[16] The third volume's author, White Kennett, was an established scholar but gained fame chiefly for his Latitudinarian principles and his defense of the Whig prelates in Convocation, for which he was advanced to be Dean of Peterborough in 1708. In spite of Abel Boyer's charge[17] that a substantial portion of the third volume was cribbed from his *Life of William III*,[18] Kennett is well worth a perusal. That his careful research included the contemporary period is evidenced by the voluminous journals he prepared for the period from 1660 to 1714.[19] Though allied with the Primate, Thomas Tenison, and his Whig colleagues, Kennett may be regarded as a conservative in several important respects. His comments on Archbishop Laud and Charles I are sympathetic. His ecclesiastical politics placed him in the moderate or Latitudinarian wing of the Church, but he was nevertheless a firm defender of the episcopacy and the royal prerogative, positions which his biographer describes as "tory."[20]

Kennett's *History* became the object of a series of replies. The Duke of Leeds, Lord Treasurer to Charles II from 1673 to 1679, "finding in that history a narrative of what appear'd to be maleadministration...[published] ...some account of his transactions with France, from his own papers and letters, [and] complain'd of the mis-representation of his services made by the late historian."[21] But the most powerful rebuttal did not appear until 1740, though it was apparently written soon after Kennett's *History* appeared. This was Roger North's *Examen: or, An Enquiry into the Credit and Veracity of a Pretended Complete History; Shewing the Perverse and Wicked Design of It, and the Many Falsities and Abuses of Truth contained in It.... All Tending to Vindicate the Honour of the Late King Charles the Second, and His Happy Reign, from the Intended Aspersions of That Foul Pen.*[22] North, who with his brothers held important posts under Charles and

James, ingenuously denied his partiality, "that his taking one side may not be understood as being of a party, because it is the side of the established religion and government, and for the continuance of it in peace."[23] No such tolerance was granted to Kennett, whom he accused of "all manner of false calumny, detraction, and libel against his superiors, the same pleasure as thieves, burglars and pickpockets have in the dexterous and undiscovered practice of their art."[24] The partisan tone of these writers— the sententious Rochester, the ponderous Clarendon, the critical Kennett, and the indignant North—set the pattern for historians for the next several generations, at least so long as the Whig-Tory debate was alive.

Purely political tracts aside, the next historical work to merit attention is *The History of the Revolutions in England under the Family of the Stuarts, from the Year 1603, to 1690*. It was first published at Paris in 1694 as the third volume of *Histoire des révolutions d'Angleterre*. The author was Pierre Joseph d'Orléans, a Jesuit priest, who dedicated his book to Louis XIV. Laurence Echard, Archdeacon of Stowe, a diligent compiler of historical and topographical works, wrote the introduction to the first English edition, translated by John Stevens, which appeared in London in 1711.[25] As England was still at war with France, the publication of d'Orléans's apologia for the Stuarts, especially James II, may have seemed inappropriate. Echard made a point of drawing attention to d'Orléans's defense of the two brothers and recommended the work for "several things so new and curious in this part, as to the Revolution itself, that it is not doubted, but it will give both pleasure and instruction to a cautious reader."[26]

Echard's attention may have been drawn to d'Orléans's study during the writing of Volumes II and III of his *History of England*, which begins in 1603 and ends in 1690 with the establishment of William and Mary on the throne. These volumes were published in 1718 together with a second edition of Volume I, which had first appeared in 1707. The set of three was republished in a third edition in one massive volume in 1720.[27] It was the first full narrative history of England, for all its predecessors were composite works. For the next half-dozen years it became the standard survey, displacing the Hughes-Kennett set, which also appeared in a second edition in 1719. In his introduction to the third volume Echard promised a fourth on the reign of William III. An apparent installment appeared in 1725 with his *History of the Revolution and the Establishment of England in the Year 1688*.[28] Although he had already covered much of the same ground in the third volume of the *History*, he "ventur'd upon it in this single volume...having since then new assistances and inducements."[29] William A. Aiken has demonstrated that Echard was able to draw upon the reminiscences of several public figures who observed and participated in the events he described.[30] One of his most important informants was Daniel, second Earl of Nottingham, who served Charles II, William III, Anne, and George I in ministerial posts. Nottingham, the butt of Swift's invective,[31] was the most important layman in the Church of England for more than two generations, and his High-Church views are neatly complemented by those of the Archdeacon.

The replies were not long in coming from those of other persuasions, such as the renowned Dissenter Edmund Calamy, who had chronicled the trials of his co-religionists in the period of the great persecution after the Restoration. The title of his critique speaks for itself: *A Letter to Mr. Archdeacon Echard, upon the Occasion of His History of England: Wherein the True Principles of the Revolution Are Defended, Clear'd from Aspersions; and a Number of Historical Mistakes Rectify'd* (1718).[32] Calamy did not charge Echard with "the tediousness and voluminousness of Hollingshed and Speed, or with the brevity and confinedness of Milton and Daniel."[33] His chief criticisms were reserved for his being too kind to Charles II and James II and for Echard's comments on religion. Calamy believed that "a considerable number of your readers…are of opinion, your history had not wanted any of its ornaments, if you had either been less favourable to the papists, or less eager in your reflections upon the dissenters."[34] This was the crux of the matter. The manner in which Echard ignored or deprecated harsh treatment of the Dissenters, dismissed the Popish plot as a sham, and failed to treat in a proper light the Savoy conference at the Restoration and other negotiations with the Non-conformists during the century filled Calamy with indignation. Nevertheless Echard's *History*, with the apparent approbation of George I, who gave the writer a gift in response to the dedication of the second and third volumes, was generally accepted as standard and authoritative. But the dominance of this Tory version of the Stuarts was short-lived. The next decade-plus saw the publication of three major new histories that all gave unremitting support to the Whig view of recent events and defended the Revolution for that act of salvation which was Whig gospel.

Of the three surveys the one which enjoyed the greatest success in terms of number of copies sold, editions published, continuations offered, and longevity as a staple survey was the *History of England* by the Huguenot Paul de Rapin-Thoyras. Rapin had come to England with William of Orange, had served for several years in the army, and then had gone into the service of the Earl of Portland as governor to his heir. On leaving Portland's service he settled first at The Hague and then at Wesel, where he spent the last two decades of his life on his *History*. Though designed for foreigners and written without access to printed and manuscript sources in England, it enjoyed a phenomenal popularity, going through many French and English editions. The English translation was undertaken by Nathaniel Tindal, a clergyman, and began to appear in 1726, three years after the first publication of the French volumes. Although Rapin's work ran only to the Revolution, its popularity encouraged one continuation in French and two in English.

If Rapin was relatively detached in his outlook, this perspective could hardly be ascribed to two other historians who followed him. The first was Gilbert Burnet, Bishop of Salisbury, whose *History of His Own Time* was published posthumously (Burnet died in 1715) in two large folios in 1724 and 1734.[35] Burnet was an eager Whig partisan. Exiled from his native Scotland, he too had come over with William of Orange but had gone on to became a pugnacious and active bishop in the Church of England, to the dismay and disapproval of Anglicans and Presbyterians alike. Swift was one of his fiercest critics, and his many annotations in his own copy of Burnet's *History* reflect the repugnance which so characterized the attitude of High-Churchmen to the Bishop.[36] Burnet was a man of great energy and genuine scholarship. To the less prejudiced his commentary on the later seventeenth century is of great value, and it is justly famous. Its publication had been eagerly awaited for a quarter of a century, since extracts had circulated as early as 1700 in manuscript and in print from 1715, though unauthorized.[37] The first volume produced a rash of critics and commentators.[38] Almost without exception they tended to support the Tory position of Echard rather than the forthright Whig views of Burnet.

At this point we may note that another Whig memoir of the late Stuart period was composed sometime in the 1720s or early 1730s, though it did not appear in print until 1787. This was *The History of Great Britain from the Revolution in 1688, to the Accession of George the First* by Alexander Cunningham.[39] Cunningham was a Scot with close connections to many of the most prominent politicians of his time. His position as tutor to the second Duke of Argyle and his appointment to minor diplomatic posts in the reigns of William III and George I gave him a familiarity with the Continent and English interests there. Due to the paucity of personal papers to survive, his reasons for writing his narrative are obscure, but his great aversion to Bishop Burnet may have prompted him to write a corrective to the more famous cleric. Also, he may have written to tout his own contributions to the political transactions of the first decade of the eighteenth century. Whatever the reason, his firsthand knowledge of political intrigues is helpful.

The honest Whiggery of Burnet was much intensified in the many writings of John Oldmixon, the most consistently, indeed, vehemently if not hysterically Whig historian of the Augustan period. He was also one of Swift's most vociferous, if not most sophisticated, antagonists in the last years of Anne's reign, assisting Arthur Maynwaring in the *Medley*'s debate with Swift's *Examiner* and rebutting Swift's tracts in other publications.[40] Oldmixon's continuing animosity to the Irish cleric is evident in more than a few places in his later historical writings, especially his *History of England* (below). Oldmixon first took on all the later writers in 1724–26 in his two-volume *Critical History of England*.[41] The subtitle clearly illustrates his purpose: *The Errors of the Monkish Writers, and Others before the Reformation, Are Expos'd and Corrected. As Are Also the Deficiency and Partiality of Later Historians. And Particular Notice Is Taken of The History of the Grand Rebellion. And Mr. Echard's History of England. To Which Are Added Remarks on Some Objections Made to Bishop Burnet's History of His Times.* The intemperate Oldmixon drew the heat of so many responses that he tried again in 1727 to denigrate the Tory writers, especially Clarendon, in his *Clarendon and Whitlock Compared*.[42] But his greatest effort was reserved for yet another folio trilogy *History of England* which appeared successively in 1730, 1735, and 1739.[43] The first two volumes dealt with the Stuarts (and George I), the last with the Tudors.

The culmination of the battle of the tomes came in the 1740s. It was the ghost of Rapin, or rather the real presence of a supplement, that was the most successful. The most important, *The Continuation of Mr. Rapin de Thoyras's History of England*, is that ascribed to Nathaniel Tindal, the translator of Rapin's volumes into English. Recent scholarship has shown that the continuation was compiled not by Tindal but by the editor and antiquary Thomas Birch, Tindal serving primarily as his editor.[44] Moreover, Birch's *Continuation*, which covered the period from the Restoration to the reign of George II, was a patent government commission. The direction came from the Lord Chancellor, Philip Yorke, Earl of Hardwicke, his brother Charles, and Horace Walpole, the studious son of Sir Robert Walpole. As heirs to another distinguished chancellor, Lord Somers, the Yorke brothers also possessed Somers's library, which included Somers's own papers, a valuable resource for any historian of the period. Birch and Tindal were commissioned to write the history of the post-Restoration period with the primary goal of recording the constitutional accomplishments of the Whigs at the Revolution and their successful efforts to preserve them against Tory attacks until the accession of George I secured them.

The most detailed account of Restoration England to appear was that of James Ralph, an American. His two folios published 1744–46 display careful and extensive research into and use of the printed literature up to that time, and Volume II, which covers William's reign, is still of value as a guide to the Williamite press.[45] Like Birch, he, too, was acting on commission, but this time from the opposition Whigs. His principal backer was George Bubb Dodington, a key adviser to Frederick, Prince of Wales. Ralph's history of the last four decades of the seventeenth century was intended by Dodington and his colleagues as a companion to and continuation of William Guthrie's folio *General History of England*, which adopts the "Country" themes of the opposition, both Whig and Tory, to Walpole.[46] His history illustrates once again that the court Whig view of the late seventeenth century was not nearly so dominant as one might have expected in the half-century of the Whig supremacy.

Even more pronounced in its conservative bias was the Jacobite Thomas Carte's *History of England*,[47] which he had carried down to 1648 in four massive folios at the time of his death in 1757. His sponsors included a number of leading Jacobites.

The appearance in 1754 of the first volume of David Hume's politic and unexceptional survey[48] marked an end to the partisanship which had characterized Augustan historical writing on the later Stuarts. Hume was to remain the standard narrative until the next century.

Augustan historical writing on the later Stuarts is not limited to large-scale surveys of the seventeenth century or even of the whole history of the country. Jonathan Swift's *History of the Four Last Years of the Queen* was the first effort to write a comprehensive history for a major part of the reign of Queen Anne, for the contemporary annalists Abel Boyer and David Jones offered only a chronicle, and one year at a time.[49] Certainly in its purpose and outlook as a Tory apologia, Swift's tract may properly be regarded as the precursor of Thomas Salmon's account (below), which was to become the most popular and most widely accepted interpretation of the tumultuous events which climaxed Anne's reign.

Though the title under which it finally appeared was acceptable to Swift, his *History* was less ambitious than the name suggests. It was intended as a defense of the Treaty of Utrecht and was rather a history of the Parliament that sat from 1710 to 1713 and the diplomatic negotiations leading to the treaty. Swift hoped that the publication of his tract while the peace treaty was under review in Parliament would reinforce the ministry's proposals. But he was dissuaded from publishing it both then and later in the 1720s and the 1730s, when he again sought to have it printed. Though it has the advantage of being written by one close to the principal ministers, it was a highly partisan political tract. The provocative nature of many of his remarks, such as those against the Duke of Marlborough, was thought to do more harm than good.[50]

It fell, therefore, to David Jones to publish a survey of Anne's reign by recasting his annals into a single narrative, though in an unlikely form. In the 1690s he had seen through the press three editions of the *Detection of the Court and State of England* by Roger Coke. In 1719 he extended this work to 1714 in a fourth and final edition, enlarging the work by another volume in the process.[51] The new volume is devoted almost wholly to Anne's reign and is regularly referred to by scholars, incorrectly, as Coke's work. Coke died before Anne came to the throne, and the portion covering Anne's reign was compiled in its entirety by Jones. Once again a history must be described as mildly Whiggish, although Jones was careful to the point of blandness and occasionally deprecated Whig excesses. Generally, however, he wrote approvingly of the Marlborough-Godolphin ministry. In not a few pages his comments on events are the only original sections, for Jones (and to a lesser extent Boyer) cribbed his annals and his addition to Coke largely out of the pages of the monthly *Present State of Europe: or, The Historical and Political Mercury*, itself no more than a translation of the *Mercure historique et politique* published at The Hague.

Two years later, in 1721, the presently least known but for Augustan readers probably the most influential and certainly the most popular history of Anne's reign appeared, *The Life of Her Late Majesty Queen Anne, as Well before Her Accession to the Throne as After*.[52] Printed in two octavo volumes for Charles Rivington at the Bible and Crown in St. Paul's Church-Yard, it was published anonymously. The few references I have seen to it tend to identify it with Boyer's folio *History* of 1722 (below), the next survey of the period to appear. Yet a quick perusal of its pages shows that it is a thorough-going Tory account, an original work not over-indebted to its predecessors. Indeed, its consistently high-flying, High-Church commentary finds its parallel only in the writings of the most vehement Tories, Jacobites and Non-jurors included. No opportunity is lost to denigrate the Whigs and excoriate statesmen identified with them. The old canard about Sir Cloudesley Shovell and his officers' being intoxicated the night his fleet ran aground in the Scilly Isles is exhumed, though it was and is universally accepted that smugglers set out false lights to lead him off course so that they could rob his ships when they wrecked. The achievements of the Duke of Marlborough, who only won a victory every other year, are found wanting in comparison with those of Sir George Rooke and the Earl of Peterborough. The whole work is a classic running exposition of the Tory "blue water" concept of British foreign policy. But the anonymous writer's greatest eloquence is reserved for matters affecting religion: he displays his hatred and contempt for Dissenters, whether native, Huguenot, or Palatine, while staunchly defending the Church of England and the monopoly of offices reserved for its adherents. It is an inflammatory, provocative work. The question of its authorship piques one's curiosity. A comparison with Volume II of Thomas Salmon's *Review of the History of England* (1724), also printed for Rivington, soon suggests an answer.

Salmon was an industrious drudge who churned out many volumes of topographical and historical works in the 1720s and 1730s. They achieved a high degree of popularity and went through numerous editions. In 1722 he had published an octavo *Review of the History of England, as Far as It Relates to the Titles and Pretension of Our Several Kings, and Their Respective Characters from the Conquest to the Revolution*. It was republished in 1724 with a second volume "containing the transactions and occurrences of the three last reigns; viz. King James II, King William III, and Queen Anne" (title-page).[53] The interpretive comments which constitute the most original writing in the anonymous 1721 *Life* are repeated almost verbatim in the 1724 *Review*. The main distinction between the 1721 *Life* and its reduced version in Volume II of the *Review* is the omission of much of the derivative material. This consisted essentially of standard accounts of the war in Europe, speeches and letters, lists of legislative enactments and appointments, and the like.[54]

The influence of Salmon's history of Anne's reign has been missed by historians because so few of the editions of his text bear his name. Other than the truncated version in the *Review*, the only one recognized as coming from his pen is that in the two volumes devoted to the history of England which appeared as Volumes XXV and XXVI of his *Modern History* in 1734 and 1735.[55] The *Modern History* is an extended commentary on world travel literature, a subject in which Salmon had some expertise from his previous career in the army and his extensive travels abroad. The two volumes devoted to England differ in focus and content. Although ostensibly covering the whole range of recorded English history, the first is devoted primarily to the later Stuarts. The second volume is devoted to Anne's reign and is again essentially the original comments found in the 1721 *Life* and repeated in Volume II of the *Review*. It is an interpretive work, eschewing the documents and letters which clog the *Life* and so many contemporary histories. Its main new feature is that Salmon "annexe[s] some political remarks on Bishop Burnet's History of the reign of Queen Anne" (title-page). The second volume of Burnet's autobiographical work, which covers Anne's reign, had appeared only in 1734, a decade after the first volume. It was logical then that Salmon, who had felt impelled to comment on the first volume in the two volumes of the *Impartial Examination* (see n. 53), now saw fit to add briefer comments on the second Burnet volume, this time appending them to his third traversal of Anne's reign. The new comments found in the *Modern History* were, if possible, more high-flying than those in the 1721 or 1724 texts. The comments are grouped together for each year following the account of events for each regnal year. The common thread of Salmon's version of the events of Anne's reign found in all three texts, 1721, 1724 and 1735, two of which bear his name, reinforces the attribution of the 1721 *Life* to his pen. It is well to remember that both Salmon's father Thomas and his brother Nathaniel were clergymen. All three were historians, the father primarily a musicologist, the brother essentially an antiquary interested in Roman and medieval Britain. Thomas shared with Nathaniel his High-Church position and aversion to the undiluted Whiggery of Bishop Burnet.

To the Tory histories of Salmon and the Whiggish history of Jones may be added Boyer's substantial folio, *The History of the Life and Reign of Queen Anne* (1722).[56] The most Whiggish in tone, it is drawn, as is Jones's, from his annual volumes, although considerably re-written and augmented. It is not unlikely that Salmon added the second volume to the *Review* in 1724 to rebut Boyer. Salmon's justification implies it, but is also strangely prescient when one considers how the Whig view of the later Stuarts has so prevailed in later historical writing:

The principal design of it is to prevent, if possible, partial relations being convey'd down to posterity as uncontested truths, for our present set of historians seem all to write in one strain, and to court one interest; and their concurrent testimony may, perhaps, be of such weight with the next age, as to make their relations entirely relied on, if they are not animadverted upon while the several facts and circumstances are fresh in our memories.[57]

The publication in 1724 of volume one of Burnet diverted attention for a time to the Restoration period. In 1729, at the end of the decade, there appeared *Memoirs of Queen Anne*, by Gibson, a writer known only by his surname.[58] Devoted mainly to the four last years of her reign, it is a strong Whig attack on the Tory ministry of Robert Harley, Earl of Oxford. At last Oldmixon had an ally. If one did not know that Swift's history of the same period was not published until 1758, one might have thought Gibson's *Memoirs* a reply. As Swift does not seem to have attempted to exhume his aborted *History* until 1728, the Gibson volume did follow at a curiously appropriate time.

The decade of the 1730s saw the rapid development of a new marketing device, the publication of books or sets in fascicles or serials. History was especially popular, and history titles in parts were often sold in conjunction with newspapers. One has only to recall Bolingbroke's *Remarks on the History of England* and his *Dissertation upon Parties*, both of which appeared first in the pages of the *Craftsman*, to see the attraction of this medium.[59] The party wars of the later Stuarts were still live issues with the subjects of George II. The excesses of the Whigs and the Jacobite flirtations of the Tories were constantly paraded for their propaganda value. The Tory memoirs of John Reresby, dating from the Restoration, appeared in print in 1734 for the first time, to be employed as election material. Both Sir Robert Walpole and the opposition led by Bolingbroke and Pulteney made frequent use of history to buttress their positions. Both laid claim to the legacy of the Revolution and the Country opposition to Charles II and James II.[60]

James Ralph did not treat Anne's reign in his *History of England* (above) and reserved his venom for Walpole to two shorter books.[61] He did direct his attention to the Queen's administration, however, in an answer to the autobiographical account of the octogenarian dowager Duchess of Marlborough, the most redoubtable Whig of all. The *Account of the Conduct of the Dowager Duchess of Marlborough, from Her First Coming to Court, to the Year 1710*,[62] though ghost-written for her by Nathaniel Hook, showed that age had not lessened the furies, described by Swift,[63] which had ever possessed her. Along with Henry Fielding[64] and others Ralph rushed to the defense of Anne and Queen Mary in *The Other Side of the Question: or, An Attempt to Rescue the Characters of the Two Royal Sisters...in a Letter to Her Grace*.[65]

Salmon's several versions of Anne's reign, to be found in his 1721 *Life*, the 1724 *Review*, and the 1735 *Modern History*, take their final shape in another 1735 publication, *The Life and Reign of Her Gracious Majesty Queen Anne....*[66] Boyer's *History of the Life and Reign of Queen Anne* was also republished in 1735 under an altered title but without other changes.[67] Together Salmon and Boyer furnished the basis of a whole series of histories of Anne's reign which appeared in the 1730s and 1740s. In 1738 the 1735 edition of Salmon reappeared anonymously as *The Life and Reign of...Queen Anne* with some minor omissions, such as listing acts passed and other details of this kind.[68] Most of the diatribes upon Burnet are faithfully repeated. In the same year Paul Chamberlen published his *Impartial History of the Life and Reign*.[69] Described by William T. Morgan as "one of the better contemporary histories of the period,"[70] it turns out, upon inspection, to be a verbatim reprinting of the 1722 Boyer with some minor abridgments. Another anonymous folio *History* of 1740[71] is also a Salmon product, this time a reprint of the 1721 version. Gibson's *Memoirs* of 1729 were reprinted in 1742.

The next series of histories of Anne's reign returned to Salmon. These include four editions of *An Impartial History of the Life and Reign of her Late Majesty Queen Anne* which credit Conyers Harrison as the compiler. There are two London printings for 1744 and Cambridge printings for both 1744 and 1745.[72] Harrison did no more than reprint the 1738 version in abridged form. He omitted the inflammatory diatribes against Burnet which first appeared in the 1735 version. He also reduced the text for the period after 1707 to little more than a hundred pages, in contrast to over five hundred for the preceding years (the pagination varies from edition to edition). The most notable cuts occurred at the end, for the years 1712–14 are treated in just a few pages. These four editions of "Harrison" were all printed by R. Walker. Another 1744 edition bears the imprint of R. Offtey at London but is the same "Harrison" text.[73] Other variants have been reported, but the general pattern is not altered.[74] From the appearance of the second and more Tory version of 1735, Salmon's *Life* dominated the field for a decade or more.

The success of Salmon's *Life* was phenomenal, unequaled by any other survey of the reign. Indeed, the Cambridge edition of 1744 and 1745 was distributed free as a supplement to the *Cambridge Journal and Weekly Flying Post*, as an inducement to subscribers.[75] The fact that Boyer's history did not even sell out in its first edition, and the remaining stock was reissued thirteen years later; that Kennett went through only two editions, and those before any competitors were available; that Oldmixon's *History of the Stuarts* was not republished; and that only the moderate Rapin and the unashamed Tory apologists Echard and Salmon went through repeated editions, gives us new cause for reflection on the attitudes of Augustan Englishmen to the Revolution as well as to the Hanoverian Succession and intervening events. A recent commentator on Swift notes that the polemical writings to which he contributed were primarily written for "confirming the faithful and encouraging the waverers, not converting the opponent."[76] If this be true, then the great quantity of Salmon's texts which reached the public, a quantity overwhelming in comparison with any other account of Anne's reign published in the early Hanoverian period, is a striking testimony to the hold Tory concepts and views still had on the general public.

In dealing with the nature, extent, and inspiration of the histories of the later Stuarts, specifically Queen Anne, that appeared in the reigns of the first two Georges, we have given more attention to the interpretive content than to the purely factual content of the works considered. But certainly a prime interest of contemporary historical writings to us now is their value as historical sources. Boyer and Jones both drew heavily upon contemporary newspapers, broadsides, pamphlets, and monthly periodicals. I would estimate that more than three-quarters of their material was drawn verbatim from other printed sources. But this does not mean they should be ignored. Boyer in particular had excellent sources. He based much of his annuals, his history, and his monthly *Political State of Great Britain* (which began in 1711) on a manuscript newsletter which he distributed.[77] His Huguenot connections also gave him unrivaled access to Continental newswriters.[78] His reports on parliamentary sessions have special value. He attended sessions to take notes for publication in his works, and he had the assistance of "several publick-spirited members, who have either communicated to me many remarkable speeches on important occasions, or procured me opportunities of being an ear-witness to their debates."[79] Boyer, Burnet, Oldmixon, Cunningham, and Jones all provide original, unique material of proven reliability. All the other works I have cited are essentially derived from four of these writers.[80] The Birch-Tindal *Continuation*, for example, is especially indebted to Burnet. Because of their originality Boyer, Burnet, and Oldmixon are the most cited by modern scholars. This utilization may be responsible in part for our tendency to view the Whig interpretation as the prevailing one.

What do these writers have to tell us about the Augustan concept of history? To begin with, most of these men wrote for profit. They were writers by profession, Cunningham and Burnet excepted, and Burnet was a prolific pamphleteer and respected historian. But even more, they were trying to respond to a sustained demand for a recapitulation and interpretation of the momentous events that closed the seventeenth century in England. The permanency of the Revolution settlement and the Hanoverian Succession were in some doubt until the middle of the century and the last Jacobite invasion in 1745. The nature of authority in the state, the role of the Church, and England's intervention in Europe were all subjects of enduring interest and continuing debate. These writers intended their works both to satisfy the demand for information and at the same time to justify a particular party or interpretation of events. The first objective we can identify with narrative history. The flood of histories which appeared in the Augustan period certainly established narrative history, particularly of contemporary or near contemporary history, as a popular genre. The second objective relates directly to the history of political theory and to historiography. Gibson stated forthrightly in his preface that he presumed "this essay will meet with the more favorable reception, that our deliverance from these past dangers, was such as ought to be held in perpetual remembrance by all who wish the true welfare of their country."

A touchstone for determining basic political beliefs, the trial of Dr. Sacheverell provided as detailed and full an exposition as one can find of the ideological viewpoints that divided Augustan England.[81] Salmon took particular offence at the way the Whig ministry put down the mobs who rioted during the trial. "This is a specimen what fine work a Whig-principle will make when reduc'd to practice.... Surely 'tis with an ill grace when a Whig complains of a practice which is the natural result of his favourite principle."[82] Gibson deplored the Sacheverell sermon, as by it "those in power were in all places represented as persons who countenanced schism, and all manners of irreligion."[83] Not so Salmon, who wrote, "As to the Doctor's [Sacheverell's] opinion of the danger of the Church at that time, if he did err, it was with nine parts in ten of the clergy and laity of the church of England, who really apprehended the constitution to be in danger from some of the ministry." Salmon devoted no fewer than 50 pages out of 1100 to the trial. The conflict about hereditary right and the Revolution settlement is glossed over with the statement that once the crown was settled in William and Mary, Anne, and the Electress Sophia, it was on as sound a hereditary basis as it had ever been. Rejecting the Whig interpretation of the Revolution, he went on to assert, "By this means the succession seems to be so well established, that it may bid defiance to all Whig principles....The terms abdication, and male-administration, are become useless."[84] The exhaustive narrative of Ralph is even more heavily burdened with commentary and allies itself to that of Echard in enunciating an apologia for the discredited James II and displaying a patent hostility to the Prince of Orange and his supporters. These are only a few examples, but they do provide a sobering reminder that the Whiggish views which have dominated English historical writing since the beginning of the nineteenth century do not accurately reflect contemporary public opinion in the first half of the eighteenth century. For the most part the enormous output of the eighteenth-century press is still a *terra incognita* to current scholars. One may hope that the extraordinary resources of the on-line Eighteenth-Century Short Title Catalogue will put an end to this condition.

In his *Revolution Principles: The Politics of Party 1689–1720*, John Kenyon has demonstrated convincingly that the ideology of the Whigs failed them after the Revolution.[85] In an earlier statement he commented that only the "misfortunes of the Harley ministry saved them."[86] He went on to point out that as late as 1717 the Whigs were still in a defensive position. Our own view of their immediate and lasting success, at least in terms of popular acceptance of their ideology, is patently at variance with the facts. This is demonstrated most tellingly in another historian's commentary published in the same year as Kenyon's: "Whether or not this period was one of such complete Whig supremacy in politics as older historians believed, Whiggish versions of history certainly predominated at this time."[87]

The Whig party of Anne's reign and its leaders were regarded with suspicion and continued to be criticized severely even in the later eighteenth century by Sir John Dalrymple, James Macpherson, and Thomas Somerville. Even though these three historians were supporters of the Revolution and the settlement that followed it, they found the Whig party and its leaders as reprehensible and as self-serving as their Tory opponents. This should not surprise us. We know from other studies that the Whigs were essentially a minority party even though they came to dominate the political machinery of government. The recent studies of Linda Colley and J. C. D. Clark both attest to the enduring strength of Tory ideology and even the Tory party, in spite of the Whig supremacy.[88] Herbert Butterfield has shown us that the Whig view of George III had a much briefer currency than we once thought, and that it did not prevail until well into the nineteenth century. He proved this by analyzing carefully a whole series of half-forgotten historians of the late eighteenth and early nineteenth centuries. To cite Kenyon again, Tory ideology was far more persistent and pervasive than our latter-day infatuation with Locke and his imitators would suggest. This brief survey of Augustan historians and their view of the climactic events of late Stuart England supports his conclusions.

The plenitude of accounts of Anne's reign which appeared from the 1720s through the 1740s contrasts markedly with the paucity for those of William's reign or even of his predecessors. The political inspiration for these surveys is incontestible. The disastrous, absolutist policies of Charles II and James II only proved an embarrassment for the Tories, who had to respond with apologias rather than panegyrics. They made what capital they could out of the other Stuarts, but Anne was their treasure. Her model deportment as sovereign—her morality, her piety, her concern for her country and her church—contrasted brilliantly with the unattractive popular image of the first two Georges. In like manner, from a Whig viewpoint, the solid achievements of Anne's reign—the great naval and military victories, the passage of the Union—clearly outshone the lackluster, corrupt administration of Walpole. Military histories of Marlborough and Eugene appearing in the 1730s reinforced the disparity. The Whig historians gloried in King William and the Revolution, but the unimpressive performance of his armies in the Nine Years' War would hardly have served so well to point out the shortcomings of the Hanoverians. Each party could find sustenance for its own aspirations and ideology in Good Queen Anne's glorious reign.

When contemporary history first became a popular subject, massive folios may have been the most imposing products of the genre, but it was the cheap octavos and duodecimos, oft reprinted, which attracted the large readership. The tedious narrative, criticized by Temple for its surfeit of documents and speeches, was never a popular model. But these works had served their purposes, both the temporal political one and the development of the discipline. The lacuna of broad survey works was filled, albeit not by works of any particular literary merit. Even today, however, they have value for us for factual data and as a guide to the literature and to contemporary opinion. They form the foundation upon which the later, more moderate synthetic treatments of Hume, Smollett, and others were laid. More important, because of their comprehensiveness, their visibility, and their wealth of data, they have been the most consulted by historians in the nineteenth and twentieth centuries. It is these influential works which constitute the basis for the Whig interpretation of English history. This is especially true of Rapin and the Birch-Tindal *Continuation*, which was very accessible because it went through so many editions.

Though the first comprehensive history of a major part of Queen Anne's reign to be written, Swift's *History of the Four Last Years of the Queen* was almost the last to be published. As an apologia it had lost its currency by the time he resurrected it in the 1720s and again in the 1730s. By 1758, when it finally appeared in print, the most intense era of party-oriented historical writing was over with the demise of the Whigs and Tories. Hume's urbane, moderate *History*, then in the process of appearing, was much more attuned to the Age of Reason than the partisan, polemical *History* of Swift. A quarter of a century ensued before the study of the late Stuarts was revived in the 1770s, when revolutionary activities, distrust of the central government, and renewed party conflicts recalled the similar conditions and made more timely the study of the consequences of those conflicts in Stuart England.

¹ Fussner, *The Historical Revolution: English Historical Writing and Thought, 1580–1640* (New York, 1962), and *Tudor History and the Historians* (New York, 1970); *English Historical Scholarship in the Sixteenth and Seventeenth Centuries*, ed. Fox (London, 1956); MacGillivray, *Restoration Historians and the English Civil War* (The Hague, 1974); Peardon, *The Transition in English Historical Writ-*

ing, 1760–1830 (New York, 1933); Butterfield, *George III and the Historians* (London, 1957).

² David C. Douglas, *English Scholars, 1660–1730*, 2nd ed., rev. (London, 1951).

³ The most important, because of the historical writings of the subjects, are T. E. S. Clarke and H. C. Foxcroft, *A Life of Gilbert Burnet* (Cambridge, 1907); Norman Sykes, *William Wake*, 2 vols. (Cambridge, 1957), and *Edmund Gibson* (London, 1926); and Gareth V. Bennett, *White Kennett* (London, 1957), and *The Tory Crisis in Church and State, 1688–1730: The Career of Francis Atterbury, Bishop of Rochester* (Oxford, 1975).

⁴ John V. Price, "Hume's Concept of Liberty and The History of England," *Studies in Romanticism*, 5 (1966), 139–57; D. C. Coleman, *History and the Economic Past* (Oxford, 1987), pp. 7–9.

⁵ John Rushworth, 7 vols. (London: Newcomb, 1659–1701); Rymer, 20 vols. (London: vols. I–XVII, A. and J. Churchill, 1704–1717; vols. XVIII–XX, J. Tonson, 1726–35), T148099; Birch, 7 vols. (London: Gyles, Woodward, and Davis, 1742), T160848. Numbers preceded by a T or N refer to the entries in the on-line Eighteenth-Century Short Title Catalogue maintained by the Research Library Information Network. In some cases the printing history is so complex, as in the case of Clarendon's *Rebellion*, and so many editions or variants have been recorded, that it was not possible to publish all the relevant numbers.

⁶ *An Introduction to the History of England* (London: Simpson and Simpson, 1695). In 1742 an anonymous editor could still repeat the same lament: "England, however productive of eminent writers in various kinds of literature, still remains defective in excellent historians...." *A Collection of the State Letters of the First Earl of Orrery*, preface, quoted in Mark A. Thomson, *Some Developments in English Historiography during the Eighteenth Century* (London, 1957), p. 11.

⁷ Tyrell, 3 vols. (London: Rogers et al., 1696–1704), T136504.

⁸ A. C. Elias, Jr., *Swift at Moor Park* (Philadelphia, 1982), pp. 55–66 for Temple's project, Appendix C for Swift's.

⁹ The best discussions of the clerical controversies are to be found in Bennett, *Atterbury*, and H. G. Every, *The High-Church Party, 1688–1718* (London, 1956).

¹⁰ Its publication was prompted at least in part by the success of a series of Whig memoirs—volumes by John Berkeley, Denzil, Lord Holles, and Thomas, Lord Fairfax, and two further volumes by Edmund Ludlow—which appeared in 1699. Edmund Ludlow, *A Voyce from the Watch Tower*, ed. A. B. Worden (London, 1978), p. 2.

¹¹ *Private Correspondence and Miscellaneous Papers of Samuel Pepys*, ed. J. R. Tanner, 2 vols. (New York, 1925), II, 301–02, 20 January 1703.

¹² Gilbert Burnet, *History of His Own Time*, ed. [M. J. Routh], 2nd ed. (Oxford, 1833), I, 58.

¹³ *Complete History*, 3 vols. (London: B. Aylmer, R. Bonwick, et al., 1702–06).

¹⁴ [William Newton], *The Life of the Right Reverend Dr. White Kennett, Late Lord Bishop of Peterborough* (London: Billingsley, Roberts, and Cox, 1730), T132807, p. 32.

15 Authority statement on the title-page of Vol. III. Cf. Newton, p. 33.

16 *Remarks and Collections of Thomas Hearne*, ed. C. E. Doble et al., 11 vols. (Oxford, 1885–1921), I, 282. Hearne goes on: it "is done with Dr. Kennett's usual unaccuracy, pride, injudiciousness & knavery" (p. 283).

17 *The Life and Reign of Her Late Excellent Majesty Queen Anne* (London: J. Roberts, Taylor, et al., 1722), T131168, p. iv.

18 *Life of William III* (London: S. and J. Sprint et al., 1703), T91260; 2nd ed. N19816.

19 British Library, Lansdowne MSS 1002–10. The portion for 1660–62 only was published as *A Register and Chronicle Ecclesiastical and Civil* (London: Williamson, 1728), T132809. Though a later publication project, aborted by his death, these journals illustrate Kennett's honest concern for accuracy and depth in historical writing. The initial collection of material could well have stemmed from his preparation for the *Compleat History*. Bennett, pp. 176–77, is silent on this point.

20 Newton, p. iv.

21 Newton, pp. 34–35; *Copies and Extracts of Some Letters Written to and From the Earl of Danby (Now Duke of Leeds) in the Years 1676, 1677, and 1678. With Particular Remarks upon Some of Them. Published by His Grace's Direction* (London: Nicholson, 1710), T132736; 2nd ed., N29005.

22 *Examen* (London: Gyles, 1740), T147677.

23 *Examen*, p. iv.

24 *Examen*, p. vii. The vituperation North heaps on Kennett occupies the better part of fourteen quarto pages of fine print.

25 *The History of the Revolutions* (London: E. Curll and R. Gosling, 1711), T73961.

26 *The History of the Revolutions*, "Advertisement Concerning This History."

27 *History of England. From the First Entrance of Julius Caesar* (London: Tonson, 1707), T160955; *History of England*, 3 vols., 2nd ed. (London: Tonson, 1718), N8404; *History of England* (London: Tonson, 1720), T137777.

28 *History of the Revolution* (London: Tonson, 1725), T138380.

29 *History of the Revolution*, Preface.

30 *The Conduct of the Earl of Nottingham* (New Haven, 1941), Introduction.

31 *A Hue and Cry after Dismal* (London: 1712), N16900. In [*The Prose Writings of Jonathan Swift*], ed. Herbert Davis et al., 14 vols. (1939–68; various reimpressions, sometimes corrected, Oxford, 1957–69), VI, 139–41; hereafter cited as *Prose*.

32 *Letter* (London: Clarke, 1718), T38156; 2nd ed., N11417; 3rd ed., T38157. Calamy's *Letter* inspired two further responses: Londinensis Anonymus [Thomas Lewis? Matthias Earbery?], *A Letter to Dr. Calamy* (London: Bettenham, 1718?), T38108; Philalethes [Laurence Echard? Isaac Sharpe? J. Sharpe?], *An Answer to Dr. Calamy's Letter* (London: Bettenham, 1718), T17484.

33 *Letter*, p. 7.

34 *Letter*, p. 66.

35 *History of His Own Time*, 2 vols. (London: Ward, 1724–34), T144689.

[36] *Prose*, V, 266–94. For Swift's annotations printed against their full context see also the Routh edition of Burnet.

[37] See the introduction to Helen C. Foxcroft, ed., *A Supplement to Burnet's History of My Own Time* (Oxford, 1902).

[38] They include three by John Cockburn: *A Specimen of Some Free and Impartial Remarks on Publick Affairs and Particular Persons, Occasion'd by Dr. Burnet's History of His Own Times* (London: T. Warner, 1724?), T9525; *Vindication of the Late Bishop Burnet from the Calumnies and Aspersions of a Libel Entitled, A Specimen of Some Free and Impartial Remarks* (London: J. Roberts, 1724), T50863; and *Defence of Dr. Cockburn against the Calumnies and Aspersions of a Libel* (London: T. Warner, 1724), N29022; [Hugh Tootel], *Remarks on B[isho]p Burnet's History of His Own Time* (London: A. Moore, 1724); Laurence Braddon, *Bishop Burnet's Late History Charg'd with Partiality and Misrepresentations* (London: Pickles, 1725); and Bevil Higgons, *Historical and Critical Remarks on Bishop Burnet's History of His Own Time* (London: P. Meighan, 1725), T36307; 2nd ed., 1727, T108390; 3rd ed., 1736, not yet entered in ESTC.

[39] *The History of Great Britain*, 2 vols. (London: Strahan and Cadell, 1787), T141108.

[40] Oldmixon's writings are most fully examined in Pat Rogers's unpublished dissertation, "The Whig Controversialist as Dunce: A Study of the Literary Fortunes and Misfortunes of John Oldmixon," Cambridge, 1972. One may also consult Oldmixon's autobiographical *Memoirs of the Press* (London: T. Cox, 1742), T039158.

[41] *Critical History of England*, 2 vols. (London: J. Pemberton, 1724–26), T115226; 2nd ed., 1726–30, T115225; 3rd ed., Vol. I only, 1728, T115227.

[42] *Clarendon and Whitlock Compared* (London: J. Pemberton, 1727), T53989.

[43] *History of England*, part 2 (London: John Pemberton et al., 1730), T135546; part 3 (London: Thomas Cox et al., 1735), T135575; part 1 (London: printed for T. Cox and R. Hett, 1739), T135576.

[44] I am indebted for the information that follows on the composition of the *Continuation* to the unpublished dissertation of my former student Laird Okie: "Augustan Historical Writing: The Rise of Enlightenment Historiography in England," Univ. of Kansas, 1982. It contains the most informed and most detailed account of the Rapin-inspired continuations and, as its title indicates, historical writing generally in the early Hanoverian period.

[45] *The History of England*, 2 vols. (London: Daniel Browne, 1744–46), T146950.

[46] Guthrie, 4 vols. (London: Daniel Browne, 1744–51), T138171.

[47] Carte, 4 vols. (London: Hodges, 1747–55), T101742.

[48] *The History of Great Britain*, I (Edinburgh: Hamilton, Balfour, and Neill, 1754), T82483.

[49] See Henry L. Snyder, "David Jones, Augustan Historian and Pioneer English Annalist," *Huntington Library Quarterly*, 44 (1980), 11–26.

[50] See the introduction by Herbert Davis in *Prose*, VII.

[51] *A Detection*, 3 vols. (London: Brotherton and Meadows, 1719), T144752.

52 T90438.

53 *Review of the History of England*, 2 vols. (London: Rivington, 1722–24), T152163; 2nd ed. (1724), N15001. The quotation is from the title-page of the first edition. In the same year Salmon also published another two-volume set that gave considerable space to the reigns of James II and Charles II: *An Impartial Examination of Bishop Burnet's History of His Own Times*, 2 vols. (London: Rivington and Clarke, 1724), T154521. The *Impartial Examination* seems to have been intended as a continuation of the *Review*, whose pagination it continues. (The second edition of Vol. I of the *Review* was paginated separately, befitting its separate publication earlier.) For our purposes the main interest of the *Impartial Examination* lies in its consistently Tory tone, even to the point of defending Dr. Sacheverell and dishing the Whig ministry that impeached him in 1710.

54 This material could well have been extracted from Boyer's *History of the Reign of Queen Anne, Digested into Annals* (11 vols., 1703–13), hence the confusion on the subject of authorship. As Boyer, like Jones, took material of this nature from the *Votes of the House of Commons*, the *London Gazette*, and, above all, the *Political State of Europe: or, The Historical and Political Monthly Mercury*, it is probably not right to give full credit to Boyer as the *Life*'s authority in these matters. They could have used common sources, though Boyer made them more accessible. I shall suggest that in the *Review* Salmon was recycling his own work—that is, that the *Life* is Salmon's writing.

55 *Modern History*, XXV–XXVI (London: Wotton, Shuckburgh, and Osborne, 1734–35), T139608–09.

56 (London: Roberts, 1722), T131168.

57 *Review of the History of England*, II, vii.

58 *Memoirs of Queen Anne* (London: Millar, 1729), T90442; second edition, 1742, T90443. I do not know the source of the attribution. It is so listed in all standard bibliographical works and catalogues. If it is correct, then the writer may well be the William Gibson who published *A History of the Affairs of Europe, from the Peace of Utrecht to the Conclusion of the Quadruple Alliance* (London: Batley, 1725), T94743.

59 This was especially true with provincial newspapers. See John Feather, *The Provincial Book Trade in Eighteenth-Century England* (Cambridge, 1985), pp. 21, 36.

60 See Quentin Skinner, "The Principles and Practice of Opposition: The Case of Bolingbroke versus Walpole," in Neil McKendrick, ed., *Historical Perspectives* (London, 1974); Isaac Kramnick, *Bolingbroke and His Circle: The Politics of Nostalgia in the Age of Walpole* (Cambridge, 1968); and John P. Kenyon, *The History Men* (London, 1983), pp. 39–41.

61 *A Critical History of the Administration of Sir Robert Walpole* (London: Hinton, 1743), T132722, and *Of the Use and Abuse of Parliaments*, 2 vols. (London, 1744), T131624.

62 *An Account of the Conduct* (London: Bettenham, 1742), N16618.

[63] "Three Furies reigned in her Breast, the most mortal Enemies of all softer Passions: which were, sordid Avarice, disdainful Pride, and ungovernable Rage." *The History of the Four Last Years of the Queen*, in *Prose*, VII, 8.

[64] *A Full Vindication of the Duchess Dowager of Marlborough* (London: Roberts, 1742), T89744.

[65] *The Other Side of the Question* (London: Cooper, 1742), T95227.

[66] *The Life and Reign* (London: Walker, 1735), T149724.

[67] *The History of Queen Anne* (London: T. Woodward et al., 1735), T122942.

[68] *The Life and Reign* (London: Printed for the Compiler, 1738), T89138.

[69] *Impartial History*, Part 1, no more published (London: W. Lloyd, 1738), T55565.

[70] *Bibliography of British History*, 5 vols. (Bloomington, IN., 1934–42), III, 27.

[71] *History* (London: Printed and Sold by the Booksellers in Town and Country, 1740), T89116.

[72] *Impartial History* (London: R. Walker, 1744), T89457; (London, R. Walker, 1744), T154530; (Cambridge: printed by R. Walker and T. James and deliver'd gratis to the customers of the Cambridge Journal, 1744), T154529; (Cambridge: printed by R. Walker and T. James and deliver'd gratis to the customers of the Cambridge Journal, 1745), N17112.

[73] *Impartial History* (London: R. Offtey, 1744), T32960.

[74] The precise number of texts or even editions is impossible to state with complete accuracy because of the incomplete nature of the bibliographical sources. I have recorded here those entered in the on-line file of the Eighteenth-Century Short Title Catalogue, as they are verified entries. As that file grows the information will become yet more complete.

[75] Roy M. Wiles, *Serial Publication in England before 1750* (Cambridge, 1957), p. 340; see also details from the colophons quoted in n. 72.

[76] F. P. Lock, *Swift's Tory Politics* (London, 1983), p. 20.

[77] See Henry L. Snyder, "Newsletters in England, 1689–1715, with Special Reference to John Dyer—A Byway in the History of England," *Newsletters to Newspapers: Eighteenth-Century Journalism*, Donovan H. Bond and W. Reynolds McLeod, eds. (Morgantown, WV, 1977), p. 8 and throughout.

[78] For Boyer and his connections one must consult a number of illuminating articles by Graham C. Gibbs, which include: "The Contribution of Abel Boyer to Contemporary History in England in the Early Eighteenth Century," *Clio's Mirror: Historiography in Britain and the Netherlands*, A. C. Duke, C. A. Tamse, eds. (Zutphen, Netherlands, 1985), pp. 87–108; "Abel Boyer Gallo-Anglus Glossographus et Historicus, 1667–1729: His Early Life, 1667–1689," *Proceedings of the Huguenot Society of London*, 22 (1978), 87–98; "Abel Boyer Gallo-Anglus Glossographus et Historicus, 1667–1729: From Tutor to Author, 1689–1699," *Proceedings of the Huguenot Society of London*, 24 (1983), 46–59; "The Role of the Dutch Republic as the Intellectual Entrepot of Europe in the Seventeenth and Eighteenth Centuries," *Bijdragen en Mededelingen betreffende de Geschiedenis der Nederlanden*, 86 (1971), 323–49.

[79] Boyer, *History of the Life*, p. iv; Historical Manuscripts Commission, House of Lords Manuscripts, IX, 106–07.

[80] I except Cunningham, because his work was not published until late in the century.

[81] See Geoffrey Holmes, *The Trial of Doctor Sacheverell* (London, 1973).

[82] Salmon, *Life*, II, 214.

[83] Gibson, p. 72.

[84] Salmon, *Life*, Preface.

[85] (Cambridge, 1977).

[86] Kenyon, "The Revolution of 1688: Resistance and Contract," in McKendrick, p. 69.

[87] R. C. Richardson, "The Eighteenth Century: The Political Uses of History," *The Debate on the English Revolution* (New York, 1977), p. 40.

[88] Linda Colley, *In Defiance of Oligarchy: The Tory Party, 1714–60* (Cambridge, 1982); and J. C. D. Clark, *The Dynamics of Change: The Crisis of the 1750s and English Party Systems* (Cambridge, 1982).

Contributors

Carl P. Daw is a lecturer in English at the University of Connecticut and Episcopal chaplain to students there. He prepared the Scolar facsimile edition of Swift's *Miscellanies in Prose and Verse, 1711* and has written numerous essays on Swift.

J. A. Downie is Principal Lecturer in English at Goldsmiths' College, University of London. He is author of *Robert Harley and the Press* and *Jonathan Swift: Political Writer*.

Frank H. Ellis is Mary Augusta Jordan Professor Emeritus at Smith College and Five College Graduate Professor at the University of Massachusetts. He is editor of *A Discourse of the Contests and Dissentions between the Nobles and the Commons in Athens and Rome*; of *Poems on Affairs of State*, Vol. VI (1697–1704) and Vol. VII (1704–1714) and of *Swift vs. Mainwaring: The Examiner and the Medley*.

John Irwin Fischer is Professor of English at Louisiana State University. He is author of *On Swift's Poetry* and co-editor of *Contemporary Studies of Swift's Poetry*.

Charles H. Peake (d. 1988) was Professor of English at Queen Mary College, University of London. He was author of *James Joyce: The Citizen and the Artist* and editor of *Poetry of Landscape and the Night.*

Hermann J. Real is Professor of English at the Westfälische Wilhelms-Universität, Münster. He is author of *Untersuchungen zur Lukrez-Übersetzung von Thomas Creech*, editor of *The Battle of the Books*, co-author of *Jonathan Swift: Gulliver's Travels*, co-editor of *Proceedings of the First Münster Symposium on Jonathan Swift*, and co-translator of *Gullivers Reisen*.

Angus Ross is Reader in English at the University of Sussex. He is, with David Woolley, editor of the Oxford Authors *Jonathan Swift* and has edited numerous other eighteenth-century texts.

Henry L. Snyder is Professor of History at the University of California, Riverside, and North American Director of the Eighteenth-Century Short Title Catalogue. He has edited *The Marlborough-Godolphin Correspondence*.

Michael Treadwell is Professor of English Literature at the University of Trent. He is author of various studies on Swift and the eighteenth-century book trade.

James Woolley is Associate Professor of English at Lafayette College. He is author of various essays on Swift and related figures.

Index

AMS Studies in the
Eighteenth Century, No. 14
ISSN: 0196-6561

Other titles in this series:

1. Paul J. Korshin, ed. *Proceedings of the Modern Language Association Neoclassicism Conferences, 1967–1968.* 1970.

2. Francesco Cordasco. *Tobias George Smollett: A Bibliographical Guide.* 1978.

3. Paula R. Backscheider, ed. *Probability, Time, and Space in Eighteeth-Century Literature.* 1979.

4. Ruth Perry. *Women, Letters, and the Novel.* 1980

5. Paul J. Korshin, ed. *The American Revolution and Eighteenth-Century Culture.* 1985.

6. G. S. Rousseau, ed. *The Letters and Papers of Sir John Hill, 1714–1775.* 1982.

7. Paula R. Backscheider. *A Being More Intense: A Study of the Prose Works of Bunyan, Swift, and Defoe.* 1984.

8. Christopher Fox, ed. *Psychology and Literature in the Eighteenth Century.* 1988.

9. John F. Sena. *The Best-Natured Man: Sir Samuel Garth, Physician and Poet.* 1986.

10. Robert A. Erickson. *Mother Midnight: Birth, Sex, and Fate in the Eighteenth-Century Novel—Defoe, Richardson, and Sterne.* 1986.

13. Richard J. Dircks, ed. *The Letters of Richard Cumberland.* 1988.